Shell Scripting Recipes

A Problem-Solution Approach

Second Edition

Chris F. A. Johnson

Jayant Varma

Apress®

Shell Scripting Recipes, Second Edition

ISBN-13 (pbk): 978-1-4842-0221-0

ISBN-13 (electronic): 978-1-4842-0220-3

Managing Director: Welmoed Spahr
Lead Editor: Louise Corrigan
Editorial Board: Steve Anglin, Louise Corrigan, Jim DeWolf, Jonathan Gennick, Robert Hutchinson, Michelle Lowman, James Markham, Susan McDermott, Matthew Moodie, Jeffrey Pepper, Douglas Pundick, Ben Renow-Clarke, Dominic Shakeshaft, Gwenan Spearing, Matt Wade, Steve Weiss
Coordinating Editor: Mark Powers
Compositor: SPi Global
Indexer: SPi Global
Artist: SPi Global

Distributed to the book trade worldwide by Springer Science+Business Media New York, 233 Spring Street, 6th Floor, New York, NY 10013. Phone 1-800-SPRINGER, fax (201) 348-4505, e-mail orders-ny@springer-sbm.com, or visit www.springeronline.com. Apress Media, LLC is a California LLC and the sole member (owner) is Springer Science + Business Media Finance Inc (SSBM Finance Inc). SSBM Finance Inc is a Delaware corporation.

For information on translations, please e-mail rights@apress.com, or visit www.apress.com.

Apress and friends of ED books may be purchased in bulk for academic, corporate, or promotional use. eBook versions and licenses are also available for most titles. For more information, reference our Special Bulk Sales–eBook Licensing web page at www.apress.com/bulk-sales.

Any source code or other supplementary material referenced by the author in this text is available to readers at www.apress.com/9781484202210. For detailed information about how to locate your book's source code, go to www.apress.com/source-code/. Readers can also access source code at SpringerLink in the Supplementary Material section for each chapter.

This book is dedicated to my parents,
who would have been quite proud to see this book.

—Jayant Varma

Contents at a Glance

Contents

About the Authors

Chris F. A. Johnson was introduced to Unix in 1990 and learned shell scripting because there was no C compiler on the system. His first major project was a menu-driven, user-extensible database system with report generator. Chris uses the shell as his primary, general-purpose programming language, and his projects have included a member database, menuing system, and POP3 mail filtering and retrieval. Chris is the coauthor of *Pro Bash Programming* (Apress, 2015). When not pushing shell scripting to the limit, he designs and codes web sites, teaches chess, and composes cryptic crosswords.

Jayant Varma is the founder of OZ Apps (`www.oz-apps.com`), a consulting, training, and development company providing IT solutions (specialization in mobile technology). He is an experienced developer with more than 20 years of industry experience spread across several countries. He is the author of a number of books on iOS development, including *Learn Lua for iOS Game Development* (Apress, 2012), *Xcode 6 Essentials* (Packt, 2015), *More iPhone Development with Swift* (Apress, 2015), and *More iPhone Development with Objective-C* (Apress, 2015). He has also been a university lecturer in Australia where he currently resides. He loves traveling and finds Europe to be his favorite destination.

Acknowledgments

I would like to thank the wonderful staff at Apress for the opportunity to update this book. Special thanks to Louise and Mark, who facilitated the quick turnaround on the book and getting it to print. Lastly, special thanks to my family for their support in getting this book completed.

—Jayant Varma

CHAPTER 1

■ ■ ■

The POSIX Shell and Command-Line Utilities

The POSIX shell is a descendant of the KornShell, which is a descendant of the Bourne shell. The basic syntax has remained the same, and Bourne shell scripts will usually run successfully in a POSIX shell. Not all of the KornShell features are included in POSIX (there are no arrays, for example), but the most important ones are. Those, which would be important to many developers, are string manipulation and arithmetic.

The scripts in this book make extensive use of features of the POSIX shell, and keep external commands to a minimum. This chapter presents an overview of the features of the POSIX shell and the external Unix commands used in this book, without going into great detail. Further information is available in the documentation for the shell and the various commands as well as on many web pages, a number of which are listed in the Appendix. We will also explain some of the idiosyncrasies used in the scripts, and present a library of functions that are used by many scripts.

Shell Commands

These descriptions are brief overviews of the built-in commands; for a complete description, see your shell's man page.

echo

The echo command prints its arguments separated by single spaces followed by a newline. If an unquoted variable contains characters present in $IFS (see "Parameters and Variables" later in this chapter), then the variable will be split on those characters:

```
$ list="a   b c d e f   g   h"
$ echo $list
a b c d e f g h
```

If the variable is quoted, all internal characters will be preserved:

```
$ echo "$list"
a   b c d e f   g   h
```

In the early days of Unix, two different versions of echo appeared. One version converted escape sequences, such as \t and \n, into the characters they represent in the C language; \c suppressed the newline, and discarded any further characters. The other used the -n option to suppress the trailing newline and did not convert escape sequences. The POSIX standard for echo says that "Implementations shall not support any options" and "If the first operand is -n, or if any of the operands contain a backslash ('\') character, the results are implementation-defined." In other words, you cannot rely on echo's behavior being one or the other. It is best not to use echo unless you know exactly what echo is going to print, and you know that it will not contain any problem characters. The preferred command is printf.

printf

This command may be built into the shell itself, or it may be an external command. Like the C-language function on which it is based, printf takes a format operand that describes how the remaining arguments are to be printed, and any number of optional arguments. The format string may contain literal characters, escape sequences, and conversion specifiers. Escape sequences (the most common ones being \n for newline, \t for tab, and \r for carriage return) in format will be converted to their respective characters. Conversion specifiers, %s, %b, %d, %x, and %o, are replaced by the corresponding argument on the command line. Some implementations support other specifiers, but they are not used in this book. When there are more arguments than spec-ifiers, the format string is reused until all the arguments have been consumed.

The %s specifier interprets its argument as a string and prints it literally:

```
$ printf "%s\n" "qwer\ty" 1234+5678
qwer\ty
1234+5678
```

The %b specifier is like %s, but converts escape sequences in the argument:

```
$ printf "%b\n" "qwer\ty" "asdf\nghj"
qwer    y
asdf
ghj
```

The %d, %x, and %o specifiers print their arguments as decimal, hexadecimal, and octal numbers, respectively.

```
$ printf "%d %x %o\n" 15 15 15
15 f 17
```

The conversion specifiers may be preceded by flags for width specification, optionally preceded by a minus sign indicating that the conversion is to be printed flush left, instead of flush right, in the specified number of columns:

```
$ printf "%7d:\n%7s:\n%-7s:\n" 23 Cord Auburn
     23:
   Cord:
Auburn :
```

In a numeric field, a 0 before the width flag indicates padding with zeroes:

```
$ printf "%07d\n" 13
0000013
```

set

In the *Oxford English Dictionary*, the longest entry is for the word *set*—thirty-two pages in my Compact Edition. In the Unix shell, the set command is really three commands in one. Without any arguments, it prints the names and values of all shell variables (including functions). With one or more option arguments, it alters the shell's behavior. Any non-option arguments are placed in the positional parameters.

Only three options to set are used in this book:

- -v: Print shell input lines as they are read.

- -x: Print commands and their arguments as they are executed.

- -f: Disable file name generation (globbing).

Given this script, which is call xx.sh,

```
echo "Number of positional parameters: $#"
echo "First parameter: ${1:-EMPTY}"
shift $(( $# - 1 ))
echo "Last parameter: ${1:-EMPTY}"
```

its output is this:

```
$ xx.sh the quick brown fox
Number of positional parameters: 4
First parameter: the
Last parameter: fox
```

If set -v is added to the top of the script, and the standard output redirected to oblivion, the script itself is printed:

```
$ xx.sh the quick brown fox >/dev/null
echo "Number of positional parameters: $#"
echo "First parameter: ${1:-EMPTY}"
shift $(( $# - 1 ))
echo "Last parameter: ${1:-EMPTY}"
```

If set -v is replaced with set -x, variables and arithmetic expressions are replaced by their values when the lines are printed; this is a useful debugging tool:

```
$ xx.sh the quick brown fox >/dev/null
++ echo 'Number of positional parameters: 4'
++ echo 'First parameter: the'
++ shift 3
++ echo 'Last parameter: fox'
++ exit
```

To demonstrate the set -f option, and the use of + to reverse the operation, run the following script in an empty directory:

```
## Create a number of files using brace expansion (bash, ksh)
touch {a,b,c,d}${RANDOM}_{e,r,g,h}${RANDOM}

## Turn off filename expansion
set -f
printf "%-22s%-22s%-22s\n" * ; echo ## Display asterisk
printf "%-22s%-22s%-22s\n" *h* ; echo ## Display "*h*"

## Turn filename expansion back on
set +f
printf "%-22s%-22s%-22s\n" * ; echo ## Print all filenames
printf "%-22s%-22s%-22s\n" *h* ; echo ## Print filenames containing "h"
```

When the script is run, this is the output:

```
$ xx.sh
*

*h*

a12603_e6243          a28923_h23375         a29140_r28413
a5760_g7221           b17774_r4121          b18259_g11343
b18881_e10656         b660_h32228           c22841_r19358
c26906_h14133         c29993_g6498          c6576_e25837
d11453_h12972         d25162_e3276          d7984_r25591
d8972_g31551

a28923_h23375         b660_h32228           c26906_h14133
d11453_h12972
```

You can use set to split strings into pieces by changing the value of $IFS. For example, to split a date, which could be 2005-03-01 or 2003/09/29 or 2001.01.01, $IFS can be set to all the possible characters that could be used as separators. The shell will perform word splitting on any character contained in $IFS:

```
$ IFS=' -/.'
$ set 2005-03-01
$ printf "%s\n" "$@"
2005
03
01
```

When the value to be set is contained in a variable, a double dash should be used to ensure that the value of the variable is not taken to be an option:

```
$ var="-f -x -o"
$ set -- $var
```

shift

The leading positional parameters are removed, and the remaining parameters are moved up. By default, one parameter is removed, but an argument may specify more:

```
$ set 1 2 3 4 5 6 7 8
$ echo "$* ($#)"
1 2 3 4 5 6 7 8 (8)
$ shift
$ echo "$* ($#)"
2 3 4 5 6 7 8 (7)
$ shift 3
$ echo "$* ($#)"
5 6 7 8 (4)
```

■ **Tip**   This is most useful when used in scripts to iterate through a number of parameters passed. Access the **$0** parameter and keep shifting till there are no more to go through. However shift removes the parameters, so be aware if you want to reuse the parameters.

Some shells will complain if the argument to shift is larger than the number of positional parameters.

type

The POSIX standard says type "shall indicate how each argument would be interpreted if used as a command name." Its return status may be used to determine whether a command is available:

```
if type stat > /dev/null 2>&1 ## discard the output
then
  stat "$file"
fi
```

If the command is an executable file, type prints the path to the file; otherwise, it prints the type of command that will be invoked: function, alias, or shell builtin. Its output is not standard across different shells, and therefore cannot be used reliably in a shell script.

The four arguments to type in the following example represent an executable file, a function, a nonexistent command, and an alias.

```
$ type ls pr1 greb ecoh
ls is hashed (/bin/ls)
pr1 is a function
pr1 ()
{
```

```
    case $1 in
        -w)
            pr_w=
        ;;
        *)
            pr_w=-.${COLUMNS:-80}
        ;;
    esac;
    printf "%${pr_w}s\n" "$@"
}
bash: type: greb: not found
ecoh is aliased to `echo'
```

Unlike most shells, bash will print the definition of a function.

getopts

The command getopts parses the positional parameters according to a string of acceptable options. If an option is followed by a colon, an argument is expected for that option, and will be stored in $OPTARG. This example accepts -a, -b, and -c, with -b expecting an argument:

```
while getopts ab:c opt
do

    case $opt in
        a) echo "Option -a found" ;;
        b) echo "Option -b found with argument $OPTARG" ;;
        c) echo "Option -c found" ;;
        *) echo "Invalid option: $opt"; exit 5 ;;
    esac
done
```

case

A workhorse among the shell's built-in commands, case allows multiple branches, and is the ideal tool, rather than grep, for determining whether a string contains a pattern or multiple patterns. The format is

```
case STRING in
    PATTERN [| PATTERN ...]) [list] ;;
    [PATTERN [| PATTERN ...]) [list] ;; ...]
esac
```

The PATTERN is a pathname expansion pattern, not a regular expression, and the list of commands following the first PATTERN that matches is executed. (See the "Patterns" section further on for an explanation of the two types of pattern matching.)

eval

The command eval causes the shell to evaluate the rest of the line, then execute the result. In other words, it makes two passes at the command line. For example, given the command:

```
eval "echo \${$#}"
```

The first pass will generate echo ${4} (assuming that there are 4 positional parameters). This will then print the value of the last positional parameter, $4.

local

The local command is used in functions; it takes one or more variables as arguments and makes those local to the function and its children. Though not part of the POSIX standard, it is built into many shells; bash and the ash family have it, and pdksh has it as a standard alias for typeset (which is also not included in POSIX). In KornShell 93 (generally referred to as ksh93), if a function is defined in the portable manner (as used throughout this book), there is no way to make a variable local to a function.

In this book, local is used only in the few scripts that are written specifically for bash, most often for setting $IFS without having to restore it to its original value:

```
local IFS=$NL
```

Parameters and Variables

Parameters are names used to represent information; there are three classes of parameters: Positional parameters are the command-line arguments, and are numbered beginning with $1; variables are parameters denoted by a name that contains only letters, numbers and underscores, and that begins with a letter or an underscore; and special parameters that are represented by non-alphanumeric characters.

Positional Parameters

Positional parameters are the command-line arguments passed to a script or a function, and are numbered beginning with 1. Parameters greater then 9 must be enclosed in braces: ${12}. This is to preserve compatibility with the Bourne shell, which could only access the first nine positional parameters; $12 represents the contents of $1, followed by the number 2. The positional parameters can be assigned new values, with the set command. (See the example under "Special Parameters.")

Special Parameters

The parameters $* and $@ expand to all the positional parameters, and # represents the number of positional parameters. This function demonstrates the features of these parameters:

```
demo()
{
  printf "Number of parameters: %d\n" $#
  printf " The first parameter: %s\n" "$1"
  printf "The second parameter: %s\n" "$2"
  printf "\nAll the parameters, each on a separate line:\n"
  printf "\t%s\n" "$@"
```

7

```
    printf "\nAll the parameters, on one line:\n"
    printf "\t%s\n" "$*"
    printf "\nEach word in the parameters on its own line:\n"
    printf "\t%s\n" $*
}
```

Here, the demo function is run with three arguments:

```
$ demo The "quick brown" fox
Number of parameters: 3
 The first parameter: The
The second parameter: quick brown

All the parameters, each on a separate line:
        The
        quick brown
        fox

All the parameters, on one line:
        The quick brown fox

Each word in the parameters on its own line:
        The
        quick
        brown
        fox
```

The decimal exit code of the previous command executed (0 for success, non-zero for failure) is stored in $?:

```
$ true; echo $?
0
$ false; echo $?
1
```

The shell's current option flags are stored in $-; the shell's process ID is in $$; $! is the process ID of the most recently executed background command, and $0 is the name of the current shell or script:

```
$ sleep 4 &
[1] 12725
$ printf "PID: %d\nBackground command PID: %d\n" $$ $!
PID: 12532
Background command PID: 12725
$ printf "Currently executing %s with options: %s\n" "$0" "$-"
Currently executing bash with options: fhimBH
```

Shell Variables

These are the variables that are assigned values at the command line or in a script. The system or the shell itself also set a number of variables; those used in this book are

- $HOME: The path name of user's home directory (e.g., /home/chris).

- $IFS: A list of characters used as internal field separators for word splitting by the shell. The default characters are space, tab, and newline. Strings of characters can be broken up by changing the value of $IFS:

```
$ IFS=-; date=2005-04-11; printf "%s\n" $date
2005
04
11
```

- $PATH: This colon-separated list of directories tells the shell which directories to search for a command. To execute a command in other directories, including the current working directory, an explicit path must be given (/home/chris/demo_script or ./demo_script, not just demo_script).

- $PWD: This is set by the shell to the pathname of the current working directory:

```
$ cd $HOME && echo $PWD
/home/chris
$ cd "$puzzles" && echo $PWD
/data/cryptics
```

standard-vars—A Collection of Useful Variables

My standard-vars file begins with these lines:

```
NL='
'
CR='
'
TAB=' '
```

You might be able to guess that these three variables represent newline, carriage return, and tab, but it's not clear, and cannot be cut and pasted from a web site or newsgroup posting. Once those variables are successfully assigned, however, they can be used, without ambiguity, to represent those characters. The standard-vars file is read by the shell and executed in the current environment (known as *sourcing*, it is described later in the chapter) in most of my shell scripts, usually via standard-funcs, which appears later in this chapter.

Create the file with the following script, then add other variables as we found them useful:

```
printf "%b\n" \
    "NL=\"\n\"" \
    "CR=\"\r\"" \
    "TAB=\"\t\"" \
    "ESC=\"\e\"" \
    "SPC=\"\040\"" \
    "export NL CR TAB ESC SPC" > $HOME/scripts/standard-vars-sh
```

The -sh extension is part of the system used for working on scripts without contaminating their production versions. It is explained in Chapter 20.

Patterns

Two types of patterns are used in shell scripts: pathname expansion and regular expressions. Path-name expansion is also known as globbing, and is done by the shell; regular expressions are more powerful (and much more complicated), and are used in external commands such as sed, awk, and grep.

Pathname Expansion

Pathname expansion uses three special characters to tell the shell to interpret an unquoted string as a pattern:

- The asterisk (*) matches any string, including an empty one. By itself, an asterisk matches all files in the current directory, except those that begin with a dot.

- A question mark (?) matches any single character. By itself, a question mark matches all files in the current directory whose name is a single character, other than a dot.

- An opening bracket, ([), when matched with a closing bracket, (]), matches any of the characters enclosed. These may be individual characters, a range of characters, or a mixture of the two.

These patterns can be combined to form complex patterns for matching strings in case statements, and for building lists of files. Here are a few examples executed in a directory containing these files:

a	b	c
d	ee	ef
eg	eh	fe
ff	fg	fh
ge	gf	gg
gh	he	hf
hg	hh	i_158_d
i_261_e	i_502_f	i_532_b
i_661_c	i_846_g	i_942_a
j_114_b	j_155_f	j_248_e
j_326_d	j_655_c	j_723_g
j_925_a	k_182_a	k_271_c
k_286_e	k_292_f	k_294_g

To display all files with single-character names:

```
$ echo ?
a b c d
```

The next example prints all files whose names end with f:

```
$ echo *f
ef ff gf hf i_502_f j_155_f k_292_f
```

All files containing a number whose first digit is in the range 3 to 6 can be shown with:

```
$ echo *_[3-6]*
i_502_f i_532_b i_661_c j_326_d j_655_c
```

Regular Expressions

When I started writing shell scripts, I had problems with grep. I used the asterisk as a wildcard, expecting it to match any string. Most of the time, all was well, but occasionally grep would print a line I didn't want. For instance, when I wanted lines that contained call, I might get calculate as well, because I used 'call*' as the search pattern.

At some point, it dawned on me that the patterns used by grep were not the wildcards I had been using for years to match files, but regular expressions, in which * stood for "zero or more occurrences of the preceding character or range of characters". To match any string, the pattern is .*, as the period matches any character, and the combination matches "zero or more occurrences of any character." As with pathname expansion, [...] matches any of the characters enclosed in the brackets.

To match non-empty lines, search for any single character; that is, a dot:

```
$ printf "%s\n" January February March "" May June July | grep .
January
February
March
May
June
July
```

To print lines containing a b or a c, brackets are used:

```
$ printf "%s\n" January February March " " May June July | grep '[bc]'
February
March
```

In addition, the caret, ^, matches the expression only at the beginning of a line, and the dollar sign, $, matches only at the end of a line. Combining the two, ^...$, matches only the entire line. By anchoring the match to the beginning of the line, we can match lines with a as the second letter (the first letter can be anything):

```
$ printf "%s\n" January February March " " May June July | grep '^.a'
January
March
May
```

Using both the caret and the dollar sign, we can match lines beginning with J and ending with y:

```
$ printf "%s\n" January February March " " May June July | grep '^J.*y'
January
July
```

There are various flavors of regular expressions, including basic (BREs) and extended (EREs). The Perl language has its own set (which has been incorporated into Python), but the basics are common to all versions.

Regular expressions can be very complex (the example in the "Notes" to the `printat` function in Chapter 12 is daunting at first glance, but actually fairly simple), and are sometimes described as "write only"; once a regex (or regexp, the common abbreviations for regular expression) is written, it can be very hard to read it and understand how it works. A.M. Kuchling put it well in his *Regular Expression HOWTO*[1] (replace *Python* with whatever language you are using):

> *There are also tasks that can be done with regular expressions, but the expressions turn out to be very complicated. In these cases, you may be better off writing Python code to do the processing; while Python code will be slower than an elaborate regular expression, it will also probably be more understandable.*

If you want to delve deeper into regular expressions, the classic book from O'Reilly, sed & awk, has a very good section, and they are covered comprehensively in the Apress book, *Regular Expression Recipes: A Problem-Solution Approach*. There are also some links in the Appendix to online resources. In this book, you will find very few regular expressions, and none that cannot be easily understood.

Parameter Expansion

At its most basic, parameter expansion substitutes the value of the variable when it is preceded by a dollar sign ($). The variable may be enclosed in braces (`${var}`), and if the variable is a positional parameter greater than 9, the braces must be used. You can use three other forms of expansion within the braces: Bourne, POSIX, and shell specific.

The original Bourne shell parameter expansions tested whether the variable was set or empty, and acted on the results of that test. The KornShell added expansions to return the length of the variable's contents, and to remove the beginning or end of the value if it matched a pattern; these have been incorporated into the POSIX standard. KornShell 93 (`ksh93`) added the searchand-replace and substring capabilities that have also been included in `bash`.

The Bourne Shell Expansions

The original Bourne shell expansions have two forms. With a colon, they test whether a variable is null or unset; without the colon, the test is only whether the variable is unset.

${var:-DEFAULT}

If $var is unset or null, the expression expands to `DEFAULT`; otherwise, it expands to the contents of the variable:

```
$ var=
$ echo ${var:-y}
y
$ var=x
$ echo ${var:-y}
x
```

---

[1]http://www.amk.ca/python/howto/regex/regex.html

Without the colon, the variable must be unset, not just null, for DEFAULT to be used (the result of the variable expansion is surrounded by slashes):

```
$ var=
$ echo /${var-y}/
//
$ unset var
$ echo /${var-y}//y/
```

${var:=DEFAULT}

The only difference between this and the previous expansion is that this also assigns a value to var:

```
$ var=
$ echo "${var:=q}"
q
$ echo "${var:=z}"
q
```

${var:+VALUE}

This expansion (which was not in the very first Bourne shell) is the opposite of the previous two. If var is not null (or, without the colon, if it is set), VALUE is used. In the first example, var is unset, so the variable expands to an empty string, with or without the colon:

```
$ unset var
$ echo /${var:+X}/
//
$ echo /${var+X}/
//
```

In the next example, var is set but null. With the colon, the test is for a non-null string, so X is not printed. Without it, X is printed, because the test is for whether the variable is set.

```
$ var=
$ echo /${var:+X}/
//
$ echo /${var+X}//X/
```

Finally, when the variable is set and not null, VALUE is used, with or without the colon:

```
$ var=A
$ echo /${var:+X}//X/
$ echo /${var+X}//X/
```

A common use for this type of expansion is when building a list in which a separator character is wanted between items. If we just used concatenation, we'd end up with the separator at the beginning where it is not wanted:

```
$ for f in a b c d e
> do
>   list=$list,$f
>done
$ echo $list
,a,b,c,d,e
```

With this expansion, we can insert the separator only if $list is not empty:

```
list=${list:+$list,}$f
```

This is equivalent to the following:

```
if [ -n "$list" ]
then
  list=$list,$f
else
  list=$f
fi
```

Using this expansion in place of the simple variable in the preceding example, there is no initial comma:

```
$ for f in a b c d e
> do
>   list=${list:+$list,},$f
>done
$ echo $list
a,b,c,d,e
```

${var:?MESSAGE}

If var is unset (or, with the colon, null), an error or MESSAGE will be printed. If the shell is not interactive (as in the case of a script), it will exit.

```
$ unset var
$ echo ${var?}
bash: var: parameter null or not set
$ echo ${1?No value supplied}
bash: 1: No value supplied
```

POSIX Parameter Expansions

The expansions introduced by ksh, and adopted by POSIX, perform string manipulations that were once the province of the expr command. In these expansions, PATTERN is a file-globbing pattern, not a regular expression.

${#var}—Length of Variable's Contents

This expansion returns the length of the expanded value of the variable:

```
$ var=LENGTH
$ echo ${#var}
6
```

${var%PATTERN}—Remove the Shortest Match from the End

The variable is expanded, and the shortest string that matches PATTERN is removed from the end of the expanded value:

```
$ var=usr/local/bin/crafty
$ echo "${var%/*}"
usr/local/bin
```

${var%%PATTERN}—Remove the Longest Match from the End

The variable is expanded, and the longest string that matches PATTERN from the end of the expanded value is removed:

```
$ var=usr/local/bin/crafty
$ echo "${var%%/*}"
usr
```

${var#PATTERN}—Remove the Shortest Match from the Beginning

The variable is expanded, and the shortest string that matches PATTERN is removed from the beginning of the expanded value:

```
$ var=usr/local/bin/crafty
$ echo "${var#*/}"
local/bin/crafty
```

${var##PATTERN}—Remove the Longest Match from the Beginning

The variable is expanded, and the longest string that matches PATTERN is removed from the beginning of the expanded value:

```
$ var=usr/local/bin/crafty
$ echo "${var##*/}"
crafty
```

Combining Expansions

The result of one expansion can be used as the PATTERN in another expansion to get, for example, the first or last character of a string:

```
$ var=abcdef
$ echo ${var%${var#?}}
a
$ echo ${var#${var%?}}
f
```

Shell-Specific Expansions, bash2, and ksh93

I use two shell-specific parameter expansions in this book, either in the bash/ksh93 versions of functions (for example, substr in Chapter 3), or in bash-only scripts.

${var//PATTERN/STRING}—Replace All Instances of PATTERN with STRING

Because the question mark matches any single character, this example converts all the characters to tildes to use as an underline:

```
$ var="Chapter 1"
$ printf "%s\n" "$var" "${var//?/~}"
Chapter 1
~~~~~~~~~
```

This expansion can also be used with a single slash, which means to replace only the first instance of PATTERN.

${var:OFFSET:LENGTH}—Return a Substring of $var

A substring of $var starting at OFFSET is returned. If LENGTH is specified, that number of characters is substituted; otherwise, the rest of the string is returned. The first character is at offset 0:

```
$ var=abcdefgh
$ echo "${var:3:2}"
de
$ echo "${var:3}"
defgh
```

Shell Arithmetic

In the Bourne shell, all arithmetic had to be done by an external command. For integer arithmetic, this was usually expr. The KornShell incorporated integer arithmetic into the shell itself, and it has been incorporated into the POSIX standard. The form is $((expression)), and the standard arithmetic operators are supported: +, -, *, /, and %, for addition, subtraction, multiplication, division, and modulus (or remainder). There are other operators, but they are not used in this book; your shell's documentation will have all the details.

The standard order of operator precedence that we remember from high school algebra applies here; multiplication and division are performed before addition and subtraction, unless the latter are grouped by parentheses:

```
$ a=3
$ echo $(( $a + 4 * 12 ))
51
$ echo $(( ($a + 4) * 12 ))
84
```

The POSIX specification allows variables in arithmetic expressions to be used without a leading dollar sign, like this: echo $((a + 4)) instead of echo $(($a + 4)). This was not clear from early versions of the standard, and a major group of otherwise POSIX-compliant shells (ash, dash, and sh on BSD systems) did not implement it. In order for the scripts in this book to work in those shells, the dollar sign is always used.

Aliases

Aliases are the simple replacement of a typed command with another. In a POSIX shell, they can only take arguments after the command. Their use in scripts and on the command line can be replaced entirely by functions; there are no aliases in this book.

Sourcing a File

When a script is executed, it can obtain the values of variables that have been placed in the environment with export, but any changes it makes to those or other variables will not be visible to the script that called it. Functions defined or changes to the current directory also will not affect the calling environment. For these to affect the calling environment, the script must be sourced. By using the dot command, the file is executed in the current shell's environment:

```
.filename
```

This technique is used throughout the book, most often to define a library of functions.

Functions

Functions group one or more commands under a single name. Functions are called in the same way as any other command, complete with arguments. They differ from ordinary commands in that they are executed in the current shell environment. This means they can see all the variables of the calling shell; they do not need to be exported. Variables set or changed in a function are also set or changed in the calling shell. And, most of all, a function that does all its work with shell commands and syntax is faster than an external command.

Functions Are Fast

In Chapter 6, the basename and dirname functions replace the external commands of the same name, and do the job in a fraction of the time. Even a function more than 70 lines long can execute much faster than an external command. In Chapter 5, the _fpmul function is faster than the calc function, which uses awk, unless there are dozens of operands.

Under normal circumstances, one wouldn't think of writing a shell function for floating-point multiplication; awk would be a better choice for that. I (Chris) wrote _fpmul as a personal challenge, just to show that it could be done. Now that it's done, and it has proved to be faster than other methods, I do use it in scripts. A single line is all that's needed to make the function available:

```
.math-funcs
```

Other operations on decimal fractions are more complicated, and therefore aren't worth writing unless there's a specific need to do so.

Command Substitution Is Slow

When I discovered that using command substitution to store the results of a function in a variable was so slow (in all shells except ksh93) that it severely reduced the advantage of using functions, I started looking for ways to mitigate the phenomenon. For a while I tried using a variable to tell a function whether to print the result:

```
[ ${SILENT_FUNCS:-0} = 1 ] || echo "${_FPMUL}"
```

This worked, but I found it ugly and cumbersome; when I didn't want a function to print anything, I had to set SILENT_FUNCS to 1 usually by preceding the call with SILENT_FUNCS=1. Occasionally, I could set it at the beginning of a section of code and have it in force for all subsequent function calls. I was well into writing this book when the solution occurred to me, and I had to backtrack and rewrite parts of earlier chapters to incorporate it.

Whenever a function returns a value (other than an exit status), I now write two functions. One has the expected behavior of printing the result; the other, which begins with an underscore, sets a variable that is the function's name (including the underscore) converted to uppercase. To illustrate, here is a pair of functions to multiply two integers:

```
_mul()
{
    _MUL=$(( "$1" * "$2" ))
}

mul()
{
    _mul "$@" && printf "%s\n" "$_MUL"
}
```

I can now print the result of the multiplication with

```
$ mul 12 13
156
```

Or, I can store the result in a variable with

```
$ _mul 12 13
$ product=$_MUL
```

The extra few milliseconds it takes to use command substitution . . .

```
$ time mul 123 456
56088
Real: 0.000 User: 0.000 System: 0.000
$ time { q=$(mul 123 456); }
Real: 0.005 User: 0.001 System: 0.003
```

. . . may not seem significant, but scripts often loop hundreds or even thousands of times, and may perform several such substitutions inside a loop. The result is a sluggish program.

Using the Functions in This Book

The functions are used in three ways: at the command line, as commands in scripts, and as a reference. For use at the command line, the source of some of the function libraries are in the shell startup file; others are loaded at the command line when needed. In scripts, usually a single function library is sourced, and it will load any other libraries it needs. At other times, the function library serves as a reference, and the code is copied, sometimes modifying it, into the body of another script or function. You might want to follow this as your strategy or could have something completely different.

The functions in this book are mostly stored in libraries of related functions. You may find a different structure more suited to your coding style. If so, go ahead and reorganize them. We would recommend that you avoid having the same function in more than one library, unless the subsequent versions offer additional features that are not usually needed. The first library in this book is a collection of functions that are used in many scripts. All are used in at least one script in the book.

standard-funcs: A Collection of Useful Commands

The functions in this library encapsulate commonly used tasks in a consistent interface that makes using them easy. When you might need to get a keystroke from the user, you can call get_key; to display a date, use show_date; want to exit from a script because something has failed, use die. With menu1, display anything from one-line to full-screen menu and execute a command based on the user's response.

After defining the functions, the library loads standard_vars shown earlier in this chapter:

```
. standard-vars
```

1.1 get_key—Get a Single Keystroke from the User

In some circumstances, such as when asking a user to select from a menu, only a single key needs to be pressed. The shell read command requires a newline before it exits. Is there a way to read a single key?

How It Works

The bash read command has an option, -n, to read only a specified number of characters, but that is lacking in most other shells. The portable way uses stty to turn off the terminal's buffering, and to set the minimum number of characters required for a complete read. A single character can then be read by dd.

Usage

```
get_key [VAR]
```

If a variable is specified, the key will be read into that variable. If not, it will be in $_KEY.

The Script

```
get_key()
{

    [ -t 0 ] && { ## Check whether input is coming from a terminal
        [ -z "$_STTY" ] && {
            _STTY=$(stty -g) ## Store the current settings for later restoration
        }

        ## By default, the minimum number of keys that needs to be entered is 1
        ## This can be changed by setting the dd_min variable
        ## If the TMOUT variable is set greater than 0, the time-out is set to
        ## $TMOUT seconds
        if [ ${TMOUT:--1} -ge 0 ]
        then
            _TMOUT=$TMOUT
            stty -echo -icanon time $(( $_TMOUT * 10 )) min ${dd_min:-1}
        else
            stty -echo -icanon min ${dd_min:-1}
        fi
}

## Read a key from the keyboard, using dd with a block size (bs) of 1.
## A period is appended, or command substitution will swallow a newline
_KEY=$(dd bs=1 count=1 2>/dev/null; echo .)
_KEY=${_KEY%?} ## Remove the period

## If a variable has been given on the command line, assign the result to it
[ -n "$1" ] &&
        ## Due to quoting, either ' or " needs special treatment; I chose '
        case $_KEY in
            "'") eval "$1=\"'\"" ;;
            *) eval "$1='$_KEY'" ;;
        esac
        [ -t 0 ] && stty "$_STTY" ## reset terminal
        [ -n "$_KEY" ] ## Succeed if a key has been entered (not timed out)
}
```

Notes

The get_key function is often redefined in other scripts to allow entry of cursor and function keys—and even mouse clicks. For an example, which is too long to include in this book, see the mouse_demo script on my web site.[2]

1.2 getline—Prompt User to Enter a Line

For interactive scripts, I like the editing capabilities that bash's readline library offers, but I still want the script to work in other POSIX shells. I want the best of both worlds!

How It Works

The getline function checks for the existence of the $BASH_VERSION variable, and uses the readline library if it is set. If not, a POSIX read command is used.

Usage

```
getline "PROMPT" [VAR]
```

If no VAR is given, the line is read into the _GETLINE variable. If the variable name used is password, the keystrokes will not be echoed to the terminal.

The Script

```
_getline()
{
    ## Check that the parameter given is a valid variable name
    case $2 in
        [!a-zA-Z_]* | *[!a-zA-Z0-9_]* ) die 2 "Invalid variable name: $2" ;;
        *) var=${2:-_GETLINE} ;;
    esac

    ## If the variable name is "password" do not turn on echoing
    [ -t 0 ] && [ "$2" != "password" ] && stty echo
    case ${BASH_VERSION%%.*} in
        [2-9]|[1-9][0-9])
                read ${TMOUT:+-t$TMOUT} -ep "$1: " -- $var
                ;;
          *) printf "%s: " "$1" >&2
            IFS= read -r $var
            ;;
    esac
    [ -t 0 ] && stty -echo ## turn echoing back off
}
```

[2]http://cfaj.freeshell.org/src/scripts/mouse-demo-sh

1.3 press_any_key—Prompt for a Single Keypress

Despite the now-trite comment, "But my keyboard doesn't have an ANY key," it is often desirable to pause execution of a script until the user presses a key with the message "PRESS ANY KEY TO CONTINUE."

How It Works

The get_key function (shown two functions previously) provides the mechanism to read a single keypress, and printf and carriage returns display and erase the message.

Usage

```
press_any_key
```

At one time, this script accepted an argument: the name of a variable in which to store the key. It was never used, so it was removed. If you do want the keystroke, you can get it from the $_KEY variable set by get_key.

The Script

```
press_any_key()
{
    printf "\r <PRESS ANY KEY> "        ## Display the message
    get_key                             ## Get the keystroke
    printf "\r                    \r"    ## Erase the message
}
```

1.4 menu1—Print a Menu and Execute a Selected Command

Over the years, I have written many menu scripts, but when I needed a simple, easily adaptable menu, none fit the bill. All I wanted was a simple script that could display a menu, and execute a command based on the user's selection.

How It Works

The menu1 (so called to prevent conflict with an existing menu program) function displays the $menu variable, which should be set by the calling script. This can be anything from a one-line menu to a full screen. The user selects by number, and the corresponding argument to menu1 is executed with eval. A 0, q, or a newline exits the menu.

Usage

```
menu="MENU" menu1 CMD1 CMD2 ...
```

Two optional variables control the behavior of the function. If $_MENU1 is not null, the function will exit after a single successful loop. If $pause_after is not null, the script will pause, and the user will be prompted to press_any_key.

Here is a simple session; the characters in bold are the user's input, which do not actually appear when the script is run.

```
$ menu=" 1. Yes 2. No ?"
$ menu1 "echo YES" "echo NO"
 1. Yes 2. No ? 3
          bash: Invalid entry: 3
 1. Yes 2. No ? 2
NO
 1. Yes 2. No ? 1
YES
 1. Yes 2. No ? q
```

This is a slightly fancier version, with a two-line menu, that exits after one command:

```
$ menu="$NL Do you want to see today's date?$NL 1. Yes 2. No ?"
$ menu1 "date" ":"

 Do you want to see today's date?
  1. Yes    2. No ? y
        bash: Invalid entry: y

Do you want to see today's date?
 1. Yes    2. No  ?
Mon Feb 7 08:55:26 EST 2005
```

For more elaborate menus using this function, see the conversion script in Chapter 5.

The Script

```
menu1()
{
    m1_items=$#  ## Number of commands (i.e., arguments)
    while :      ## Endless loop
    do
     printf "%s " "$menu"    ## Display menu
     get_key Q               ## Get user's choice
     case $Q in
         0|q|""|"$NL" )
                   printf "\n"; break ;;    ## Break out
         [1-$m1_items])                     ## Valid number
                   printf "\n"
                   ( eval "\$$Q" )          ## Execute command
                   case $pause_after in     ## Pause if set
                       *?) press_any_key
                           ;;
                   esac
                   ;;
```

```
            *) printf "\n\t\a%sInvalid entry: %s\n" "${progname:+$progname: }" "$Q"
               continue
               ;;
        esac

        [ -n "$_MENU1" ] && break ## If set, exit after one successful selection
done
}
```

1.5 arg—Prompt for Required Argument If None Supplied

You may have a number of scripts that take an argument. You might want a simple method to check whether an argument is present, and prompt the user for one if there isn't.

How It Works

The arguments to the script are passed using "$@" to arg; if there is an argument, it is stored in $_arg; if not, the user is prompted (with the value of $prompt) to enter an appropriate value.

Usage

```
arg "$@"
```

The best illustration of this function comes from Chapter 5, where the conversion functions all use it. Here, for example, is the script to convert from ounces to grams (the actual calculation is done by _oz2g):

```
oz2g()
{
    units=grams
    prompt=Ounces arg "$@"
    _oz2g $arg
     printf "%s%s\n" "$_OZ2G" "${units:+ $units}"
}
```

When run without an argument, arg prompts for input. If the $units variable has been set by the calling script, it is printed:

```
$ oz2g
Ounces? 23
652.05 grams
```

And with one, there is no prompt, and no units are printed because arg empties $units when there is an argument:

```
$ oz2g 2
56.7
```

The Script

```
arg()
{
    case $1 in
        "") printf "%s? " "$prompt" >&2  ## Prompt for input
            stty echo                     ## Display characters entered
            read arg < /dev/tty           ## Get user's input
            ;;
        *) arg="$*"     ## Use existing arguments
           units=       ## For use with the conversion script, Chapter 5
           ;;
    esac
}
```

1.6 die—Print Error Message and Exit with Error Status

When a fatal error occurs, the usual action is to print a message and exit with an error status. It would be nice to make this exit routine uniform across all scripts. This is similar to what's available in Perl or PHP.

How It Works

The die function takes an error number and a message as arguments. The first argument is stored in $result, and the rest are printed to the standard error.

Usage

```
die NUM [MESSAGE ...]
```

This function is usually used when an important command fails. For example, if a script needs certain directories, it may use checkdirs (introduced later in this chapter) and call die when one cannot be created:

```
checkdirs "$HOME/scripts" "$HOME/bin" || die 13 "Could not create $dir"
```

The Script

```
die() {
    result=$1
    shift
    printf "%s\n" "$*" >&2
    exit $result
}
```

1.7 show_date—Display Date in D[D] MMM YYYY Format

Much of the time, the display_date function from the date-funcs library in Chapter 8 is overkill, and all you might want is a simple function to convert a date, usually in ISO format, into a more humanreadable form.

How It Works

By expanding the IFS variable to include the hyphen, period, and slash, as well as a space, most popular date formats can be split into their separate components. By default, the elements are expected in year-month-day order, but, by setting the DATE_FORMAT variable to dmy or mdy, the other common formats can also be accommodated.

Usage

```
_show_date YYYY-MM-DD ## Result is stored in $_SHOW_DATE
show_date YYYY-MM-DD ## Result is printed
```

So long as you remember that the year 05 is two millennia in the past, you should have little trouble with this function. Here are a few examples:

```
$ show_date 2005.04.01
1 Apr 2005
$ DATE_FORMAT=dmy show_date 04-01-2005
4 Jan 2005
$ DATE_FORMAT=mdy show_date 04/01/2005
1 Apr 2005
```

The Script

```
_show_date()
{
    oldIFS=$IFS      ## Save old value of IFS
    IFS=" -./"       ## Allow splitting on hyphen, period, slash and space
    set -- $*        ## Re-split arguments
    IFS=$oldIFS      ## Restore old IFS

    ## If there are less than 3 arguments, use today's date
    [ $# -ne 3 ] && {
        date_vars  ## Populate date variables (see the next function)
        _SHOW_DATE="$_DAY $MonthAbbrev $YEAR"
        return
    }
    case $DATE_FORMAT in
        dmy) _y=$3      ## day-month-year format
            _m=${2#0}
            _d=${1#0}
            ;;
        mdy) _y=$3      ## month-day-year format
            _m=${1#0}
            _d=${2#0}
            ;;
         *) _y=$1       ## most sensible format
            _m=${2#0}
            _d=${3#0}
```

```
            ;;
    esac

    ## Translate number of month into abbreviated name
    set Jan Feb Mar Apr May Jun Jul Aug Sep Oct Nov Dec
    eval _m=\${$_m}
    _SHOW_DATE="$_d $_m $_y"
}

show_date()
{
    _show_date "$@" && printf "%s\n" "$_SHOW_DATE"
}
```

1.8 date_vars—Set Date and Time Variables

You need to set variables with elements of the current date and time. It's possible to do it like this, but it is very inefficient, and if it's run at the wrong instant (such as just before midnight), the results would be incorrect if the date changed between setting, for example, DAY and HOUR, because $HOUR and $MINUTE would refer to the day after $DAY:

```
YEAR=$(date +%Y)
MONTH=$(date +%m)
DAY=$(date +%d)
HOUR=$(date +%H)
MINUTE=$(date +%M)
SECOND=$(date +%S)
```

How It Works

Combining the shell command, eval, and the date utility's format string, it can all be done in a single command; date is called with a format string that produces shell code to set all the variables, and eval executes it.

Usage

```
date_vars [DATE OPTIONS]
```

The output of the date command in the date_vars function looks like this:

```
DATE=2005-02-05
YEAR=2005
MONTH=02
DAY=05
TIME=22:26:04
HOUR=22
MINUTE=26
SECOND=04
datestamp=2005-02-05_22.26.04
```

```
                DayOfWeek=Sat
                DayOfYear=036
                DayNum=6
                MonthAbbrev=Feb
```

This is interpreted as a shell command by eval to set the variables.

While date_vars is usually called without any arguments, it can be used with whatever options your date utility provides. For example, if you have GNU date, you can use the -d option to use a date other than the current one:

```
date_vars -d yesterday
```

The Script

```
date_vars()
{
    eval $(date "$@" "+DATE=%Y-%m-%d
                      YEAR=%Y
                      MONTH=%m
                      DAY=%d
                      TIME=%H:%M:%S
                      HOUR=%H
                      MINUTE=%M
                      SECOND=%S
                      datestamp=%Y-%m-%d_%H.%M.%S
                      DayOfWeek=%a
                      DayOfYear=%j
                      DayNum=%w
                      MonthAbbrev=%b")

    ## Remove leading zeroes for use in arithmetic expressions
    _MONTH=${MONTH#0}
    _DAY=${DAY#0}
    _HOUR=${HOUR#0}
    _MINUTE=${MINUTE#0}
    _SECOND=${SECOND#0}

    ## Sometimes the variable, TODAY, is more appropriate in the context of a
    ## particular script, so it is created as a synonym for $DATE
    TODAY=$DATE

    export DATE YEAR MONTH DAY TODAY TIME HOUR MINUTE SECOND
    export datestamp MonthAbbrev DayOfWeek DayNum
}
```

1.9 is_num—Is This a Positive Integer?

When a script needs an integer, and the method of input is not under the scripter's control (as when a user is asked for input), the value should be verified, and rejected if it is not what is required.

How It Works

This function itself is limited to verifying positive integers, and checks for any non-digit characters. Negative integers can be accepted by calling the function without a leading negative sign on the argument.

Usage

```
is_num INT
```

The verification is registered entirely by the function's return code:

```
$ is_num 33 && echo OK || echo NO GO
OK
$ var=-33
$ is_num "$var" && echo OK || echo NO GO
NO GO
```

A negative integer may be allowed by the caller by stripping any leading minus sign:

```
$ is_num "${var#-}" && echo OK || echo NO GO
OK
```

The Script

```
is_num()
{
    case $1 in
        *[!0-9]*) return 5 ;; ## Fail is any character is not a digit from 0 to 9
    esac
}
```

Notes

I once used a more elaborate version that would accept negative integers as well as a verbose option, -v, which would print the results. Here it is; use whichever you prefer.

```
is_num() {
    case ${1#-} in
        -v) isnum_verbose=1
            shift
            ;;
        *) isnum_verbose=0 ;;
    esac
    case $1 in
        *[!0-9]*) case $isnum_verbose in
                      1) printf "Not a number: %s\n" $1 >&2 ;;
```

```
                       esac
                       return 5
                       ;;
    esac
}
```

1.10 abbrev_num—Abbreviate Large Numbers

When printing numbers in a confined space, such as a listing of mailbox contents in Chapter 10, printing them in a shortened form allows more room for other matter. You might like to convert 123456 to 123K, and 456789123 to 456M into Human readable form.

How It Works

The suffix, K, M, or G, is determined by the length of the number, and the number is divided by 1000, 1000000, or 1000000000 as required. The result is always a maximum of four characters.

Usage

```
_abbrev_num NUM ## Result is stored in $_ABBREV_NUM
abbrev_num NUM ## Result is printed
```

Four-digit numbers are not converted, as they are no longer than the maximum:

```
$ abbrev_num 4321
4321
```

Longer number are converted (and rounded to the nearest unit):

```
$ abbrev_num 123456
123K
$ abbrev_num 234567890
235M
```

The Script

The numbers are rounded up by adding 500, 500000, or 500000000 before dividing.

```
_abbrev_num() {
    case ${#1} in
    1|2|3|4) _ABBREV_NUM=$1 ;;
    5|6) _ABBREV_NUM=$(( ($1 + 500) / 1000 ))K ;;
    7|8|9) _ABBREV_NUM=$(( ($1 + 500000) / 1000000 ))M ;;
    10|11|12) _ABBREV_NUM=$(( ($1 + 500000000) / 1000000000 ))G ;;
    *) _ABBREV_NUM="HUGE" ;;
    esac
}
```

```
abbrev_num()
{
     _abbrev_num "$@" && printf "%s\n" "$_ABBREV_NUM"
}
```

Notes

These abbreviated numbers are sometimes referred to as "human-readable," but they can be less useful than the full number when it comes to comparing relative sizes. The abbreviated form cannot be sorted, and the length of a number gives a graphic representation of its size. That representation is helped when thousands separators are used, and for that we need a function: commas.

1.11 commas—Add Thousands Separators to a Number

Large numbers are easier to understand when thousands separators are inserted. Can that be done in a script?

How It Works

POSIX parameter expansion can give the length of a variable and remove three digits; this, plus concatenating the parts interspersed with commas, provides all that is necessary.

Usage

```
_commas NNN           ## Result is stored in $_COMMAS
commas NNN [NNN ...] ## Result[s] is/are printed
```

The underscore version of the function accepts only a single argument and stores it in _COMMAS, but the other accepts multiple arguments and prints the results one to a line.

```
$ commas $(( 2345 * 43626 )) 3.14159265 299792458
102,302,970
3.14159265
299,792,458
```

The Script

```
_commas() {
    _COMMAS=             ## Clear the variable for the result
    _DECPOINT=.          ## Character for decimal point; adjust for other locales
    _TH_SEP=,            ## Character for separator; adjust for other locales
    case $1 in
        "$_DECPOINT"*) _COMMAS=$1 ## Number begins with dot; no action needed
            return
            ;;
        *"$_DECPOINT") ## Number ends with dot; store it in $c_decimal
            c_num=${1%"$_DECPOINT"}
            c_decimal=.
```

```
            ;;
        *"$_DECPOINT"*) c_num=${1%"$_DECPOINT"*} ## Separate integer and fraction
            c_decimal=$_DECPOINT${1#*"$_DECPOINT"}
            ;;
         *) c_num=$1 ## No dot, therefore no decimal
            c_decimal=
            ;;
esac

while :
do
    case $c_num in
        ## Three, two or one digits [left] in $num;
        ## add them to the front of _COMMAS and exit from loop
        ???|??|?) _COMMAS=${c_num}${_COMMAS:+"$_TH_SEP"$_COMMAS}
                break
                ;;
        *) ## More than three numbers in $num
        left=${c_num%???} ## All but the last three digits

        ## Prepend the last three digits and a comma
        _COMMAS=${c_num#${left}}${_COMMAS:+"$_TH_SEP"$_COMMAS}
        c_num=$left ## Remove last three digits
        ;;
    esac
  done

  ## Replace decimal fraction, if any
  _COMMAS=${_COMMAS}${c_decimal}
}
commas()
{
    for n
    do
        _commas "$n" && printf "%s\n" "$_COMMAS"
    done
}
```

1.12 pr1—Print Arguments, One to a Line

When you want to pipe a list of words to a command one at a time, it means you must use a for loop or pipe the items to tr -s ' ' '\n'. Is there a better way?

How It Works

If there are more arguments than format specifiers in its format string, printf will reuse that string until all the arguments have been processed. If the format string contains one format specifier and a newline, each argument will be printed on a new line.

Usage

```
pr1 [-w] ITEM ...
```

With pr1, you can print a list of directories beginning with s, one to a line, without calling ls, and pipe it through awk to get the names without the full path. This is accomplished by setting the field separator to a slash, and printing the penultimate (NF-1) field:

```
$ pr1 ~/work/s*/ | awk -F/ '{print $(NF-1)}'
screenshots
sounds
src
stocks
sun
sus
sysadmin
system
```

Even using the external printf, if your shell does not have it built in, pr1 is considerably faster than echoing the list to ls -1 or xargs -n1.

By default, arguments will be truncated to the width of the screen. To prevent that, use the -w option.

The Script

```
pr1()
{
    case $1 in
        -w) pr_w= ;;
        *) pr_w=-.${COLUMNS:-80} ;;
        esac
        printf "%${pr_w}s\n" "$@"
}
```

1.13 checkdirs—Check for Directories; Create If Necessary

I often need to know whether all the directories a script uses exist, and create them if they do not.

How It Works

The checkdirs function checks whether each of its arguments is an existing directory, and attempts to create it if it doesn't; it prints an error message if a directory does not exist and cannot be created. If any directory could not be created, it returns an error status.

Usage

```
checkdirs DIRPATH ...
```

Only the existence of a directory is checked for, not the ability to read it or write into it. In this example, /bin exists, but it is unlikely that an ordinary user has the permission to write to a file inside it.

```
$ checkdirs /qwe /bin uio /.autofsck || echo Failed
mkdir: cannot create directory `/qwe': Permission denied
mkdir: `/.autofsck' exists but is not a directory
Failed
```

The Script

```
checkdirs() {
  checkdirs=0 ## Return status: success unless a check fails
  for dir ## Loop through the directory on the command line
  do
    [ -d "$dir" ] &&      ## Check for the directory
            continue ||    ## If it exists, proceed to the next one
    mkdir -p "$dir" ||     ## Attempt to create it
        checkdirs=1        ## Set error status if $dir couldn't be created
  done
  return $checkdirs        ## Return error status
}
```

1.14 checkfiles—Check That a Directory Contains Certain Files

With bash or ksh93, you can use brace expansion to combine multiple filenames with a directory and check for the existence of each one:

```
$ for file in /bin/{bash1,bash2,bash3,bash4,bash5}
> do
>     [ -f "$file" ] || return 5
> done
```

Other POSIX shells do not have this syntax, so you need another method of combining directory and filename and checking them.

How It Works

The directory given as the first argument is prepended to each of the other arguments in turn. The resulting path is checked, and the function returns with an error as soon as a given file does not exist.

Usage

```
checkfiles DIR FILE ...
```

The function fails if a file does not exist, and the name of the first nonexistent file will be in $_CHECKFILE.

```
$ checkfiles /bin bash1 bash2 bash3 bash4 bash5 ||
> printf "%s\n" "$_CHECKFILE does not exist"
bash4 does not exist
```

The Script

```
checkfiles()
{

    checkdict=$1                          ## Directory must be first argument
    [ -d "$checkdict" ] || return 13     ## Fail if directory does not exist
    shift                                 ## Remove dir from positional parameters
    for _CHECKFILE                        ## Loop through files on command line
    do
        [ -f "$checkdict/$checkfile" ] || return 5
    done
}
```

1.15 zpad—Pad a Number with Leading Zeroes

When a one-digit number needs to be zero-padded to two digits, such as when building an ISO date, it's easy to do with parameter expansion. For example, month may be a single digit or two digits, and may or may not have a leading zero. This expansion will ensure it is two digits, with a leading 0 if necessary: month=0${month#0}. When more than one digit may have to be prepended and the number's length is variable, a more flexible method is needed.

How It Works

The obvious method is to use $(printf "%0%${width}d" "$NUM"), but command substitution takes a long time in all shells except ksh93. The brute-force method of adding a zero in a loop until the desired size is reached is faster unless the amount of padding is large. The definition of large may vary from shell to shell and system to system; on my system with bash it is approximately 50.

Usage

```
_zpad NUM PADDING [CHAR]    ## Result is stored in $_ZPAD
zpad NUM PADDING [CHAR]     ## Result is printed
```

NUM is the number to be padded; PADDING is the desired number of digits in the result:

```
$ zpad 5 4
0005
```

The optional CHAR is a character to use for the padding instead of 0.

```
$ zpad 23 5 x
xxx23
```

The Script

```
_zpad()
{
```

```
        _ZPAD=$1
        while [ ${#_ZPAD} -lt $2 ]
        do
              _ZPAD=${3:-0}$_ZPAD
        done
}

zpad()
{
        _zpad "$@" && printf "%s\n" "$_ZPAD"
}
```

1.16 cleanup—Remove Temporary Files and Reset Terminal on Exit

Your scripts often could do unfriendly things to the terminal like change the colors, change the prompt, change some settings. These are all right so long as the script is running, but when control returns to the command line, it may be almost unusable. When the scripts exits, this terminal needs to be reset.

In addition, the scripts may create temporary files that shouldn't be left lying around when it is finished. These need to be removed.

How It Works

The trap command tells the shell to execute certain commands when a signal is received. If a trap is set on the EXIT signal, the specified commands will be executed whenever the script finishes, whether by a normal completion, and error, or by the user pressing Control+C. The cleanup function is designed for that purpose.

Usage

```
trap cleanup [SIGNALS]
```

The signal will usually be EXIT, and you could have the standard-funcs library set this trap when it is sourced.

The Script

```
cleanup()
{
    ## delete temporary directory and files
    [ -n "$tempfile_dir" ] && rm -rf "$tempfile_dir"

    ## Reset the terminal characteristics
    [ -t 0 ] && {
        [ -n "$_STTY" ] && stty $_STTY || stty sane
    }
    exit
}
trap cleanup EXIT ## Set trap to call cleanup on exit
```

The Unix Utilities

With a few exceptions, the external commands used in this book are standard on all Unix systems. Here we provide a quick look at most of the utilities you'll see in this book. For more complete information, see their man pages or the POSIX specification (see the Appendix for the web site, or Chapter 19 for a script to view the POSIX man pages).

cat: Concatenate Files to the Standard Output

The command cat is best known for and used more often than not to display the contents of a file to the screen. Users can overuse it and in many cases the commands can work without using cat, some examples can include

```
cat "$1" | sed 's/abc/ABC/g"
```

could easily be used simply as

```
sed '/s/abc/ABC/g' "$1"
```

or

```
cat /etc/passwd | grep "$USER"
```

could be used as

```
grep "$USER" /etc/passwd
```

In a script, valid uses for cat include these two tasks:

- To provide more than one filename as input to a command that can only take a single file on the command line, or can only read the standard input. This often appears as cat "$@" | CMD, which will concatenate any files given as arguments, and read the standard input if no files are given.

- To send an unmodified file, along with the output of one or more commands, to the input of another command.

sed: A Text Stream Editor

Many new to scripting rarely use sed for more than relatively simple tasks (if they use). It is a very powerful, non-interactive text editor, but it uses cryptic, single-letter commands. The scripts, which also use the inherently hard-to-read regular expressions, can easily become difficult to maintain.

One main use for sed is for search and replace. To change all lines that start with /bin to /usr/bin in the file script.sh and store the result in newscript.sh, use this command:

```
sed 's|^/bin|/usr/bin|' script.sh > newscript.sh
```

The usual delimiter after the s (substitute) command is the slash, but any character can be used. Since the slash is in the strings being used, it either must be escaped, or another character must be used; here the the pipe symbol is used.

A command in a sed script can be limited to certain lines or certain ranges of lines. To define this address space, either a number (to match a line number) or a regular expression may be used. To limit the changes to the first ten lines, and changing all instances of John to Jack:

```
sed '1,10 s/John/Jack/g'
```

To change the first instance of one only on lines containing a number of at least two digits: sed '/[0-9] [0-9]/ s/one/1/'

When no file is supplied on the command line, the standard input is used. All output is sent to the standard output.

awk: Pattern Scanning and Processing Language

The awk programming language can do many of the same things as sed, but it uses a much more legible syntax. Like sed, it processes a file line by line, operating on lines that match a pattern. When no pattern is associated with an action, it is performed on all lines; when no action is associated with a pattern, the default action is to print the line.

To print only non-blank lines, a regular expression consisting of a single dot matches those lines which contain any character (pr1, from the standard-funcs library earlier in this chapter, prints each argument on a separate line):

```
$ pr1 a b c "" e f | awk '/./'
a
b
c
e
f
```

To print the last field lines that begin with a number (NF is an awk variable that contains the number of fields on the current line; the dollar sign specifies a field on the line), use this:

```
awk '/^[0-9]/ {print $NF}'
```

The fields are, by default, separated by whitespace characters. The field separator can be changed either on the command line with the -F CHAR option, or in the script in a BEGIN block:

```
$ awk 'BEGIN { FS = ":" }
/chris|cfaj/ {print $1, $NF}' /etc/passwd
chris /bin/bash
cfaj /usr/local/bin/pdksh
```

grep: Print Lines Matching a Regular Expression

Like awk and sed, grep reads the standard input if no files are specified, and can accept multiple files on the command line. The regular expression can be as simple as a string (i.e., a regular expression that matches only itself):

```
$ grep '^c' /etc/passwd
jayant:x:501:501:Jayant C Varma:/home/jayant:/bin/bash
chris:x:503:503:author:/home/chris:/usr/local/bin/pdksh
```

date: Show or Set the System Date

The flexibility of date is in the format string, which determines what information about the current date and time will be printed, and how it will be printed. The format string begins with a + and can contain literal strings and specifiers for the elements of the date and time. A good example is in the date_vars function in the standard-funcs library, shown previously.

Setting the system date must be done by the superuser, and doesn't figure in any of the scripts in this book.

tr: A Character Translation Utility

Often developers ask why tr cannot change one string to another; the reason is that it is a *character translation utility*; use sed or awk to change strings. The tr utility only converts characters in the first string with the corresponding characters in the second string:

```
$ echo abcdefgascdbf | tr abc 123
123defg1s3d2f
```

With the -d option, it deletes (or rather omits) characters:

```
$ echo abcdefgascdbf | tr -d abc
defgsdf
```

See the man page for full details and other options.

wc: Count Characters, Words, and Lines in a File

By default, wc prints the number of lines, words, and characters in a file, followed by the filename. The information printed can be selected with the -l, -w, and -c options. If any option is given, only the information requested is printed: wc -l prints only the number of lines, and wc -cw prints the number of characters and the number of words.

When no filename is given, wc reads the standard input, and, naturally, prints no filename. To store information from wc in a variable, use input redirection instead of giving a filename:

```
$ wc -l FILE
3419 FILE
$ wc -l < FILE
3419
```

Some versions of wc print spaces before the size. These can cause problems when using the result as a number in calculation. There are various ways to remove the leading spaces. You could try using shell arithmetic:

```
var=$(( $(wc -l < FILE) ))
```

file: Determine the File Type

The file command uses "magic" files that contain rules for classifying files.

```
$ file /etc/passwd /bin/ls ./ean13.ps
/etc/passwd: ASCII text
/bin/ls:    ELF 32-bit LSB executable, Intel 80386, version 1 (SYSV), for GNU/
Linux 2.2.5, dynamically linked (uses shared libs), stripped
./ean13.ps: ASCII English text, with CRLF line terminators
```

ls: Sort and Provide Details About Files

If ls is called with arguments, it lists the files, or the contents of directories, supplied on the command line. Without any arguments, it lists the names of files and directories in the current directory. This example lists files and directories in the current directory that begin with letters in the range a to m; the -d option tells it just to print the names of directories, not their contents, and -F prints a classification character after the names of certain types of files (in this example, slashes indicate directories).

```
$ l$ ls -d -F [a-m]*
actions    ean13.ps      file2            liblcms1_1.12-2ubuntu1_i386/
acute      enzyme.dat    firefox-installer/   max/
bin        enzymes.tar   gle-log          mc-chris/
ch8.doc    file1         lfy/             menulog.
```

To me, the most important options are -l, which prints details about the files instead of just the names, and -t, which prints the most recently modified files first. Many more options are available; as usual, see the man page for details.

uniq: Remove Consecutive Duplicate Lines

For uniq to remove all duplicate lines from a file, it must first be sorted; otherwise, only consecutive duplicate lines are removed (see unique in Chapter 19 for a script to remove duplicate lines from an unsorted file). Since the sort command has a -u option that removes duplicate lines, uniq is more often used with -c for counting the number of instances of each line (the {a..g} construction was introduced in bash3, and expands to a b c d e f g):

```
$ pr1 $(( $RANDOM % 2 )){a..g} $(( $RANDOM % 2 )){a..g} | sort | uniq -c
      2 0a
      1 0b
      1 0c
      2 0d
      1 0g
      1 1b
      1 1c
      2 1e
      2 1f
      1 1g
```

sudo: Execute Commands as the Superuser

The file, /etc/sudoers, contains rules that give users permission to run commands as other users, usually as root. Permission can be given to selected users to run only certain commands or all commands, with or without a password being required, by prefacing it with sudo.

split: Divide a File into Equal-Sized Pieces

By default, split divides a file into separate files of 1,000 lines each, using xaa, xab, and so on as the filename of the split files. The user can choose to split a file by any number of bytes or number of lines. The name and length of the extension can also be set with command-line options. With -l for line count, or -b for byte count and file for the filename prefix.

which: Show the Full Path to a Command

We have generally avoided which, partly because Bourne-type shells have the built-in type command, and partly because historically it was a csh script that did not work in a Bourne-type shell. In recent years, however, which is a compiled command on most systems and works with all shells. The advantage it has over type is that it prints only the path to the command; type's output is not standard, and usually includes more than just the path.

gs, gv: Render, Convert, or View PostScript and PDF Files

Ghostscript is used by several commands to render PostScript programs; You could use gv to view PS and PDF files, and ImageMagick's convert to convert from one format to another.

Summary

There's more to the shell than is described in this chapter. It is only intended to explain some of the commands and concepts used in this book's scripts, not be a tutorial on how to write shell scripts. Throughout the book, the scripts are commented to describe what is going on, but they do not always explain the syntax itself. This chapter has provided those explanations.

■ ■ ■

## CHAPTER 2

Playing with Files: Viewing, Manipulating, and Editing Text Files

Text files are a mainstay of Unix operating systems. From the password file, /etc/passwd, to server configuration files, such as httpd.conf (exact location varies, depending on the system), a computer's behavior is controlled by text files. But what is a text file? E-mail and Usenet messages are text files; HTML web pages are text files; shell scripts are text files; log files are text files. Text files are human-readable and can be edited with any text editor. They can, of course, be viewed, manipulated, and edited with shell scripts.

A Unix operating system does not distinguish between text files and binary files. All files are binary files—text files are just a subset. According to the Single UNIX Specification (SUS) glossary, a text file

> *contains characters organised into one or more lines. The lines must not contain NUL characters and none can exceed {LINE_MAX} bytes in length, including the newline character*[1]

NUL is ASCII 0, a byte in which all bits are set to 0, and LINE_MAX, the maximum number of characters permissible on a line, is system-dependent; it is 2,048 on the Linux and FreeBSD systems I use.

Many of the text files on a Unix system use a well-defined format. Some of these are covered in other sections of the book, as are scripts to convert text to other formats. This chapter presents scripts that deal with arbitrarily formatted (or unformatted) text files.

End of the Line for OS Differences: Converting Text Files

Files are often moved from one operating system to another. It's a lot easier now than it used to be. Gone are the days when each computer manufacturer used a different character encoding. The 8-bit Commodore computers I owned in the dim, distant past had the upper- and lowercase characters reversed (well, sort of, but that's another story). IBM mainframe computers used the Extended Binary-Coded Decimal Interchange Code (EBCDIC) character set. Nowadays, the American Standard Code for Information Interchange (ASCII) is the basis for all coding. There are a number of extensions, but the first 128 characters are immutable. Almost.

---

[1]http://www.opengroup.org/onlinepubs/007908799/xbd/glossary.html#tag_004_000_306

There are differences between the newline characters on different systems.

- Unix systems use NL (the newline character, which is ASCII 10, octal \012, hexadecimal 0x0a, also called a linefeed, LF) to end a line.

- Windows uses the CR/LF pair (CR is a carriage return, ASCII 13, octal \015, hexadecimal 0x0d, or to use the form most often seen, ^M).

- Macintosh uses CR.

While many applications can deal with different line endings, there are many, probably more, that cannot. Most systems already have commands to take care of it, dos2unix and unix2dos being the most common, along with the GNU command recode. If you don't have those commands, the replacements for them are provided in this section, along with converters for Macintosh files.

In all the scripts in this section, the result is stored in a temporary file created by mktemp (if you don't have the command, there's a script to replace it), then mved over the original file.

2.1 dos2unix—Convert Windows Text Files to Unix

MS-DOS and Windows systems use a CR/LF combination at the end of each line. Unix systems use only LF. Depending on how files are copied from one system to another, the line endings may or may not be converted. A script copied from Windows could look like this in a text editor:

```
#! /bin/sh^M
echo "Defenestration required"^M
exit^M
```

Many programs will complain if a file has incorrect line endings. Some will just not work. A shell script with carriage returns may fail at the very first line, with an error message:

```
: bad interpreter: No such file or directory
```

If there's a carriage return at the end of the shebang line (e.g., #! /bin/sh^M), the operating system will look for an interpreter whose name ends with a CR, and will (almost certainly) not find one. The script will not run.

How It Works

This script uses sed to remove the carriage returns. On a string, or a few lines, you could remove the CRs in the shell itself (line=${line%$CR}), but sed is faster on all but very short files.

Carriage returns are legitimate characters in text files, even in shell scripts. In some scripts, a literal CR is assign to a variable, so that it is not removed by a conversion program. This script removes carriage returns from line endings but leaves them anywhere else on a line.

Usage

```
dos2unix FILE [...]
```

The Script

```
CR=$(printf "\r") ## or source standard-vars
progname=${0##*/}
tempfile=$(mktemp $progname.XXXXXX) || exit 5
for file
do
    sed "s/$CR$//" "$file" > "$tempfile" &&
    mv "$tempfile" "$file"
done
```

2.2 unix2dos—Convert a Unix File to Windows

Under Windows, a file with Unix line endings (just LF), may look even stranger than a Windows file on Unix:

```
#! /bin/sh
        echo "Defenestration required"
                                exit
```

■ **Tip**   While some methods of copying from one system to another will do the conversion, it could be safer to convert a file explicitly before copying.

How It Works

This script adds a carriage return to the end of each line so that all lines have a CR/LF pair. Existing CRs will not be duplicated.

Usage

```
unix2dos FILE [...]
```

The Script

```
progname=${0##*/}
CR=$(printf "\r")
tempfile=$(mktemp $progname.XXXXXX) || exit 5
for file
do
    sed -e "s/$/$CR/" -e "s/$CR$CR$/$CR/" "$file" > "$tempfile" &&
    mv "$tempfile" "$file"
done
```

2.3 mac2unix—Convert Macintosh Files to Unix

Macintosh files use a carriage return instead of a linefeed as the line terminator. To a Unix system, these files appear as a single long line. Since they have no linefeed characters, they are not valid Unix text files.

On Mac OS/X, which is Unix-based, you may need to do conversions even if you're not copying to another system. Shell scripts need Unix line endings, and many Unix tools on OS/X require LF, not CR, between lines.

How It Works

Mac files can present even more problems than Windows files. Since there are no line feeds, the entire file is on a single line. Many Unix text utilities will not operate on long lines.

This script uses tr, which has no such limitations since it reads and translates individual characters.

Usage

```
mac2unix FILE [...]
```

The Script

```
progname=${0##*/}
tempfile=`mktemp $progname.XXXXXX` || exit 5
for file
do
    tr '\015' '\012' < "$file" > "$tempfile" &&
    mv "$tempfile" "$file"
done
```

2.4 unix2mac—Convert Unix Files to Mac Format

Mac OS/X sometimes requires Unix-type line endings. In such cases, no changes to the Unix line endings are necessary. For the other times (and for pre-OS/X systems), conversion must be done.

How It Works

Since this conversion is a simple one-to-one character translation, tr is the obvious tool to use. This script converts linefeeds to carriage returns, i.e., from Unix to Mac format.

Usage

```
unix2mac FILE [...]
```

The Script

```
progname=${0##*/}
tempfile=$(mktemp $progname.XXXXXX) || exit 5
for file
do
    ## Old versions of tr do not understand \r and \n
    ## the octal codes work on all versions
    tr '\012' '\015' < "$file" > "$tempfile" &&
    mv "$tempfile" "$file"
done
```

2.5 dos2mac—Convert Windows Files to Macintosh

To convert MS-DOS/Windows files to Macintosh format, the LF must be removed.

How It Works

A lazy way could be to combine two existing scripts like:

```
dos2unix "$@"
unix2mac "$@"
```

It is more efficient, however, just to remove the linefeeds with tr.

Usage

```
dos2mac FILE [...]
```

The Script

```
progname=${0##*/}
tempfile=$(mktemp $progname.XXXXXX) || exit 5
for file
do
    tr -d '\012' < "$file" > "$tempfile" &&
    mv "$tempfile" "$file"
done
```

2.6 mac2dos—Convert Macintosh Files to Windows

To prepare a Mac file for use on Windows, the carriage returns must be converted to CR/LF pairs.

How It Works

The obvious tool is sed, but some versions are limited in the maximum line length they can process, and an entire Mac file looks like a single line. To get around this, mac2dos first uses tr to convert the CRs to LFs.

Usage

```
mac2dos FILE [...]
```

The Script

```
progname=${0##*/}
tempfile=`mktemp $progname.XXXXXX` || exit 5
for file
do
    { tr '\015' '\012' < "$file" || continue; } |
        sed -e "s/$/$CR/"  > "$tempfile" &&
            mv "$tempfile" "$file"
done
```

Displaying Files

There are many ways to display a file. The simplest is cat, which copies a file or files to stdout. The POSIX specification for cat only requires one option, -u, which may be ignored.

Two common pagers, more and less, enable a user to scroll through the file one screen at a time. To print a file with page breaks or multiple columns, there's pr. The following scripts display the contents of files in different ways.

2.7 prn—Print File with Line Numbers

"I want to number the lines of a file."

"So do I, but I don't want blank lines numbered."

"I want the blank lines numbered, but I want consecutive blank lines to be suppressed; I just want one blank line when there are more, one after another, in the file."

How It Works

Many versions of cat can do all that, but some cannot, and line numbering is not required by the POSIX standard for cat. There are other commands that can print a file with line numbers: less and pr. Not all versions of pr support line numbering, though POSIX requires it.

This script adds options that are present in some versions of cat: squeeze adjacent blank lines; do not number blank lines; start numbering a number other than 1. And one that might not be seen elsewhere: truncate lines that exceed the terminal width.

Usage

```
prn [-b][-s][-n N][-t] [FILE ...]
```

If no file is given on the command line, standard input will be used. There are five options:

- b: Do not number blank lines.

- s: Squeeze multiple consecutive blank lines into one.

- n NUM: Start numbering with NUM.

- N NUM: Numbering will be NUM characters wide.

- -t: Truncate the lines to the width of the screen or window.

```
$ printf "%s\n" "the" "quick" "brown" "fox" "" "jumped" "over" | prn -b
    1 the
    2 quick
    3 brown
    4 fox

    5 jumped
    6 over
$ prn -tN 2 kjv.txt | head
 1 Genesis:01:001:001:In the beginning God created the heaven and the earth.
 2 Genesis:01:001:002:And the earth was without form, and void; and darkness was
 3 Genesis:01:001:003:And God said, Let there be light: and there was light.
 4 Genesis:01:001:004:And God saw the light, that it was good: and God divided t
 5 Genesis:01:001:005:And God called the light Day, and the darkness he called N
 6 Genesis:01:001:006:And God said, Let there be a firmament in the midst of the
 7 Genesis:01:001:007:And God made the firmament, and divided the waters which w
 8 Genesis:01:001:008:And God called the firmament Heaven. And the evening and t
```

The Script

```
progname=${0##*/}
version=1.0

die() {
    error=$1
    shift
    printf "%s: %s\n" "$progname" "$*" >&2
    exit $error
}
```

```
blank=1
truncate=0
suppress=0
nwidth=5
cchar=
last=
opts=bstn:N:
n=1
while getopts $opts var
do
  case $var in
      b) blank=0 ;;
      s) suppress=1 ;;
      n) case $OPTARG in
          *[!0-9]*) die 5 "Numeric value required"
         esac
         n=$OPTARG
         ;;
      N) case $OPTARG in
          *[!0-9]*) die 5 "Numeric value required"
         esac
         nwidth=$OPTARG
         ;;
      t) truncate=1 ;;
  esac
done
shift $(( $OPTIND - 1 ))

if [ $truncate -eq 1 ]
then
  width=$(( $COLUMNS - ${nwidth} + 1 ))
  fmt="%${nwidth}d %-${width}.${width}s\n"
else
  fmt="%5d %s\n"
fi

cat ${1+"$@"} | {
  while IFS= read -r line
  do
    case $line in
      "") [ "$last" = "" ] && [ $suppress -eq 1 ] && continue
          [ $blank -eq 0 ] && {
              echo
              last=$line
              continue
          } ;;
    esac
    printf "$fmt" $n "$line" last=$line
    n=$(( $n + 1 ))
  done
}
```

2.8 prw—Print One Word per Line

For various reasons, you might sometimes need to print all words in a file on separate lines. Some of those reasons are shown in other scripts in this book (wfreq, for example, which appears later in the chapter).

How It Works

As often happens when I commit a relatively simple task to a file, I think of embellishments. Originally designed solely to pipe a file, one word at a time, to other scripts, prw has been somewhat enhanced. One can now specify more than one word per line, and specify the width of the column used for each word. The words can be printed flush left or flush right within that width.

Input can be one or more files, or the standard input if no file is given on the command line.

Usage

prw [OPTIONS] [FILE ..]

- -n NUM: Print NUM words per line.
- -w NUM: Use NUM columns per word.
- -W NUM: Print words flush right in NUM columns.

Here are a few examples:

```
$ prw $HOME/.bashrc | head -8
#
~/.bashrc:

executed
by
bash(1)
for
non-login
shells.

$ echo "the quick brown fox jumps over the lazy dog" | prw -n 2 -w 20
the                 quick
brown               fox
jumps               over
the                 lazy
dog
$ echo "Now is the time for all good men to come to the aid of the party" |
    prw -n 3 -W 15
          Now            is            the
         time           for            all
         good           men             to
         come            to            the
          aid            of            the
        party
```

The Script

```
die() {
    printf "%s: %s\n" "$progname" "$*" >&2
    exit $1
}

NL=`
`
version="1.0"
progname=${0##*/}
num=0
flush_r=-
err1="Numeric value required"

while getopts Vn:w:W: var
do
  case $var in
      n) case $OPTARG in
           *[!0-9]*) die "$err1" ;;
         esac
         num=$OPTARG
         ;;
      w) case $OPTARG in
           *[!0-9]*) die 1 "$err1" ;;
         esac
         width=$OPTARG ;;
      W) case $OPTARG in
           *[!0-9]*) die 1 "$err1" ;;
         esac
         width=$OPTARG
         flush_r= ;;
      V) printf "%s: %s\n" "$progname" "$version"; exit ;;
  esac
done
shift $(( $OPTIND - 1 ))

fmt=%${width:+$flush_r$width.$width}s
n=0
while [ $(( n += 1 )) -lt $num ]
do
  fmt="${fmt:+$fmt }%${width:+$flush_r$width.$width}s"
done

cat ${1+"$@"} |
  while read -r line
  do
    printf "${fmt:-%s}\n" ${line}
  done
```

2.9 wbl—Sort Words by Length

By their very nature, shell scripts are often specialized for very esoteric purposes. There are many such scripts. Who else would want to sort a list of words by their lengths?

In fact, someone in the `comp.unix.shell` newsgroup asked how to sort the output of `ls` by length of filename. Why did they want that? no idea; perhaps it was a homework exercise. But there was a script lying around that did the job.

My reason for having it relates to one of my professions (Chris): I compose cryptic crosswords for a magazine and a newspaper. Having words sorted by length is an absolute necessity for finding words to fit in a crossword grid. It also accounts for the number of scripts in this book that play with words (and can be used to help solve crossword puzzles or to set them).

How It Works

By printing the words one each, flush right on very wide lines, `sort` will, in effect, sort by word length. The leading spaces are then trimmed. The original script was a one-liner, but some options have been added.

Usage

```
wbl [-ufr][-R RANGE] [FILE ...]
```

All of the four options may be used at once:

- `-u`: Eliminate duplicates.

- `-f`: Make the sort case insensitive (A equals a).

- `-r`: Reverse the sorting order, print longest words first.

- `-R "RANGE"`: Accept all characters in RANGE as part of a word. The default is "[A-Z][a-z]"; to include hyphenated words as a single word, use "[A-Z][a-z]-". Note that a hyphen must not appear at the beginning of RANGE, nor between two characters that are not the boundaries of a range.

```
$ printf "%s\n" the quick brown fox jumps over the lazy dog | wbl -u
dog
fox
the
lazy
over
brown
jumps
quick
```

The Script

```
range=[a-z][A-Z]
opts=
while getopts ufrR: var
do
  case $var in
      u) opts="$opts -u" ;;
      f) opts="$opts -f" ;;
      r) opts="$opts -r" ;;
      R) range=$OPTARG ;;
  esac
done
shift $(( $OPTIND - 1 ))

## convert any character that is not a letter to a newline
out=$(cat ${1+"$@"} | tr -cs "$range" "[\012*]")

## print all the words flush right across 99 columns
out=$(printf "%99s\n" $out | sort $opts)

## print all the words without the leading spaces
printf "%s\n" $out
```

Formatting File Facts

One can use many commands to get information about a file. Some are universal; some are limited to certain operating systems. The nicest (I have come across) is GNU stat, which is standard on recent GNU/Linux systems. It allows you to select the information you want and the format of the output. Others include ls, wc, and file.

The scripts in this section combine these commands and others to give you even more information about a file or files.

2.10 finfo—File Information Display

One often wants more information about a file than any single utility provides, but combining the output of multiple commands can be tricky.

How It Works

Much of the information about a file can be gleaned from the output of ls -l. The finfo command parses the output of that command, then uses wc and file to get more information about the file.

Usage

```
finfo [OPTIONS] FILE [...]
```

The options are as follows:

- -z: Do not show files of zero length.

- -D: Do not show directories.

- -H: Do not print header (in summary mode).

- -s: Show summary, one line per file.

- -c: Clear screen between files (expanded mode).

- -h: Print usage information and exit.

- -V: Print script's version and exit.

If you want a summary of your files, use finfo -s:

```
LINES   WORDS   SIZE FILE NAME        FILE TYPE
   27     185   1265 Ack.shtml         HTML document text
   10      76    528 bio.txt           ASCII English text
  105     284   2148 cpsh-sh           a sh script text executable
   63     133   1164 dehex-sh          Bourne-Again shell script text executable
   16      46    330 dos2mac-sh        a sh script text executable
```

If you want each file's information in a separate section, use finfo without any options (except the file pattern), for example:

```
$ finfo Ack.shtml

         Name: Ack.shtml
         Type: HTML document text
        Inode: 611116
         Size: 1265
        Lines: 27
        Words: 185
  Owner:group: chris:chris
  Permissions: -rw-rw-r--
         Date: Aug 12 15:51
```

The Script

```
file_info()
{
    ifile=$1
    [ -r "$ifile" ] || return 5
    [ -d "$ifile" ] && [ $nodirs -ge 1 ] && return 1
    set -- `wc "$file" 2>/dev/null` `file
    "$file"`
    lines=$1
    words=$2
    size=$3
    shift 5
```

```
    file_type=$*
    case $file in
      *[-.]sh) desc=`grep -i "description=" "$file"`
               desc=${desc#*description=}
               desc=${desc%%$NL*}
               ;;
      *) desc= ;;
    esac
}

NL=
progname=${0##*/}
version=1.0
cu_up="\e[A" ## ANSI code to move cursor up one line
summary=0
clear=0
noheader=0
empty=0
nodirs=0

opts=csHVz

while getopts $opts var
do
  case $var in
      c) clear=1 ;;
      D) nodirs=1 ;;
      H) noheader=1 ;;
      s) summary=1 ;;
      z) empty=1 ;;

      V) printf "%s\n" "$progname, version $version" ; exit ;;
  esac
done
shift $(( $OPTIND - 1 ))

_ll=6
_wl=6
_cl=7
_fl=25
_tl=$(( $COLUMNS - $_ll - $_wl - $_cl - $_fl - 4 ))
_sfl=$(( $COLUMNS - 15 ))

## create a bar wide enough to fill the width of the screen or window
bar=------------------------------------------
while [ ${#bar} -lt ${COLUMNS} ]
do
    bar=$bar$bar$bar
done
## or you can use the repeat function from the next chapter
## bar=$(repeat --- $COLUMNS)
```

```
[ $noheader -eq 0 -a $summary -eq 1 ] && {
  printf "\n%${_ll}s %${_wl}s %${_cl}s %-${_fl}.${_fl}s %-${_tl}.${_tl}s\n" \
      LINES WORDS SIZE "FILE NAME" "FILE TYPE"
  printf "%${COLUMNS}.${COLUMNS}s" "$bar"
}

#############################################################################

## If you are using an older version of Solaris or SunOS,
## in which ls -l doesn't print the group, uncomment the following line
## ls_opt=-g
#############################################################################

ls -il $ls_opt "$@" |
 while read inode perms links owner group size month day time file
 do
   [ $empty -eq 1 -a ${size:-0} -eq 0 ] && continue

   ## Extract file name if it's a symbolic link;
   ## this will fail in the unlikely event that
   ## the target of the link contains " -> "
   ## See Chapter 6 for a script to fix badly formed filenames
   case $perms in
       l*) file=${file% -\> *} ;;
   esac
   file_info "$file" || continue
   if [ $summary -ge 1 ]
   then
     printf "%${_ll}d %${_wl}d %${_cl}d %-${_fl}.${_fl}s %-${_tl}.${_tl}s\n" \
            $lines $words $size "$file" "$file_type"
   else
     [ $clear -ge 1 ] && printf "${CLS:=`clear`}"
     printf "\n\n"
     printf "        Name: %-${_sfl}.${_sfl}s\n" "$file"
     printf "        Type: %-${_sfl}.${_sfl}s\n" "$file_type"
     printf "        Inode: %-${_sfl}.${_sfl}s\n" "$inode"
     [ -n "$desc" ] &&
     printf " Description: %-${_sfl}.${_sfl}s\n" "$desc"
     printf "        Size: %-${_sfl}.${_sfl}s\n" "$size"
     printf "       Lines: %-${_sfl}.${_sfl}s\n" "$lines"
     printf "       Words: %-${_sfl}.${_sfl}s\n" "$words"
     printf " Owner:group: %-${_sfl}.${_sfl}s\n" "$owner:$group"
     printf " Permissions: %-${_sfl}.${_sfl}s\n" "$perms"
     printf "        Date: %-${_sfl}.${_sfl}s\n" "$month $day $time"
     printf "\n\n   Press ENTER (q=Quit)\r"
     read x </dev/tty
     case $x in
         q|Q) break;;
     esac
     printf "$cu_up%${COLUMNS}.${COLUMNS}s\n" "$bar"
   fi
 done
```

57

2.11 wfreq—Word Frequency

What is the most frequently used word in the file? How can I get a list of all the words and the number of times they appear?

How It Works

Use wfreq to get a list of all the words and their frequency in one or more files. If no file is given on the command line, standard input is counted.

Usage

wfreq [FILE ...]

The Script

```
prw ${1+"$@"} |
    tr -cd 'a-zA-Z-\n' |
        sort |
            uniq -c |
                sort -n
```

2.12 lfreq—Letter Frequency

Shell scripts can be good for providing interesting tidbits of information, like printing the number of instances of each letter of the alphabet in a piece of text.

How It Works

When a friend asked whether it was true that certain letters occurred in my crossword puzzles more frequently than would be expected in normal text, I wrote the first version of this script. After running a few puzzles through it, I was somewhat surprised that, despite the small sample (150 to 160 letters per puzzle), the range was consistent with typical distribution in the English language.

Usage

lfreq [FILE ...]

A sample cryptic crossword grid shows a fairly normal distribution of letters for the English language:

```
$ grid='
SOMEBODY.ABUSES
Y.Y.A.I...E.E.I
PROGRESS.TRIPOD
H.P.T.C...E.A.E
OXIDE.OVERTHROW
N.A.N.N.D...A.A
....DETRIMENTAL
T.T.E.I.F.N.E.K
REARRANGING....
O.P...U.C.R.N.T
PHENOMENA.ARENA
I.S.M...T.I.W.N
CUTTER.WINNIPEG
A.R.G...O.E.U.L
LAYMAN.INEDIBLE'
$ echo "$grid" | lfreq-sh | column
```

1 F	3 B	4 L	5 M	10 O
15 A				
1 K	3 C	4 U	6 D	11 T
16 N				
1 V	3 H	4 Y	6 P	13 I
22 E				
1 X	3 W	5 G	6 S	13 R

The Script

```
NL='
'
sed -e "s/./\\${NL}&/g" ${1+"$@"} |
    sort |
      grep . |
        uniq -c |
          sort -n
```

Notes

Since this script was written to analyze the letters in a crossword grid in which all the letters are capital, upper- and lowercase letters are not combined.

If you want to count upper- and lowercase as the same letter, add this line before sort:

```
tr '[a-z]' '[A-Z]' |
```

Another method is to add the -f option to sort and the -i option to uniq.

If you like, you can also add accented characters to the translation mix. Newer versions of tr will do it (if the locale is set correctly) with this:

```
tr '[:lower:]' '[:upper:]' |
```

2.13 fed—A Simple Batch File Editor

One frequently needs to make a change over one or more files. It can be tedious work when done manually, but a script can do it in the blink of an eye.

How It Works

While a simple script cannot duplicate all the complexities of awk or sed, some common tasks are easily automated. The file editor, fed, can do simple tasks: It can delete lines, or perform a search and replace. It can operate on one or more files. Test mode shows the differences between the file and the edited version instead of replacing the original file.

Usage

```
fed [OPTIONS] FILE [...]
```

- -d RE: Delete lines containing regular expression, RE, replace them with STR if -r is used.

- -s RE: Search pattern (regular expression).

- -r STR: Replace search pattern with STR.

- -t: Test mode—show changes that would be made (using diff) instead of replacing the file.

Here are a few examples:

```
## Delete all lines beginning with an octothorpe (#)
## in files whose names end with .txt
fed -d '^#' *.txt

## Replace all lines beginning with an octothorpe (#) with "## Comment deleted"
## in all files whose names end with .sh
fed -d '^#' -r "## Comment deleted" *.sh

## Replace all instances of 4 consecutive lower case letters with a single "X"
fed -s '[a-z][a-z][a-z][a-z]' -r X *.txt

## Delete all lines containing a number, but just show the changes
## that would be made, leaving the original files intact
fed -td "[0-9]" $FILES
```

Remember to quote spaces and wildcard characters in any of the strings (and the patterns if the characters are to be matched literally).

The Script

```
escape_slash() {
    string=$1
    case ${BASH_VERSION%%.*} in
        "") string= ;;
        [2-9] | [1-9][0-9]) string=${string//\///\\/} ;;
        *) string=`echo "$string" | sed 's|/|\\/|g'` ;;
    esac
}

version="1.0"
progname=${0##*/}
delete_str=
replace_str=
search_str=
test=0
sed_cmd=

while getopts vVh-:s:r:d:t var
do
  case $var in
    d) search_str=.*$OPTARG.* ;;
    r) replace_str=$OPTARG ;;
    s) search_str=$OPTARG ;;
    t) test=1 ;;
    v) verbose=$(( $verbose + 1 )) ;;
  esac
done
shift $(( $OPTIND - 1 ))

case $verbose in
    2) set -v ;;
    3) set -x ;;
esac

[ -n "$search_str" ] && {
  escape_slash "$search_str"
  search_str=$string
  escape_slash "$replace_str"
  sed_cmd="-e 's/$search_str/$string/g'"
}

[ -z "$sed_cmd" ] && { usage; exit 5; }
```

```
tempfile=`mktemp $progname.XXXXXX` || exit 5
for file
do
  eval "sed $sed_cmd \"$file\" > $tempfile"
  if [ $test -ge 1 ]
  then
    printf "\n%s:\n" "$file"
    diff "$file" "$tempfile" || printf "\n"
  else
    mv "$tempfile" "$file"
  fi
done
[ -f "$tempfile" ] && rm "$tempfile"
```

Summary

These scripts have looked at generic text files. The contents have been irrelevant (line endings are formatting, rather than content in our opinion). Some of these, because they are not specific to any one file format, will show up in other chapters as commands used by those scripts.

Many other scripts throughout the book deal with file manipulation, from standard Unix configuration files to obscure formats for crossword puzzles. Some will be used to extract and present information from files, others will manipulate the files themselves, or create new ones.

Besides being useful on their own, these scripts can be modified to apply to different situations. Feel free to experiment, but, as always, experiment on copies of your files!

■ ■ ■

## CHAPTER 3

String Briefs

When I was introduced to Bourne shell scripting, I took to it immediately, despite some obvious deficiencies in the language. One of the features missing was string manipulation. It existed, but almost everything had to be done with external commands that were loaded from the disk each time. The KornShell introduced a number of parameter expansion modifiers that drastically reduced the number of calls to external commands. These were copied by other shells and incorporated into the POSIX standard.

To take full advantage of the POSIX features, all these scripts are presented as functions that are comprised in two libraries, char-funcs and string-funcs. Sourcing these files in your .profile makes them available at the command line. (Replace .profile with whatever file your shell uses.) Many of these functions, however, will rarely be used except in larger scripts, and they will be used in programs that appear later in the book. Strings are generally a subset of characters allowed in text files. For most practical purposes, they contain only printable characters. Most of the functions in this chapter are intended for use only with ASCII characters in the range 1 to 126, though most will work with an extended ASCII character set.

Traditionally, each character that appears on the screen is contained in an 8-bit byte. Since each bit can be either 1 or 0, a byte has 256 possible values. The ASCII character set is a set of 7-bit numbers, containing 128 possible values, that represent control codes, letters, numbers, and punctuation. The characters 0 to 31 are control codes, 48 to 57 are the digits 0 to 9, 65 to 90 are the capital letters, and 97 to 122 the lowercase letters. Punctuation is scattered through the remaining values in the 0-to-127 range.

The remaining 128 values, from 128 to 255, are used in various "extended ASCII" codings, such as the DOS line-drawing characters or the ISO 8559-1 LATIN-1 character set, which contains the accented characters used by western European languages.

Character Actions: The char-funcs Library

Many operations are required on individual characters — the building blocks of strings. In this section you are presented with functions that convert to and from numeric values, that capitalize letters and that find the next character in sequence. These functions convert single characters. All work with multiple arguments, but may not be efficient when used on a large number of them. Their operations are all done on single characters, not strings. If an argument has more than one character, only the first is used.

3.1 chr—Convert a Decimal Number to an ASCII Character

As this chapter was being put together (first edition), someone in the comp.unix.shell newsgroup asked how to convert a number to its character representation. The ASCII character 65 is a capital A; 32 is a space; 49 is a 1. That's all very well, but how does one convert 65 to A?

63

How It Works

I posted a function that I have been using for a long time. I thought that it would be good to include it here, along with a number of other conversion functions. Unfortunately, I ran into problems when I tested it with other shells, and on other systems. (Chris)

■ **Note**   While Chris started off with the 8-bit Commodore, my 8-bit machine was the Sinclair ZX Spectrum. One of the things that I recollect about the simplest way to turn capitalization on or off was to alter the 6th bit. The 6th bit is 25 which is 32. Upper case A is ASCII 65 and lower case a is ASCII 97.

I wrote about half a dozen variations, but only one worked on all systems and with all shells. Surprisingly, considering that it uses an external program, awk, it is faster than most shell-only solutions.

Usage

```
chr [-s S][-n] NN [...]
```

The arguments are integers between 1 and 255 inclusive, and are converted to the corresponding ASCII character. The -s option is followed by a separator string that is printed after each character. By default, there is no separator, and the characters are run together as a word.

The -n option suppresses the final new line, a useful feature when called multiple times from another script.

```
$ chr 115 99 114 105 112 116 script
$ chr $(( 119 - 32 )) 114 105 116 101 114
Writer
$ chr -s . 72 65 76
H.A.L.
```

The Script

```
chr()
{
    ## defaults can be changed by command-line options
    sep=      ## nothing is inserted between characters
    nl='\n'   ## a new line is printed after all arguments are processed

    ## Parse command-line options
    OPTIND=1
    while getopts s:n var
    do
      case $var in
        s) sep=$OPTARG ;; ## separator string to place between characters
        n) nl= ;;         ## suppress newline
      esac
      done
      shift $(( $OPTIND - 1 ))
```

```
    ## pipe arguments, 1 to a line, into awk, which converts the numbers
    ## into the equivalent character
    printf "%s\n" "$@" | awk '{printf "%c%s", $1, sep}' sep="$sep"
    printf "%b" "$nl"
}
```

3.2 asc—Convert a Character to Its Decimal Equivalent

What number represents the ASCII character M? What is *? How can I find the ASCII code for any given character?

How It Works

The POSIX specification of the printf command has the answer:

> *If the leading character is a single-quote or double-quote, the value shall be the numeric value in the underlying codeset of the character following the single-quote or double- quote.*

For the sake of convenience, I have encapsulated the code in the asc function.

Usage

asc C [...]

Only the first character of each argument is converted.

```
$ asc asc
97
$ asc a serious question
97
115
113
```

Remember to quote characters that have special meaning to the shell:

```
$ asc "*"
42
```

The Script

```
asc()
{
    ## loop through the arguments on the command line
    for char
    do
```

```
    ## print the ASCII value of the first character of $char
    printf "%d\n" "'$char" 2>/dev/null
  done
}
```

Notes

Possible additions to asc include specifying a separation character, as demonstrated in the chr function; the $sep variable would replace \n:

```
printf "%d${sep:-\\n}" "'$char"
```

The function could then be called with

```
$ sep=' ' asc A C E
65 67 69
```

3.3 nxt—Get the Next Character in ASCII Sequence

Generating the next number in sequence is easy; just add one to the previous number. It is not as simple to do the same thing with letters, such as when naming a series of files. If you have file pic1a, the next file will be pic1b; if you have piano-P.ogg, then it would be piano-Q.ogg. If you need to change only one or two files, you wouldn't mind a bit of typing; if you have hundreds (or even dozens) of files, you will need a script to do it.

How It Works

There are various ways to do it, and you'll find other methods later in the book. For now, we'll use the nxt function. This script allows you not only to derive the next letter (or other character) in sequence, but also to return a character any number of places forward—or backward—in the ASCII character set.

Usage

```
nxt [+|-N] C
```

By default, nxt delivers the next higher character, but, with an optional argument, it can print a character at any offset from the one given. Here are some examples:

```
$ nxt H
I
$ nxt +5 a
f
```

A negative offset prints earlier characters:

```
$ nxt -9 n o w
e
f
n
```

Since the output of nxt is produced by the chr function, it is handy to have a method to specify options to control the way that function prints its results. The is done with the chr_opts variable. If we are converting several characters, it is likely that we do not want the default behavior:

```
$ nxt H A L
I
B
M
```

Rather, all the letters should appear on the same line. To do that, we want nxt to call chr with the -n option. With the -s option, we can specify a separator character for chr to print after each conversion. By defining chr-opts ahead of nxt on the same line, its value will only apply during the call to nxt:

```
$ chr_opts="-ns." nxt H A L
I.B.M.
```

The Script

```
nxt()
{
    ## The default increment is 1, the next character
    inc=1
    case $1 in
        [+-]*[!0-9]*) ;;        ## no increment is specified, so use the default
        [+-][0-9]*) inc=$1      ## increment line may be positive or negative
                shift           ## remove increment from positional parameters
                ;;
        *) ;;
    esac
    for asc in $(asc $*)        ## loop through the converted arguments
    do
     chr $chr_opts $(( $asc + ${inc#+} )) ## convert incremented number to character
    done
    printf "\n"
}
```

3.4 upr—Convert Character(s) to Uppercase

Even though most shells have command-line key combinations that convert a word to capital letters, or just capitalize the first letter, these do not operate on the contents of variables; they change the actual characters on the command line; that is, the name of the variable, not its contents. To convert the contents of a variable, a script (or other utility) is needed.

How It Works

In the ASCII character set, capital letters are 32 characters to the left of the lowercase letters. The nxt command (described previously) with an option of -32 will convert a letter to uppercase. Or use upr, which is faster, uses only the first letter if a word is given as an argument, and only converts lowercase letters.

Using the convention described in Chapter 1, this command comes as a pair of functions. One begins with an underscore, and stores the result in a variable; the second calls the first and prints the contents of that variable. In upr as in a number of other such paired functions, the second function can take multiple arguments.

Usage

```
_upr c
upr c [...]
```

Here's an example:

```
$ upr a b c
A
B
C
```

Since upr only converts the first character, it is easy to capitalize words:

```
$ b=bash
$ _upr $b
$ printf "%c%s\n" "$_UPR" "${b#?}"
Bash
```

The Script

```
_upr()
{
    ## a look-up table is the fastest method
    case $1 in
        a*) _UPR=A ;;          b*) _UPR=B ;;
        c*) _UPR=C ;;          d*) _UPR=D ;;
        e*) _UPR=E ;;          f*) _UPR=F ;;
        g*) _UPR=G ;;          h*) _UPR=H ;;
        i*) _UPR=I ;;          j*) _UPR=J ;;
        k*) _UPR=K ;;          l*) _UPR=L ;;
        m*) _UPR=M ;;          n*) _UPR=N ;;
        o*) _UPR=O ;;          p*) _UPR=P ;;
        q*) _UPR=Q ;;          r*) _UPR=R ;;
        s*) _UPR=S ;;          t*) _UPR=T ;;
        u*) _UPR=U ;;          v*) _UPR=V ;;
        w*) _UPR=W ;;          x*) _UPR=X ;;
        y*) _UPR=Y ;;          z*) _UPR=Z ;;
        *) _UPR=${1%${1#?}} ;;
    esac
}
```

```
upr()
{
    _UPR=
    ## convert character[s] to upper case
    for chr
    do
        _upr "$chr"
        printf "%s${sep:-\\n}" "$_UPR"
    done
    printf "${_UPR:+\n}"
}
```

Notes

As scripts go, _upr is inelegant, but it is fast, and once it is hidden away in a library, you never need see it again. A shorter but slower solution is to use a wrapper for the nxt function:

```
upr()
{
    ## loop through the command-line arguments
    for chr
    do
      case $chr in
          [a-z]*) chr_opts="-n" nxt -32 "$chr" ;;
          *) printf "%c${sep}" "$chr" 2>/dev/null ;;
      esac
    done
}
```

3.5 lwr—Convert Character(s) to Lowercase

The tr command can convert characters to lowercase, but an external command is an inefficient way to convert a single character. A shell function is much faster.

How It Works

A simple look-up table is the fastest way to convert a single character from uppercase to lowercase.

Usage

```
_lwr C      ## sets the _LWR variable
lwr C [...] ## prints the result(s)
```

If you want to assign the result to a variable, use the underscore version:

```
$ _lwr X
$ var=$_LWR
```

The second version is for printing the result:

```
$ lwr W
w
```

The Script

```
_lwr()
{
    _LWR=
    case $1 in
        A*) _LWR=a ;;          B*) _LWR=b ;;
        C*) _LWR=c ;;          D*) _LWR=d ;;
        E*) _LWR=e ;;          F*) _LWR=f ;;
        G*) _LWR=g ;;          H*) _LWR=h ;;
        I*) _LWR=i ;;          J*) _LWR=j ;;
        K*) _LWR=k ;;          L*) _LWR=l ;;
        M*) _LWR=m ;;          N*) _LWR=n ;;
        O*) _LWR=o ;;          P*) _LWR=p ;;
        Q*) _LWR=q ;;          R*) _LWR=r ;;
        S*) _LWR=s ;;          T*) _LWR=t ;;
        U*) _LWR=u ;;          V*) _LWR=v ;;
        W*) _LWR=w ;;          X*) _LWR=x ;;
        Y*) _LWR=y ;;          Z*) _LWR=z ;;
        *) _LWR=${1%${1#?}} ;;
    esac
}

lwr()
{

    ## convert character[s] to lower case
    for chr
    do
     _lwr "$chr" && printf "%s" "$_LWR"
    done
    printf "${_LWR:+\n}"
}
```

Notes

This more compact version, using the nxt function from earlier in the chapter, may look better, but is far slower.

```
lwr()
{
    ## convert character[s] to lower case
    for chr
    do
```

```
      case $chr in
          [A-Z]*) chr_opts="-n" nxt +32 "$chr" ;;
          *) printf "%c " "$chr" ;;
      esac
    done
}
```

String Cleaning: The string-funcs Library

Extracting, removing, and replacing sections of a string are everyday tasks. The functions in the previous section operated on characters; in this section, they act on whole strings. (Most of these functions come in pairs, one which performs the operation and stores it in a variable, the other calling the first function and printing the result; this is described in more detail in Chapter 1.)

3.6 sub—Replace First Occurrence of a Pattern

Replacing one word or character with another is a most basic operation. When changing an entire file, the Unix command sed is the obvious method to use. If you are making the change in a single line, or even a single word, sed, because it is an external command, is slower than a shell function.

How It Works

If you use the sub function, the parameter expansion capability of the POSIX shell is utilized, and no external command is necessary. Not only that, but it cuts down on the amount of typing you have to do. As an added bonus, you can use a wildcard pattern to select the text to be replaced.

Usage

```
sub STRING PATTERN [TEXT]
```

If a string matching PATTERN is found within STRING, its first occurrence will be replaced by TEXT. To see how it works, first assign a value to the variable, string:

```
string="The quick brown fox"
```

Here's a sample showing the commands as typed, along with the result:

```
$ sub "$string" quick nervous
The nervous brown fox
$ sub "$string" " " "_"
The_quick brown fox
```

By not supplying a replacement text, the PATTERN will be deleted instead of replaced; more accurately, it will be replaced by a null string.

```
$ sub "$string" "quick "
The brown fox
```

71

The Script

```
_sub()
{
    _SUB=$1
    [ -n "$2" ] || return 1 ## nothing to search for: error
    s_srch=${2} ## pattern to replace
    rep=$3 ## replacement string
    case $_SUB in *$s_srch*)      ## if pattern exists in the string
            sr1=${_SUB%%$s_srch*}  ## take the string preceding the first match
            sr2=${_SUB#*$s_srch}   ## and the string following the first match
            _SUB=$sr1$rep$sr2      ## and sandwich the replacement string between them
            ;;
            *) return 1 ;; ## if the pattern does not exist, return an error code
    esac
}

sub()
{
    _sub "$@" && printf "%s\n" "$_SUB"
}
```

Notes

Both bash2+ and ksh93 have an additional form of parameter expansion that can make this function much shorter:

```
_sub() {
    _SUB=${1/$2/$3}
}
```

A corollary function, rsub, replaces the last instance of the pattern instead of the first:

```
_rsub()
{
    str=$1
    [ "$2" ] || return 1
    s_srch=${2}
    rep=$3
    case $str in *$s_srch*)
            sr1=${str%$s_srch*}
            sr2=${str##*$s_srch}
            _RSUB=$sr1$rep$sr2
            ;;
            *) _RSUB=
                false ;;
    esac
}
```

```
rsub()
{

    _rsub "$@" && printf "%s\n" "$_RSUB"
}
```

3.7 gsub—Globally Replace a Pattern in a String

Globally replacing a text pattern in a string with another is a simple job for a POSIX shell. No external command is required.

How It Works

The gsub function uses the same syntax as the previous script, sub, but it doesn't stop after one replacement.

Usage

```
gsub STRING PATTERN [TEXT]
```

If a string matching PATTERN is found within STRING, all occurrences will be replaced by TEXT. We'll trap a fox in the variable, string, to demonstrate:

```
string="The quick brown fox"
```

Often useful for fixing filenames, this command replaces all the spaces in string with underscores:

```
$ gsub "$string" " " "_"
The_quick_brown_fox
```

Not supplying a replacement text causes all occurrences of PATTERN to be deleted instead of replaced.

```
$ gsub "$string" " "
Thequickbrownfox
```

Using a wildcard pattern will replace all substrings that match. For example, to change any letter from a to m with Q:

```
$ gsub "$string" "[a-m]" Q
TQQ quQQQ Qrown Qox
```

The wildcard can be negated, so that all characters except those in the pattern will be changed or deleted:

```
$ gsub "$string" "[!a-m]"
heickbf
```

How many os are there in the string? By deleting everything that is not an o, we can count what's left:

```
$ _gsub "$string" "[!o]"
$ echo ${#_GSUB}
2
```

The Script

```
_gsub()
{
    ## assign the string to sr2; this will be gobbled up with each substitution
    sr2=$1

    ## return an error if there is no pattern specified
    [ -n "$2" ] || return 1
    ## assign the search pattern to s_srch
    s_srch=${2}

    ## assign the replacement text, if any, to rep
    rep=$3

    ## sr1 will hold the portion of the string that has been processed
    sr1=

    ## loop until sr2 no longer contains the search pattern
    while :
    do
      case $sr2 in
         *$s_srch*)

             ## add the string up to the match,
             ## and the replacement text, to sr1
             sr1=$sr1${sr2%%$s_srch*}$rep

             ## remove up to the match from sr2
             sr2=${sr2#*$s_srch}
             ;;
        *) break ;;
      esac
    done
    _GSUB=$sr1$sr2
}

gsub()
{
    _gsub "$@" && printf "%s\n" "$_GSUB"
}
```

Notes

The added capabilities of bash2+ and ksh93 can reduce _gsub to a single line:

```
_gsub() { _GUSB="${1//$2/$3}"; }
```

3.8 repeat—Build a String of a Specified Length

Occasionally you need a character, or a string, repeated a certain number of times. Perhaps it's only for printing a line of dashes across the width of your screen, or for drawing patterns, but the need arises more often than one might expect (for example, see the substr function later in this chapter).

How It Works

With the repeat function, strings can rapidly be built up to any desired length. Because the string triples in length each time through the while loop, even long strings are produced very quickly.

Usage

```
_repeat [-n] STRING LENGTH ## result is stored in $_REPEAT
repeat [-n] STRING LENGTH ## result is printed
```

This function produces a string of LENGTH characters, or, if the -n option is used, with LENGTH repetitions of STRING. Here are a couple of examples, with the results:

```
$ repeat = 30
==============================
$ _repeat -n '/\' 20
$ printf "%s\n" "$_REPEAT"
/\/\/\/\/\/\/\/\/\/\/\/\/\/\/\/\/\/\/\/\
```

Here, repeat is used in a bricklaying demonstration:

```
$ _repeat -n '____|' 20
$ printf "%80.80s\n" "$_REPEAT" "${_REPEAT#???}" "$_REPEAT" "${_REPEAT#???}"
```

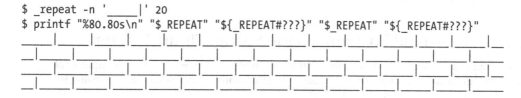

The Script

```
_repeat()
{
    ## If the first argument is -n, repeat the string N times
    ## otherwise repeat it to a length of N characters
    case $1 in
        -n) shift
            r_num=$(( ${#1} * $2 ))
            ;;
        *) r_num=$2
            ;;
    esac
    _REPEAT=$1
    while [ ${#_REPEAT} -lt ${r_num} ]
    do
        _REPEAT=$_REPEAT$_REPEAT$_REPEAT
    done
    while [ ${#_REPEAT} -gt $r_num ]
    do
        _REPEAT=${_REPEAT%?}
    done
}

repeat()
{
    _repeat "$@" && printf "%s\n" "${_REPEAT}"
}
```

Notes

I have tried concatenating more instances of $_REPEAT at one time, and found that, using bash on my system, three is the optimum number in each iteration of the while loop. This may vary from shell to shell and system to system, as it depends on the string handling functions used by the shell. Try it with more, if you like; your system may behave differently.

3.9 index, rindex—Find Position of One String Within Another

When asked to provide a script to convert an abbreviated month name (Jan, Feb, etc.) to the number of the month, one method w to use a single string containing all the months, and parameter expansion to determine the location of the month within the string:

```
mm=JanFebMarAprMayJunJulAugSepOctNovDec
idx=${mm%%$monthname*}
month=$(( (${#idx} + 3 ) / 3 ))
```

With the question "Does string A contain String B?, and if it does, at what index in the string?, these questions let to the resulting function and is been used in a number of scripts (later) in the book.

How It Works

Depending on whether you want the position of the first occurrence or the last, or even just whether it is there or not, one of the index or rindex functions will provide the answer. These functions determine the position of the substring in the main string; index finds the position of the first occurrence, and rindex, the position of the last.

Usage

```
_index STRINGA STRINGB
index STRINGA STRINGB
_rindex STRINGA STRINGB
rindex STRINGA STRINGB
```

If STRINGB is not contained in STRINGA, both functions print 0; otherwise, they print the position of the first or last occurrence of STRINGB.

```
$ str="to be or not to be"
$ index "$str" be
4
$ rindex "$str" to
14
```

If you only want to know whether a match was found, you can discard the output of these functions, and check the return code:

```
$ if _index qwerty z
> then
> echo String found
> else
> echo String not found
> fi
String not found
$ _index qwerty r
$ [ $? -eq 0 ] && echo String found || echo String not found
String found
```

we could have used _rindex in these examples, but in a lazy way, _index is shorter.

The Script

If you use the %% parameter expansion operator, the string to the left of the substring is extracted, and its length plus one is the position of the substring.

```
_index()
{
    case $1 in
        *$2*) ## extract up to beginning of the matching portion
            idx=${1%%$2*}
            ## the starting position is one more than the length
```

```
                _INDEX=$(( ${#idx} + 1 )) ;;
        *) _INDEX=0; return 1 ;;
    esac
}

index()
{
    _index "$@" && printf "%d\n" "$_INDEX"
}
```

If you use % instead of %%, the last occurrence of the substring is found, and the length of the string up to that point, plus one, is the position of the last occurrence of the substring.

```
_rindex()
{
    case $1 in
        *$2*) ## extract up to beginning of the last matching portion
                idx=${1%$2*}
                ## the starting position is one more than the length
                _RINDEX=$(( ${#idx} + 1 )) ;;
        *) _RINDEX=0; return 1 ;;
        esac
}

rindex()
{
    _rindex "$@" && printf "%d\n" "$_RINDEX"
}
```

3.10 substr—Extract a Portion of a String

The POSIX parameter expansion operators, ${var%xx} and ${var#xx}, work on the beginning and end of strings. However, scripts often need to take chunks out of the middle of a string. For example, a program spits out the date and time in the format 20050312204309. You need the month and the day. How do you extract them using only shell commands?

Consider another scenario: An identification number contains a classification in the second and third characters from the end of a number that may have anywhere from 7 to 20 letters and digits. What do you use to pull that classification out of the larger number?

How It Works

The substr function can extract any number of characters from anywhere in the string. (It uses a previous function, repeat, to build the wildcard string of questions marks used in the parameter expansion.)

Usage

```
substr STRING FIRST [LENGTH]
```

The string that substr returns begins at the FIRST character of STRING. If FIRST is negative, the position is counted from the end of the string. If the value of FIRST is greater than the length of the string, an error is returned.

Here are the answers to the problems I've posed. To extract the month and day from the string containing the date and time:

```
$ _substr 20050312204309 5 2
$ month=$_SUBSTR
$ _substr 20050312204309 7 2
$ day=$_SUBSTR
$ printf "Month: %d\nDay: %d\n" ${month#0} ${day#0}
Month: 3
Day: 12
```

To extract the characters from the end of a string, a negative number is used for the starting position:

```
$ id=AZ3167434G34
$ substr "$id" -3 2
G3
```

The Script

First the beginning of the string has to be removed so that the desired portion starts the new string. Then parameter expansion is used to remove the unwanted portion from the end of the string.

```
_substr()
{
    _SUBSTR=

    ## store the parameters
    ss_str=$1
    ss_first=$2
    ss_length=${3:-${#ss_str}}

    ## return an error if the first character wanted is beyond end of string
    if [ $ss_first -gt ${#ss_str} ]
    then
      return 1
    fi

    if [ $ss_first -gt 1 ]
    then
      ## build a string of question marks to use as a wildcard pattern
      _repeat "?" $(( $ss_first - 1 ))
```

```
      ## remove the beginning of string
      ss_str=${ss_str#$_REPEAT}
    elif [ ${ss_first} -lt 0 ] ## ${#ss_str} ]
    then
      ## count from end of string
      _repeat "?" ${ss_first#-}

      ## remove the beginning
      ss_wild=$_REPEAT
      ss_str=${ss_str#${ss_str%$ss_wild}}
    fi

    ## ss_str now begins at the point we want to start extracting
    ## so print the desired number of characters
    if [ ${#ss_str} -gt $ss_length ]
    then
      _repeat "${ss_wild:-??}" $ss_length
      ss_wild=$_REPEAT
      _SUBSTR=${ss_str%${ss_str#$ss_wild}}
    else
      _SUBSTR=${ss_str}
    fi
}
substr()
{
    _substr "$@" && printf "%s\n" "$_SUBSTR"
}
```

Notes

As has been demonstrated in other scripts, a shorter, faster version is available for bash2+ and ksh93.

```
substr()
{
    if [ $2 -lt 0 ]
    then
      printf "%s\n" "${1:$2:${3:-${#1}}}"
    else
      printf "%s\n" "${1:$(($2 - 1)):${3:-${#1}}}"
    fi
}
```

3.11 insert_str—Place One String Inside Another

In many places (especially filenames), dates appear as a 10-digit number representing the year with four digits, and the month and day with two digits each. Say your preferred format for storing a date is YYYY-MM-DD, you will need a method of inserting hyphens after the fourth and sixth digits.

How It Works

Using the _substr function, insert_str splits the string into two pieces and sandwiches the insert between them.

Usage

```
_insert_str STRING INSERT [POSITION]
insert_str STRING INSERT [POSITION]
```

POSITION is the character position in the STRING at which to place INSERT, counting from 1. To convert a date in YYYYMMDD format to international format (YYYY-MM-DD), hyphens must be added at positions 7 and 5:

```
$ date=20050315
$ _insert_str "$date" - 7
$ insert_str "$_INSERT_STR" - 5
2005-03-15
```

The Script

```
_insert_str()
{
    _string=$1 ## The (soon-to-be) container string
    i_string=$2 ## The string to be inserted
    _pos=${3:-2} ## default to inserting after first character (position 2)

    ## Store the string up to the position of the insert
    _substr "$_string" 1 $(( $_pos - 1 ))
      i_1=$_SUBSTR

    ## Store the string that will go after the insert
    _substr "$_string" $_pos
    i_2=$_SUBSTR

    ## Sandwich the insert between the two pieces
    _INSERT_STR=$i_1$i_string$i_2
}

insert_str()
{
    _insert_str "$@" && printf "%s\n" "$_INSERT_STR"
}
```

Notes

For bash2+ and ksh93, there is a faster version:

```
_insert_str()
{
    _string=$1
    i_string=$2
    i_c=${3:-2} ## use default if position not supplied
    i_1=${_string:0:i_c-1}
    i_2=${_string:$i_c}
    _INSERT_STR=$i_1$i_string$i_2
}
```

Summary

These character and string functions only scratch the surface of the manipulations possible with the shell, and many more appear later in the book. In this chapter you are presented with basic functions that provide building blocks for more complex scripts. We have already seen functions used in other functions (_repeat in _substr, and _substr in -insert_str, for example); a great deal more will be provided as the book progresses.

CHAPTER 4

■ ■ ■

What's in a Word?

The most popular page on Chris' web site (http://cfaj.freeshell.org/) is the WordFinder. It has programs for finding words that fit a pattern in a crossword grid (or on a Scrabble board).It can find anagrams, including anagrams of the word if another letter is added to it, or if one is removed from it. It can find words that begin with, end with, or contain any sequence of letters (see Figure 4-1).

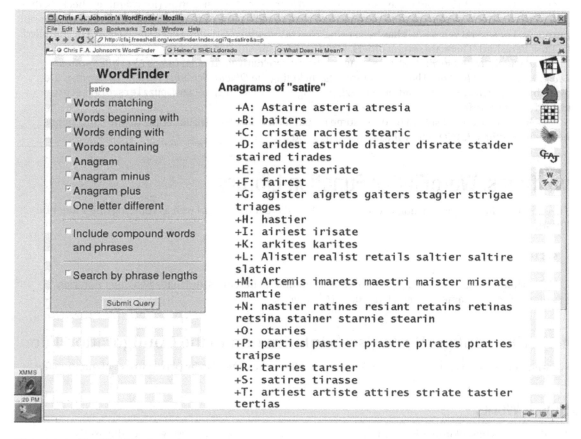

Figure 4-1. *The WordFinder web page*

These began life as C programs on his Commodore Amiga, almost 20 years ago. Combined with macros in a text editor, they constituted his system for composing crossword puzzles. Then, at a time when he couldn't afford to replace it, his hard drive crashed. Though he had everything backed up to floppy disks, and the Amiga could be run from floppies, but his word lists wouldn't fit on a floppy. Even if they had, it would have been excruciatingly slow to use.

A few weeks before the crash, he had built his first web site (the official site of the 1996 Canadian Closed Chess Championships). It was running on a Unix machine, and he had shell access. The C source code from the Amiga was uploaded to the website, and most of it compiled without a hitch. What didn't, was rewritten as shell scripts. When this was moved to its current location a couple of years later, he wrote everything as a shell script and added some new features.

Some time thereafter, the Amiga was retired and GNU/Linux was the new desktop. The central crossword program he uses is still written in C, but any new utilities are shell scripts, often accessed through emacs macros. This chapter provides a collection of scripts for playing with words.

Finding and Massaging Word Lists

Most of the scripts in this chapter use a word list. Unix systems usually come with a word list in /usr/share/dict or /usr/local/dict, but these lists are designed for system administration (for example, checking that passwords are not based on dictionary words) and spell checking; they vary greatly in size and fitness for our purposes. For several years Chris has been using *The UK Advanced Cryptics Dictionary* (*UKACD*), compiled by Ross Beresford. There are several others, some larger, some smaller.

The widely available files, web2.txt and web2a.txt, are derived from *Webster's New International Dictionary, Second Edition*. These and more lists, including the *Official Scrabble Players' Dictionary*, are available for download on the National Puzzlers' League web site, http://www.puzzlers.org/secure/wordlists/dictinfo.php.

Before any of these lists can be used, some preparation is needed. These scripts do the conversions necessary for the *UKACD*, and will work with any word list.

wf-funcs: WordFinder Function Library

This library defines a few functions needed by the WordFinder utilities, as well as sourcing other function libraries with

```
. string-funcs
```

This library, described in Chapter 3, defines a number of functions and loads two other libraries, standard-funcs (Chapter 1), and char-funcs (Chapter 3).

4.1 write_config—Write User's Information to the Configuration File

WordFinder needs to know where to look for its word files. These need to be placed in a configuration file.

How It Works

The directories that WordFinder needs are stored in $configfile; write_config stores the user's information in that file, which may be the default, $HOME/.config/wordfinder.cfg, or one specified on the command line of the calling script.

Usage

```
write_config
```

There are no options or arguments to this function, which is normally called by wf-setup.

The Script

```
write_config()
{
    {
        printf "\n%s\n" "## This file"
        printf "configfile=\"%s\"\n" "$configfile"
        printf "\n%s\n" "## Directory containing main word lists"
        printf "dict=\"%s\"\n" "$dict"
        printf "\n%s\n" "## Directory where user places word files"
        printf "%s\n" "## (may be the same as \$dict)"
        printf "userdict=\"%s\"\n\n" "$userdict"
    } > "$configfile"
}
```

4.2 do_config—Check For and Source Default Configuration File

If no configuration file is supplied on the command line, the WordFinder utilities need to use a default file. If the file does not exist, it needs to be generated.

How It Works

If the default configuration file, $HOME/.config/wordfinder.cfg, does not exist, the user is asked whether it should be created. If the user chooses *Yes*, the wf-setup script is run. The file is then sourced, if it exists.

Usage

```
do_config || exit 5
```

If the function fails, the normal action is to exit the script with an error.

The Script

```
do_config()
{
    [ -d $HOME/.config ] || mkdir $HOME/.config || return 9
    wf_cfg=${wf_cfg:-$HOME/.config/wordfinder.cfg}
    [ -f "$wf_cfg" ] && . "$wf_cfg" || {
```

```
        ## if stdin is not connected to a terminal,
        ## check for the files and return success or failuure
        [ -t 0 ] || {
            [ -d /usr/share/dict ] && { dict=/usr/share/dict; return; }
            [ -d /usr/local/dict ] && { dict=/usr/local/dict; return; }
            return 2
        }
        printf "\n %s: could not find config file, %s\n" "$progname" "$wf_cfg"
        printf " Do you wish to run the setup program now [Y/n]? "
        get_key Q
        case $Q in
            ""|y|Y|"$NL") wf-setup ;;
            *) printf "\n"; return 5 ;;
        esac
        . "$wf_cfg"
    }
}
```

4.3 set_sysdict—Select the Dictionary Directory

The directory that contains the word lists will usually be /usr/share/dict or /usr/local/dict, but if the user doesn't have permission to write to one of those directories, another directory must be used.

How It Works

If either of the usual dictionary locations is found, the user is asked whether to use that directory or choose another.

Usage

```
set_sysdict || exit 5
```

If the function fails, the calling script should usually exit with an error.

The Script

```
set_sysdict()
{
    ## The dict directory is normally in one of two places.
    ## If either is found, it becomes the default directory
    for sysdict in /usr/share/dict /usr/local/dict ""
    do
      [ -d "${sysdict}" ] && break
    done
```

```
## The user is asked to confirm the directory already found,
## or choose a different one.
while :
do
 printf "Enter name of directory for word lists${sysdict:+ ($sysdict)}: "
 read d
 if [ -n "$d" ] && [ -d "$d" ]
 then
   sysdict=$d
   break
 elif [ -z "$d" ]
 then
   break
 else
   printf "%s does not exist\n" "$d"
 fi
done
echo "Main wordlist directory: $sysdict"
}
```

4.4 mkwsig—Sort Letters in a Word

How can you tell if one word is an anagram of another? How can you find anagrams of a word?

How It Works

If word A is an anagram of word B, then sorting the letters of each word alphabetically will produce identical results. The letters of both *TRIANGLE* and *INTEGRAL*, when sorted, yield *AEGILNRT*. The same is true of *RELATING*, *ALTERING*, *ALERTING*, and (yes, it is a word) *TANGLIER*. They are all anagrams of each other.

The function, mkwsig, converts the letters of a word to uppercase and sorts them. This works well for dealing with one word at a time, but it is really slow when processing 200,000 words, as when building the file necessary to find anagrams. The wf-setup script at the end of this section uses it (and points to a faster alternative), but go out to dinner while waiting for it to finish.

Usage

```
mkwsig WORD
```

This function is used primarily by the anagram script, but it can be used on its own (and, of course, in other scripts):

```
$ mkwsig dared
ADDER
```

The Script

```
## The assignment to NL is not necessary if standard-vars has been sourced

NL='
'
mkwsig()
{

    echo "$1" |              ## The word is supplied on the command line
      tr '[a-z]' '[A-Z]' |   ## Convert all letters to upper case
        sed "s/./&\\$NL/g"   ## Put each letter on a separate line
        sort |               ## Sort the letters alphabetically
          tr -d '\012'       ## Remove the newlines
}
```

4.5 wf-clean—Remove Carriage Returns and Accents

The *UKACD* file has CR/LF line endings and accented characters. It also contains compound words. We need to clean up the file and split it into two files.

How It Works

This script uses tr to convert accented characters to ASCII, then sed removes the carriage returns and deletes words that begin or end with characters other than letters. These are prefixes, suffixes, and contractions (such as *'tis*). The resulting file is split into two files, singlewords and compounds.

Usage

```
wf-clean [FILE]
```

If no FILE is given on the command line, the user is prompted to enter a filename.

The Script

```
description="Convert accented characters to ASCII and remove carriage returns"
progname=${0##*/}

. standard-vars ## load variable definitions, including CR

die()
{
  exitcode=$1
  shift
  if [ "$*" ]
  then
```

```
    echo "$*"
  fi
  exit ${exitcode:-1}
}

file=${1:-`printf "Enter file name: " >&2;read file; echo $file`}
[ -f "$file" ] || die 5 "$progname: File ($file) does not exist"
w
## set list of accented characters and their equivalent ASCII character
accents="ÀÁÂÃÄÅÇÈÉÊËÌÍÎÏ_ÑÒÓÔÕÖØÙÚÛÜ_àáâãäåçèéêëìíîïñòóôõöøùúûü_"
ascii="AAAAAACEEEEIIIIDNOOOOOOUUUUYaaaaaaceeeeiiiinooooooouuuuy"

## Convert accented characters to ASCII,
## remove carriage returns,
## and delete words that do not begin or end with an ASCII character
tr "$accents" "$ascii" < "$file" |
    sed -e 's/$CR//' \
        -e '/^[^a-zA-Z]/d' \
        -e '/[^a-zA-Z]$/d' > "$file.clean"

## store any words that contain non-ASCII characters in the compounds file...
grep '[^a-zA-Z]' "$file.clean" > compounds

## ... and the rest in the singlewords file
grep -v '[^a-zA-Z]' "$file.clean" > singlewords
```

4.6 wf-compounds—Squish Compound Words and Save with Lengths

When entered in crossword puzzles, compound words have no spaces or hyphens. Therefore, their lengths in the word list are not the same as their lengths in the puzzle grid. We need to fix that, and provide a means of retrieving the original word or phrase along with the lengths as they appear in a cryptic crossword puzzle.

How It Works

To convert phrases so that they are the same length as when in a puzzle, as well as to give the lengths as they would appear in a cryptic crossword puzzle, we squish the words together. To make the squished words more readable, the first letter after a space or hyphen has been removed is capitalized. Apostrophes are removed, but they do not affect the letter count.

The words are printed in three tab-separated fields: the squished words, the original phrase, and the word lengths. Here are a few examples:

```
AladdinsLamp        Aladdin's lamp (8,4)
blueGreenAlgae      blue-green algae     (4-5,5)
swordOfDamocles     sword of Damocles    (5,2,8)
wireHairedTerrier   wire-haired terrier  (4-6,7)
```

Usage

```
wf-compounds [FILE] [> newfile]
```

If FILE is not given, a file named compounds will be used if it exists in the current directory.

The Script

The squishing and generation of the word-lengths string is done by the squish function, which is kept in the wf-funcs library:

```
squish()
{
    phr=$1
    lengths="("
    lastleftlen=0
    while :
    do
      case $phr in
          ## remove apostrophes
          *\'*) phr=${phr%%\'*}${phr#*\'} ;;

          ## if any non-alphabetic characters still exist
          *[!a-zA-Z]*)
              ## remove non-alphabetic characters
              ## and convert following letter to upper case
              left=${phr%%[!a-zA-Z]*}
              right=${phr#$left}
              char=${right%${right#?}}
              right=${right#?}
              leftlen=$(( ${#left} - $lastleftlen ))
              lastleftlen=${#left}
              while : ## remove consecutive non-alphabetic characters
              do
                case ${right%${right#?}} in
                    [!a-zA-Z]) right=${right#?} ;;
                    *) break ;;
                esac
              done

              ## Build the lengths string, using either a comma or a hyphen
              case $char in
                  '-') lengths=$lengths$leftlen- ;;
                  *) lengths=$lengths$leftlen, ;;
              esac
              _upr "$right"
              phr=$left$_UPR${right#?}
              ;;
```

```
          ## All cleaned up; exit from the loop
          *) break ;;
      esac
    done
    lengths="${lengths}${#right})"
}
```

The wf-compounds command sources wf-funcs, which in turn sources standard-funcs (from Chapter 1) and string-funcs (from Chapter 2).

```
. wf-funcs

## If the wfconfig command does not exist, create a dummy function
type wfconfig >/dev/null 2>&1 || wfconfig() { noconfig=1; }
verbose=0
progname=${0##*/}
file=compounds

## parse command-line options
while getopts vVf: var
do
  case $var in
      f) file=$OPTARG ;;
      v) verbose=$(( $verbose + 1 )) ;;
  esac
done
shift $(( $OPTIND - 1 ))

[ -f "$file" ] || die 5 "$progname: $file not found"

## if the verbose option is used, print a dot for every 1000 words processed
case $verbose in
    [1-9]*) dotty=`repeat ".." $(( 1000 / $verbose ))`
            dot()
            {
                case $dot in
                    "$dotty")
                        dot=
                        printf "." >&2
                        ;;
                    *) dot=$dot. ;;
                esac
            }
            ;;
    *) dot() { :; } ;;
esac

## Read each line of the file, call squish(), and print the results;
## the output should be redirected to the compounds file
while IFS= read -r line
```

CHAPTER 4 ■ WHAT'S IN A WORD?

```
do
  squish "$line"
  printf "%s\t%s\t%s\n" "$phr" "$line" "$lengths"
  dot
done < $file
```

4.7 wf-setup—Prepare Word and Anagram Lists

The conversions in the previous scripts all must be performed, and the resulting files installed in the correct directory.

The wf-setup script asks the user to verify the installation directory, then pulls together the previous scripts and installs them.

Usage

```
wf-setup [-c configfile]
```

Unless you want to use a nonstandard .cfg file, just run wf-setup and answer any questions it asks.

The Script

```
description="Prepare word lists for searches and anagrams"

progname=${0##*/}

## if the command's name ends in -sh, it's the development version
## so use the development versions of the function files
case $progname in
    *sh) . wf-funcs-sh ;;
    *) . wf-funcs ;;
esac

configfile=$HOME/.config/wordfinder.cfg
wordfiles="
        singlewords
        Compounds
        singlewords.anag
        Compounds.anag
        "

while getopts Vc: var
do
  case $var in
      c) configfile=$OPTARG ;;

  esac
done
shift $(( $OPTIND - 1 ))
```

92

```
printf "\n\n"

set_sysdict || exit 5

write_config

if checkfiles ${sysdict} $wordfiles
then
  printf "\n\tAll required files found in ${sysdict}\n"
  exit
fi

[ -f $sysdict/singlewords ] || wf-clean
[ -f $sysdict/Compounds ] ||
            wf-compounds "$sysdict/compounds" > $sysdict/Compounds

## Is wordsort installed? (It is available from http://cfaj.freeshell.org)
type wordsort &&
  [ "`wordsort --version`" = "--EINORSV$TAB--version" ] &&
      ws=1 || ws=0

for file in singlewords Compounds
do
  [ -f "$sysdict/$file.anag" ] || {
      if [ "$ws" -eq 1 ]
      then
        cut -f1 "$sysdict/$file" | wordsort
      else
        while read word
        do
          mkwsig "$word"
          printf "\t%s\n" "$word"
        done < "$sysdict/$file"
    fi > "$sysdict/$file.anag"
}
done
```

Playing with Matches

Whether looking for words that fit a pattern in a grid or the letters in a word, matching words that fit various criteria is very helpful in solving crossword puzzles and other word games. It's not very sporting to use the anagram script to solve the *Daily Jumble* in the newspaper, but if you're stumped on the last word, why not?

These scripts use a configuration file, wordfinder.cfg, to find the location of the word lists. If the file doesn't exist, the user will be prompted to create it. As with all other user configuration files in this book, it is stored in $HOME/.config.

Since these scripts use grep, the full power of regular expressions is available to the user. This book is not the place to explain them, but you can find a list of resources in the Appendix.

4.8 wf—Find Words That Match a Pattern

Given a pattern of letters in a crossword grid, for example, *e.r...e*, where the dots represent empty squares, I need a list of all the words that fit that pattern.

My original wf command was written in C, and did not have all the capabilities of this very simple shell script.

Usage

```
wf [-c] PATTERN
```

Besides using dots to represent unknown letters, the search can be limited to a given set of letters in one or more positions. For example, wf ....a.f, gives this:

```
bedwarf
distaff
engraff
restaff
```

If you want to limit the output to words that begin with *a*, *d*, or *e*, you can replace a dot with those letters in brackets:

```
$ wf [ade]...a.f
distaff
engraff
```

A dot can also be replaced by a range of letters; if you want a search to match only the letters *c* to *n*, you can do this:

```
$ wf [c-n].e.n. | column
cleans   deeing   eterne   feeing   Fresno   Greene   haeing   jeeing
creant   duenna   exeunt   foehns   geeing   greens   hieing   lierne
cueing   dyeing   eyeing   frenne   gleans   greeny   hoeing   moeing
```

With the -c option, wf will search the file of compound words, Compounds, and singlewords.

The Script

```
. wf-funcs-sh

description="Find words that match a pattern"
verbose=0
version="1.0"
progname=${0##*/}
wf_cfg=${wf_cfg:-$HOME/.config/wordfinder.cfg}
compounds=

while getopts vVc var
do
```

```
  case $var in
compounds=1 ;;
   v) verbose=$(( $verbose + 1 )) ;;
   V) version; exit ;;
   *) printf "%s: invalid option: %s\n" "$progname" "$var"
   exit
   ;;
  esac
done
shift $(( $OPTIND - 1 ))

do_config || exit 5

compounds=${compounds:+$dict/Compounds}
mask=$1
{

    cat $dict/singlewords
    if [ -n "$compounds" ]
    then
        cut -f1 $dict/Compounds
    fi
} | grep -i "^$mask$" | sort -fu
```

4.9 wfb—Find Words That Begin with a Given Pattern

Give me a list of words that begin with a given set of letters.

How It Works

Another simple script, wfb searches singlewords, and optionally the Compounds file as well.

Usage

```
wfb [-c] PATTERN
```

As with wf, the PATTERN can contain dots and ranges of letters:

```
$ wfb [a-e]rn | column
arna            arnicas     arnut     erned        erning
Arnaut          Arno        arnuts    ernes        erns
Arne            Arnold      Brno      Ernest       Ernst
Arnhem          arnotto     ern       Ernestine
arnica          arnottos    erne      Ernie
$ wfb .ff[j-n] | column
afflation       afflictive  affluxions    effluence    effluxion
afflations      afflicts    effleurage    effluences   effluxions
afflatus        affluence   effleurages   effluent     offload
afflatuses      affluent    effloresce    effluents    offloaded
```

afflict	affluently	effloresced	effluvia	offloading
afflicted	affluentness	efflorescence	effluvial	offloads
afflicting	affluents	efflorescences	effluvium	
afflictings	afflux	efflorescent	effluviums	
affliction	affluxes	effloresces	efflux	
afflictions	affluxion	efflorescing	effluxes	

The Script

```
description="Find words beginning with pattern supplied on the command line"

. wf-funcs-sh

version="1.0"
progname=${0##*/}

while getopts vVc var
do
  case "$var" in
      c) compounds=1 ;;
      V) version; exit ;;
      *);;
  esac
done
shift $(( $OPTIND - 1 ))

do_config || exit 5

compounds=${compounds:+$dict/Compounds}
{
      cat $dict/singlewords
      if [ -n "$compounds" ]
      then
      cut -f1 $dict/Compounds
       fi
} | grep -i "^$1." | sort -fu
```

4.10 wfe—Find Words That End with a Given Pattern

"For the life of me, I cannot come up with the three common English words that end in *gry*. What are they?"
   "Is there a word that rhymes with *orange*?"

How It Works

Unfortunately, there is no program that will find an answer to those questions. You can try it with wfe, but, unless you have an unusual word list, you are out of luck.

On the other hand, wfe will find 31 words in the *UKACD* that end with ease.

Usage

```
wfe [-c] PATTERN
```

Besides selecting which letters to look for, all these utilities allow you to specify which letters *not* to look for. To find all words that end in *ude* but not *tude*:

```
$ wfe -c [^t]ude | column
allude          crude        exclude       intrude         prude
blude           cumLaude     extrude       magnaCumLaude   Quaalude
Buxtehude       delude       exude         obtrude         schadenfreude
choralePrelude  denude       Gertrude      occlude         seclude
claude          detrude      illude        postlude        semiNude
collude         disillude    include       preclude        subtrude
conclude        elude        interclude    prelude         summaCumLaude
coude           emeraude     interlude     protrude        transude
```

The Script

```
description="List words ending with PATTERN"

. wf-funcs-sh

version="1.0"
progname=${0##*/}
compounds=

while getopts vVc var
do
  case $var in
    c) compounds=1 ;;
    V) version; exit ;;
  esac
done
shift $(( $OPTIND - 1 ))

do_config || exit 5

compounds=${compounds:+$dict/Compounds}

{

    cat $dict/singlewords
    if [ -n "$compounds" ]
    then
       cut -f1 "$compounds"
    fi
} | grep -i ".$1$" | sort -fu
```

4.11 wfc—Find Words That Contain a Given Pattern

"I would like a list of all the words that contain the word *fast*."

How It Works

This is a simple job for grep. Put it in a script so you wouldn't have to remember which directory contains the word lists and what the filenames are.

Usage

```
wfc [-c] PATTERN
```

To find words that contain *fast*:

```
$ wfc fast | column
breakfasted      handfasts       steadfastness   unfastidious
breakfasting     headfasts       stedfasts       unsteadfastly
breakfasts       makefasts       unfasten        unsteadfastness
handfasted       shamefastness   unfastened
handfasting      sitfasts        unfastening
handfastings     steadfastly     unfastens
```

By adding the -c option, you can expand the search to include compound words and phrases:

```
 $ wfc -c fast | column
aFastBuck                        lifeInTheFastLane
BreakfastAtTiffanyS              makefasts
breakfasted                      playFastAndLoose
breakfasting                     powerBreakfasts
breakfastRoom                    pullAFastOne
breakfasts                       shamefastness
breakfastSet                     sitfasts
breakfastTable                   snapFastener
breakfastTables                  snapFasteners
breakfastTV                      steadfastly
continentalBreakfasts            steadfastness
copperFasten                     stedfasts
copperFastened                   unfasten
copperFastening                  unfastened
copperFastens                    unfastening
goFasterStripes                  unfastens
handfasted                       unfastidious
handfasting                      unsteadfastly
handfastings                     unsteadfastness
handfasts                        weddingBreakfasts
headfasts                        youCanTGetBloodOutOfAStone
heTravelsFastestWhoTravelsAlone  zipFastener
inTheFastLane                    zipFasteners
```

The Script

```
description="Find words containing the pattern given on the command line"
version="1.0"
progname=${0##*/}
compounds=
opts=c

while getopts $opts var
do
  case $var in
   c) compounds=1 ;;
   *) exit ;;
  esac
done
shift $(( $OPTIND - 1 ))

. wf-funcs

compounds=${compounds:+$dict/Compounds}
pattern=$1

{
    cat $dict/singlewords
    if [ -n "$compounds" ]
    then
        cut -f1 "$compounds"
    fi
} | grep -i ".$pattern." | sort -fu
```

Notes

Words will not match if the pattern is at the beginning or end of the word. If you want those to match, change the last line of the script to this:

```
} | grep -i "$pattern" | sort -fu
```

4.12 wfit—Find Words That Fit Together in a Grid

If you need to find words that will fit in the top corner of the grid (see Figure 4-2). The third letter in 1-DOWN must fit into a word that goes across. If you put *part* in there, there will be nothing that can complete the intersecting word.

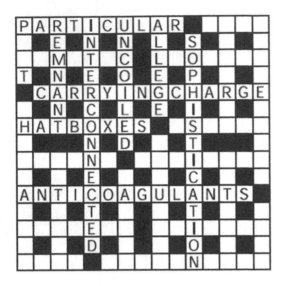

Figure 4-2. *A partially completed crossword grid*

How It Works

Specify the pattern for each word, followed by the position in the word of the intersecting letter, as arguments to wfit.

Usage

```
wfit PATTERN1 POS1 PATTERN2 POS2
```

The command for the example in the grid shown in Figure 4-2 is this:

```
$ wfit p..t 3 ..m.t.c 1
pact - cometic
Pict

pant - nematic
pent
pint
pont
punt

phot - osmotic
plot
poot
pyot

past - sematic
pest   Semitic
post   somatic
psst   somitic
```

The Script

```
## requires bash2+ or ksh93
description="Find words that fit together in a grid"
version="1.0"
progname=${0##*/}
compounds=

while getopts vVc var
do
  case $var in
    c) compounds=1 ;;
    V) version; exit ;;
    *);;
  esac
done
shift $(( $OPTIND - 1 ))

max() {
      _MAX=$1
      _MIN=$1
      shift
      for num
      do
        [ $num -gt $_MAX ] && _MAX=$num
        [ $num -lt $_MIN ] && _MIN=$num
      done
}

## fail if there are fewer than 4 arguments
[ $# -ne 4 ] && exit5

mask1=$1
mask2=$3
ltr1=$2
ltr2=$4

IFS=$' \t\n'
list1=( `wf ${compounds:+-c} "$mask1"` )
letters=`printf "%s\n" "${list1[@]}" | cut -c$ltr1 | sort -fu`

for letter in $letters
do
  maskA=${mask1:0:ltr1-1}$letter${mask1:ltr1}
  maskB=${mask2:0:ltr2-1}$letter${mask2:ltr2}
  list1=( `wf ${compounds:+-c} "$maskA"` )
  list2=( `wf ${compounds:+-c} "$maskB"` )
  [ ${#list2} -eq 0 ] && continue
  max ${#list1[@]} ${#list2[@]}
  n=0
  w1=${#list1[0]}
  w2=${#list2[0]}
```

```
  [ $verbose -ge 1 ] && echo "MAX=$_MAX MIN=$_MIN maskA=$maskA maskB=$maskB"
  while [ $n -lt $_MAX ]
  do
    if [ "${#list2[$n]}" -gt 0 ]
    then
      if [ "${#list1[$n]}" -gt 0 -a $n -eq 0 ]
      then
        printf "%${w1}s - %${w2}s\n" "${list1[n]}" "${list2[$n]}"
      else
        printf "%${w1}s %${w2}s\n" "${list1[n]}" "${list2[$n]}"
      fi
    else
      printf "%${w1}s\n" "${list1[n]}"
    fi
    n=$(( $n + 1 ))
done
    echo
done
```

Notes

This is one of the few scripts in the book that requires bash2+ or ksh93, as it uses arrays and substring parameter expansion.

4.13 anagram—Find Words That Are Anagrams of a Given Word

"I have the letters *ADGETG* left on my Scrabble rack; what six-letter words can I make with them?"

How It Works

If you ran the wf-setup script, you should have a file that has each word paired with its *signature*. Sort the letters on your rack alphabetically to create a signature (using the mkwsig function) and find words with that signature in the singlewords.anag file. Or let the anagram script do it for you.

Usage

```
anagram [-c] WORD
```

If you use the -c option, anagram will search both singlewords.anag and Compounds.anag:

```
$ anagram-sh outcast
outacts
outcast
$ anagram-sh -c outcast
actsOut
castOut
outacts
outcast
```

The Script

```
description="Find words that are anagrams of WORD on command line"
version="1.0"
progname=${0##*/}
compounds=

. wf-funcs

while getopts Vc var
do
  case $var in
    c) compounds=1 ;;
    V) printf "%s: %s\n" $progname $version; exit ;;
  esac
done
shift $(( $OPTIND - 1 ))

do_config || exit 5

pattern=`mkwsig $1`
compounds=${compounds:+$dict/Compounds.anag}

grep -i "^$pattern$TAB" $dict/singlewords.anag $compounds |
    cut -f2 |
        sort -fu
```

4.14 aplus—Find Anagrams of a Word with a Letter Added

"I am trying to solve a cryptic crossword clue. I know the answer is an anagram of *SATIRE* with *N, E, W,* or *S* added. How can I get a list of all the possible words?"

How It Works

You could use four commands: anagram satiren, anagram satiree, anagram satirew, and anagram satires. However, why not let the computer do the work with aplus? This command will find anagrams of the word with each letter of the alphabet added in turn.

Usage

aplus [-c][-l] WORD

With the -l option, aplus will just add the letters you tell it to use. The -c option includes compound words:

```
$ aplus nearly
+B: blarney
+C: larceny
+G: angerly
```

```
+I: inlayer nailery
+P: plenary
$ aplus -c -l bog nearly
+b: blarney
+o: earlyOn
+g: angerly
```

The Script

```
progname=${0##*/}
compounds=
letters=ABCDEFGHIJKLMNOPQRSTUVWXYZ

while getopts cl: var
do
  case $var in
      c) compounds=1 ;;
      l) letters=$OPTARG ;;
  esac
done
shift $(( $OPTIND - 1 ))

word=$1

while [ -n "$letters" ]
do
  _temp=${letters#?}
  l=${letters%$_temp}
  letters=$_temp
  printf "+$l:\r" >&2
  result=`anagram ${compounds:+-c} "$word$l"`
  [ -n "$result" ] && {
      printf "+%s: " "$l"
      echo $result
  }
done
```

4.15 aminus—Remove Each Letter in Turn and Anagram What's Left

Many of the cryptic crossword clues Chris writes use anagrams, sometimes of the whole word, sometimes of part of the word. Among other things, he need a program to list the anagrams of a word when letters are removed.

How It Works

The aminus script removes each letter in turn (but does not remove a letter more than once if there are duplicates), then finds the anagrams of what's left.

Usage

```
aminus [-c] WORD
```

Without the -c option that includes compound words in the result, aminus would find only *anchorites* and *antechoirs* when fed *neoChristianity*:

```
$ aminus-sh -c neoChristianity
-i: ancientHistory
-y: anchorites antechoirs chainStore
```

The Script

```
version="1.0"
progname=${0##*/}
compounds=

while getopts c var
do
  case $var in
      c) compounds=1 ;;
  esac
done
shift $(( $OPTIND - 1 ))

word=$1
done=
left=
right=$word
while [ -n "$right" ]
do
  temp=${right#?}
  l=${right%$temp}
  ## check whether the same letter has already been removed
  case $left in
      *$l*) right=$temp
            continue ;; ## don't repeat a letter
  esac

result=`anagram ${compounds:+-c} $left$temp`
[ -n "$result" ] && {
    printf "%c%s: " "-" "$l"
    echo $result
}
left=$left${l}
right=$temp
done | sort
```

Summary

From composing crossword puzzles to solving the *Daily Jumble* in your local newspaper, the scripts in this chapter can help you. If you want to know whether there was a seven-letter word on the rack you had in that Scrabble game, or whether you could have squeezed a word into _ A _ N _ _ E _ _S, the tools are here.

Some of these scripts are of most use to cruciverbalists, but many can be used by anyone who plays word games.

CHAPTER 5

■ ■ ■

Scripting by Numbers

Number crunching was once the domain of big mainframe computers hidden away in secure, air-conditioned rooms. Now, the computer on your desk (or even the one in your pocket) has more computing power than those old behemoths. The shell, with the help of external commands, can harness that power.

POSIX shells have arithmetic built in, but are limited to integers. Multiplication of decimal fractions can be done in the shell with the fpmul function, which appears in the math-funcs library described next. Other operations could also be coded with shell arithmetic, but they are more complicated, and external commands such as awk can do the job as efficiently. Similarly, there is no point to using a shell function to multiply if the result is then going to be passed to awk for addition or subtraction; let awk handle it all.

The scripts in this chapter are all relatively simple, but useful nonetheless. The majority can be used at the command line or in another script. "Number crunching" is a rather grand term for the scripts in this chapter, but they can be the basis for complex calculations.

The math-funcs Library

The math-funcs library contains a number of shell functions that will be used in many scripts. Some are also useful at the command line. For instance, Chris uses calc, a simple command-line calculator, almost every day.

Most of these functions come in pairs. One begins with an underscore and sets a variable. That variable is the name of the function converted to capital letters: _round sets the variable _ROUND. The second function calls the underscore version and prints the result.

Why two functions? In all shells except ksh93, command substitution forks a new process. In other words, command substitution is slow. It greatly diminishes the advantage of using a function instead of an external script. The difference is not significant if it is called only once, but in a script where the function is used many times or where many functions are called, it can make the difference between a quick, responsive script and a sluggish one.

To use the underscore function, call it, then either use the variable that has been set (as the argument to another command), or assign it to another variable:

```
_func arg1 arg1
printf "The answer is: %s\n" "$_FUNC"
funky=$_FUNC
```

It is much faster than command substitution:

```
printf "The answer is: %s\n" "`func arg1 arg2`"
funky=`func arg1 arg2`
```

Generally, when you want to print the result (as you would at the command line), use the plain function. Otherwise, use the underscore version.

5.1 fpmul—Multiply Decimal Fractions

Most shells cannot do floating-point arithmetic internally; an external program such as bc or awk must be used. Is there a faster way?

How It Works

In many cases, awk and bc are the best way to perform calculations with fractions, but multiplication, on its own, can be done with a function more quickly than with an external command.

Usage

```
fpmul N[.N] N[.N] [...]
_fpmul N[.N] N[.N] [...] ## the result is in $_FPMUL
```

No multiplication sign is used between the operands, although you can change a line in the function to allow them, and other non-numeric elements, to be interspersed on the command line and ignored. Normally, the command is invoked with two or more operands:

```
$ fpmul 12.345 67.89
838.10205
```

In a script, you would use the underscore version, which sets a variable rather than print the answer:

```
$ _fpmul 1.23 1.11 1.01 1.2 1.23 1.11 1.01 1.2 1.23 1.1 .2 .4
$ echo $_FPMUL
0.2963802115596415104
```

Notice the length of the fraction. On some shells, that will cause problems:

```
$ fpmul 1.23 1.11 1.01 1.2 1.23 1.11 1.01 1.2 1.23 1.1 .2 .4
fpmul: overflow error: -1711122980
```

Since fpmul uses the shell's built-in arithmetic capabilities, it is constrained by its internal limits. A shell's integer size is usually 32 bits, which means the largest number it can handle is 2,147,483,647. Versions of bash later than 2.05a, when compiled on a system that can handle them, uses 64-bit integers and has a maximum integer of 9,223,372,036,854,775,807. However, the method for multiplying decimal fractions complicates matters.

In school, more decades ago than I care to admit, I was taught a method of calculating the product of decimal fractions: remove the decimal points and multiply the resulting numbers. Get the total number of decimal places in the original fractions, and insert the decimal point that many places from the end. For example, to multiply 1.5 by 1.2, you would multiply 15 by 12 (180), and insert the decimal point 2 places from the end, giving 1.80. The fpmul function removes trailing zeros, and the answer is 1.8.

Although the final answer was less than 2, the calculation used a number as high as 180. The highest number used will grow as the number of decimal digits grows, rather than as the value of the result increases. You can see this by invoking the "show your work to the teacher" clause included in the function; it can be invoked by setting verbose to 63.

With only a few decimal places, we can see that the integers remain well within the limits:

```
$ verbose=63 fpmul 3.14 4.5
fp_tot=$(( 1 * 314 ))
fp_tot=$(( 314 * 45 ))
fp_tot=14130
14.13
```

When the number increases, even though each operand has only two digits, the integers being used in the calculations grow quickly. This calculation succeeds in bash with 64-bit integers, but fails in ash with only 32 bits:

```
bash 2.05b: $ verbose=63 fpmul 1.2 3.4 5.6 7.8 9.8 7.6 5.4
fp_tot=$(( 1 * 12 ))
fp_tot=$(( 12 * 34 ))
fp_tot=$(( 408 * 56 ))
fp_tot=$(( 22848 * 78 ))
fp_tot=$(( 1782144 * 98 ))
fp_tot=$(( 174650112 * 76 ))
fp_tot=$(( 13273408512 * 54 ))
fp_tot=716764059648
71676.4059648
ash: $ fpmul 1.2 3.4 5.6 7.8 9.8 7.6 5.4
fpmul: overflow error: -495478784
```

The Script

```
. standard-funcs

_fpmul()
{
    fp_places=
    fp_tot=1
    fp_qm=
    fp_neg=
    _FPMUL=
    for fp_n
    do
      ## 2 negatives make a positive, i.e., each negative number changes the sign
      case $fp_n in
          -*) [ "$fp_neg" = '-' ] && fp_neg= || fp_neg='-'
              fp_n=${fp_n#-}
              ;;
      esac
      ## Check for non-numeric characters
      case $fp_n in
          ## (minus signs have been removed by this point,
          ## so we don't need to include them)
          *[!0-9.]*) return 1 ;;
```

```
## Use this in place of the line above if you prefer to ignore (i.e., skip over)
## invalid arguments
##            *[!0-9.]*) continue ;;
      esac

      ## count the number of decimal places,
      ## then remove the decimal point and multiply
      case $fp_n in
         .*) fp_int=
             fp_dec=${fp_n#?}
             fp_places=$fp_places$fp_dec
             fp_n=$fp_dec
                          ;;
         *.*) fp_dec=${fp_n#*.}
              fp_int=${fp_n%.*}
              fp_places=$fp_places$fp_dec
              fp_n=$fp_int$fp_dec
              ;;
      esac

      ## remove leading zeroes
      while :
      do
        case $fp_n in
           0*) fp_n=${fp_n#0} ;;
            *) break;;
        esac
      done

      ## "Show your work to the teacher" if verbose equals 63
      [ ${verbose:-0} -eq 63 ] && printf "%s\n" "total=\$(( $fp_tot * $fp_n ))"

      ## multiply by the previous
      total fp_tot=$(( $fp_tot * $fp_n ))

      ## report any overflow error
      case $fp_tot in
         -*) printf "fpmul: overflow error: %s\n" "$fp_tot" >&2
             return 1
             ;;
      esac
   done
   [ ${verbose:-0} -eq 63 ] && printf "%s\n" "total=$fp_tot"

  ## pad the result with leading zeroes if necessary
  while [ ${#fp_tot} -lt ${#fp_places} ]
  do
    fp_tot=0$fp_tot
  done
```

```
    fp_df=
    while [ ${#fp_df} -lt ${#fp_places} ]
    do
      left=${fp_tot%?}
      fp_df=${fp_tot#$left}$fp_df
      fp_tot=$left
    done
    _FPMUL=$fp_tot${fp_df:+.$fp_df}

    ## remove trailing zeroes or decimal points
    while :
    do
      case $_FPMUL in
          *.*[0\ ]|*.) _FPMUL=${_FPMUL%?} ;;
          .*) _FPMUL=0$_FPMUL ;;
          *) break ;;
      esac
    done
}

fpmul()
{
    _fpmul "$@" || return 1
    printf "%s\n" "$_FPMUL"
}
```

Notes

The fpmul function could be improved in various ways:

- Using a variable for the decimal point would allow the script to be adjusted for use in locales where a comma (or other character) is used instead of a period.

- Instead of failing, the function could call awk or bc when there is an overflow.

- The arguments could be checked for invalid numbers.

Floating-point arithmetic is built into ksh93, so fpmul is unnecessary in such scripts. This alternative provides a KornShell drop-in function that is compatible with all scripts that use fpmul.

```
_fpmul()
{
    _FPMUL=1
    for fp_n
    do
      _FPMUL=$(( $_FPMUL * $fp_n ))
    done
}
```

5.2 int—Return the Integer Portion of a Decimal Fraction

To convert a decimal fraction to an integer in a script, the script will often put the expansion in-line, rather than call a function, but at the command line you could use an int command.

How It Works

Simple parameter expansion is all it takes to return the portion of a number that precedes the decimal point.

Usage

```
_int N[.N] ## the result is in $_INT
int N[.N]
```

The Script

```
_int()
{
    _INT=${1%%.*}
}

int()
{
    printf "%d\n" "${1%%.*}"
}
```

5.3 round—Round the Argument to the Nearest Integer

A little more complex than int, round takes the number to the nearest integer. For example, 2.3 rounds to 2, but 2.7 rounds up to 3.

How It Works

Using parameter expansion, the number is split into its integer and fractional parts. If the fractional part is less than .5, round returns the integer part; otherwise, the next higher integer is returned.

Usage

```
_round N[.N] ## the result is in $_ROUND
round N[.N]
```

The Script

```
_round()
{
    _ROUND=${1%%.*}    ## extract the integer
    case ${1#*.} in
      ## If the decimal begins with any digit from five to 9,
      ## the result is rounded up
        [5-9]*) _ROUND=$(( $_ROUND + 1 )) ;;
    esac
}

round()
{
    _round "$1"
    printf "%s\n" $_ROUND
}
```

5.4 pow—Raise a Number to Any Given Power

From finding the area of a square to turning scientific notation into a human-readable number, exponentiation (raising a number to a given power) is a fundamental mathematical operation. While this is easily handled by external utilities such as awk, you would prefer a more efficient method in most cases.

How It Works

If the exponent requested is a decimal fraction, I'm not even going to attempt to do the calculation in the shell; I'll just pass it along to awk. If the exponent is an integer, but the base contains a decimal fraction, fpmul is needed. If both the base and the exponent are integers, shell arithmetic has what it takes to produce the answer.

Usage

```
_pow BASE EXPONENT   ## The result is in $_POW
pow BASE EXPONENT    ## The result is printed
```

The base, the exponent, or both can be either an integer or a decimal fraction. These are passed, base first, without any intervening operator:

```
$ pow 12 4
20736
```

The Script

```
_pow()
{
    exp=$2
    pow_arg=

    case $exp in
        ## If the exponent contains a decimal,
        ## we'll wimp out and let awk handle it
        *.*) _POW=$(awk "BEGIN { printf \"%f\", $1 ** $2 ; exit }")
            return ;;
        ## For second and third powers, we pass the calculation to the more
        ## efficient functions defined below
        2) _square "$@"
           _POW=$_SQUARE
           return
           ;;
        3) _cube "$@"
           _POW=$_CUBE
           return
           ;;
    esac

    ## If the base contains no decimal point, we can use shell arithmetic
    case $1 in
        *.*) pow_op= ;;
          *) pow_op=" * " ;;
    esac

    ## Build the string that will be used in $(( ... ))
    ## or as the arguments to _fpmul
    while [ $exp -gt 0 ]
    do
      pow_arg="${pow_arg:+$pow_arg $pow_op} $1"
      exp=$(( $exp - 1 ))
    done
    case $pow_arg in
        *.*) _fpmul $pow_arg     ## Decimal points found
             _POW=$_FPMUL
             ;;
          *) _POW=$(( $pow_arg )) ;;
    esac
}

pow()
{
    _pow "$@" && printf "%s\n" "$_POW"
}
```

5.5 square—Raise a Number to the Second Power

Refer to 5.6, cube, which works the same way. Both scripts are described there.

5.6 cube—Raise a Number to the Third Power

Raising a number to the second or third power are special instances of pow. They are used often enough to warrant their own functions, and they can be dealt with in a simpler fashion.

How It Works

If the number contains a decimal point, use _fpmul; otherwise, use shell arithmetic. (Note that we use _fpmul, not fpmul, as there's no need to print the result; that will be done by square or cube, if needed.)

Usage

```
_square N[.N] ## the result is stored in $_SQUARE
square [N[.N]]
_cube N[.N] ## the result is stored in $_CUBE
cube [N[.N]]
```

The Script

```
_square()
{
    case $1 in
        *.*) _fpmul $1 $1              ## the base contains a decimal point
            _SQUARE=$_FPMUL
            ;;
        *) _SQUARE=$(( $1 * $1 )) ;;   ## no decimal point; use shell arithmetic
    esac
}

square()
{
    arg "$@"        ## The arg function was introduced in Chapter 1
    _square "$arg"
    printf "%s\n" "$_SQUARE"
}

_cube()
{
    case $1 in
        *.*) _fpmul $1 $1 $1
            _CUBE=$_FPMUL
            ;;
        *) _CUBE=$(( $1 * $1 * $1 )) ;;
    esac
}
```

```
cube()
{
    arg "$@"
    _cube "$arg"
    printf "%s\n" "$_CUBE"
}
```

5.7 calc—A Simple Command-Line Calculator

From mechanical calculators and slide rules, to pocket calculators and finally computers, devices for relieving the mental strain of solving mathematical problems have been with us for centuries. Every modern computer comes with at least one program that presents an on-screen version of a pocket calculator. I've tried them, but I find them slow to load and cumbersome to use. What anyone would want is something that allows you to type in "23 * 45" and gives you 1,035 without any fuss.

How It Works

The awk programming language can do any calculation one is likely to need. All that is needed is an interface to it. The calc script, which could be installed as a function, simply incorporates the expression in an awk print statement.

Usage

```
calc "EXPRESSION"
```

EXPRESSION can be any expression awk can understand. This includes using functions such as sqrt:

```
$ calc "sqrt(666)"
25.807
```

More usual is a run-of-the-mill arithmetic expression:

```
$ calc "23.45 * 11 + 65"
322.95
```

The exponentiation operator can be either a double asterisk (as seen in the square and cube functions earlier in the chapter) or the caret:

```
$ calc '23 ^ 3'
12167
```

Characters that are special to the shell must be quoted or escaped. It is recommended to always enclose the entire expression in quotes.

The Script

```
calc()
{
    awk 'BEGIN {print '"$*"'; exit }'
}
```

Adding and Averaging

These scripts all work on a list of numbers obtained from one or more files, or from the standard input. They include the four main types of averages, namely the *mean, median, mode,* and *range.* The first, total, is the simplest; it just adds them up and prints the result. The most complex is stdev, which prints the standard deviation of a set of numbers given in list or table format.

5.8 total—Add a List of Numbers

Say you have a list of numbers stored in a file, one to a line. Now you want to add them all together.

How It Works

If these numbers were all guaranteed to be integers, this could be done with shell arithmetic (see the notes). By using awk, decimal fractions can also be accommodated.

Usage

```
total [FILE ...]
```

If the numbers in the file are not one to a line, a utility such as prw (from Chapter 2) can be used:

```
prw FILE | total
```

The number of decimal places in the output can be controlled with the precision variable. The precision is expressed as a printf width modifier:

```
$ printf "%s\n" 2.345 34.56787 1.0055 | precision=.2 total
37.92
```

The value .2 indicated that the number was to be printed with two digits after the decimal point. A number before the decimal point in the precision variable denotes the total width in which the result is to be printed, and prints it flush right in that space:

```
$ printf "%s\n" 2.345 34.56787 1.0055 | precision=19.3 total
            37.918
```

The number ended at the 19th column, and used three decimal digits.

The Script

```
awk ` ## Add the value of each line to the total
    {total += $1}
        ## After all the lines have been processed, print the result
  END {printf "%" prec "f\n", total}' prec=$precision ${1+"$@"}
```

Notes

If all the numbers are integers, this script will work even when there are multiple numbers on a line:

```
echo $(( `cat ${1+"$@"} | tr -s '\012 ' '++'` 0 ))
```

5.9 mean—Find the Arithmetic Mean of a List of Numbers

A teacher calculating a student's grade average must find the arithmetic *mean*, or the sum of all the numbers divided by the number of numbers.

How It Works

The mean script takes numbers, one to a line, from one or more files, or from the standard input, and prints the arithmetic mean. There is also an option to read the input as a table, each line comprising the number and its number of occurrences.

Usage

```
mean  [-t|-T] [FILE ...]
```

The simplest use is to average a list of numbers in a file:

```
$ cat numlist
3
11
4
8
7
9
6
11
7
8
$ mean numlist
7.4
```

To average a list entered at the command line, use this:

```
$ printf "%s\n" 2 54 67 5 2 1 9 72 13 67 45 87 67 45 32 | mean
37.8667
```

Let's consider another example. If I rolled a pair of dice ten times, the results could be expressed as a table:

Table 4-1. *Ten Rolls of Two Dice*

Number	Number of Times Rolled
1	1
3	2
6	1
7	4
10	1
12	1

This table can be piped through mean with the -t option:

```
$ echo "1 1
3 2
6 1
7 4
10 1
12 1" | mean -t
6.3
```

To accommodate tables generated by uniq -c, which have the frequency before the data item, there is the -T option:

```
$ throw 10 | sort | uniq -c | mean -T
7.4
$ throw 10 | sort | uniq -c | mean -T
6.9
```

(The throw command, which appears later in Chapter 18, simulates the rolling of two six-sided dice n times.)

The Script

```
table=0

## Parse command line otions
while getopts VtT var
do
  case $var in
    t) table=1;;
    T) table=2 ;;
    V) echo $version; exit ;;
  esac
done
shift $(( $OPTIND - 1 ))
```

```
## There are three different awk programs, one for each input format
if [ $table -eq 0 ] ## One number per line
then
  awk '{ tot += $1 }              ## Add number to the total
       END { print tot / NR } ## Divide total by number of lines
     ' ${1+"$@"}
elif [ $table -eq 1 ] ## Each line has number of occurrences followed by the number
then
  awk '{
       num += $2        ## Count total number of occurrences
       tot += $1 * $2 ## Total is number multiplied by number of occurrences
       }
       END {print tot / num }' ${1+"$@"} ## Divide total by number of occurrences
elif [ $table -eq 2 ] ## Each line has number followed by the number of occurrences
then
  awk '{
       num += $1        ## Count total number of occurrences
       tot += $1 * $2   ## Total is number multiplied by number of occurrences
       }
       END { print tot / num }' ${1+"$@"} ## Divide total by number of occurrences
fi
```

5.10 median—Find the Median of a List of Numbers

A teacher wanting to know how well the class as a whole has done on a test may use the mean to get the average result, or use the *median*, which is the midpoint—the number in the middle that has the same number of items above and below it.

How It Works

When a list has an odd number of items, finding the median is easy; where there are n numbers, sort them, and the median is on line $(n + 1)/2$. It's a neat one-liner:

```
sed -n "$(( (`sort -n ${1+"$@"} | tee $tmp | wc -l` + 1) / 2 )) {p;q;}" $tmp
```

In a set with an even number of elements, the median is the arithmetic mean of the two central elements. For that, the easiest way is to pipe the sorted list through an awk script. Of course, it also works for an odd or even number of elements.

Usage

```
median [FILE ...]
```

To find the median of the numlist file (used in the previous mean example), the command is

```
$ median numlist
7.5
```

Let's consider another example. The median of 20 rolls of a pair of dice can be calculated using the following:

```
$ throw 20 | median
7
```

The Script

```
progname=${0##*/}

## Sort the list obtained from one or more files or the standard input
sort -n ${1+"$@"} |
  awk '{x[NR] = $1}     ## Store all the values in an array
        END {
          ## Find the middle number
          num = int( (NR + 1) / 2 )
          ## If there are an odd number of values
          ## use the middle number
          if ( NR % 2 == 1 ) print x[num]
          ## otherwise average the two middle numbers
          else print (x[num] + x[num + 1]) / 2
        }'
```

5.11 mode—Find the Number That Appears Most in a List

Having graded all the tests, the teacher wants to know what grade the most students achieved. This is the *mode*—the most frequently occurring value in a list.

How It Works

You can derive an approximate answer by using `sort` and `uniq -c` (and that may be adequate for your purposes), but the mode may contain none, one, or more than one value. If no value appears more than once in the data set, there is no mode; if more than one value appears with the same frequency that is higher than all the others, they are all modal values of that set of numbers.

Usage

```
mode [-t|-T] [FILE ...]
```

The teacher can pipe all the grades through mode to get the answer:

```
$ printf "%s\n" A B A B B C D F C B A C D C F C B D F C C B D C F D | mode
C
```

In the numlist file (used as an example with the mean script), three numbers have two instances (and none have more than two); therefore, mode prints all three:

```
$ mode numlist
11
7
8
```

As with the mean script, the -t and -T options accept the data in table format.

The Script

```
progname=${0##*/}
table=0            ## by default the file contains a simple list, not a table

## Parse the command-line options
while getopts tT var
do
  case $var in
      t)  table=1 ;;
      T) table=2 ;;
  esac
  done
  shift $(( $OPTIND - 1 ))

  ## There are really three separate scripts,
  ## one for each configuration of the input file
  if [ $table -eq 0 ]
  then
    ## The input is a simple list in one column
    awk '{
        ++x[$1]    ## Count the instances of each value
        if ( x[$1] > max ) max = x[$1] ## Keep track of which has the most
        }
        END {
          if ( max == 1 ) exit ## There is no mode

          ## Print all values with max instances
          for ( num in x ) if ( x[num] == max ) print num
    }' ${1+"$@"}
  elif [ $table -eq 1 ]
  then
    ## The second column contains the number of instances of
    ## the value in the first column
    awk '{ x[$1] += $2 ## Add the number of instances of each value
        if ( x[$1] > max ) max = x[$1] ## Keep track of the highest number
        }
      END { ## Print the result
          if ( max == 1 ) exit
          for ( num in x ) if ( x[num] == max ) print num
          }' ${1+"$@"}
```

```
elif [ $table -eq 2 ]
then
  ## The first column contains the number of instances of
  ## the value in the second column
  awk '{ x[$2] += $1
         if ( x[$1] > max ) max = x[$2]
       }
    END {    ## Print the result
         if ( max == 1 ) exit
         for ( num in x ) if ( x[num] == max ) print num
       }' ${1+"$@"}
fi | sort
```

5.12 range—Find the Range of a Set of Numbers

The fourth main type of average, after *mean*, *median*, and *mode*, is *range*: the difference between the highest and lowest numbers in the set.

How It Works

In the range command, an awk script reads the input and stores the highest and lowest numbers until the end of input is reached. At that point, the difference between the two is printed.

Usage

```
range [-nN] [FILE ...]
```

Using the numlist file as input, the range is 8, the difference between 11 and 3:

```
$ range numlist
8
```

We'll store a sample in the variable table:

```
$ table="11    2
          7    5
         33    1
          2    4"
```

By default, range uses the first column:

```
$ echo "$table" | range
31
```

The -n option tells range to analyze column N of the input. This example uses column 2:

```
$ printf "%s\n" "$table" | range -n2 ## uses column 2
4
```

Because the variable, table, is not quoted in the next example, each number in the table is printed on a separate line, and range reads it as a simple list:

```
$ printf "%s\n" $table | range
32
```

The Script

```
progname=${0##*/}
column=1

## Parse command-line options
while getopts Vn: var
do
  case $var in
    n) column=$OPTARG ;;
  esac
done
shift $(( $OPTIND - 1 ))

awk 'BEGIN {
      ## awk variables are initialized to 0, so we need to
      ## give min a value larger than anything it is likely to
      ## encounter
      min = 999999999999999999 }
    {
      ++x[$col]
      if ( $col > max ) max = $col
      if ( $col < min ) min = $col
    }
      END { print max - min }
' col=$column ${1+"$@"}
```

5.13 stdev—Finding the Standard Deviation

The *standard deviation* is a measure of the dispersion of a set of data from its mean. The more spread apart the data is, the greater the deviation. One use of standard deviation is in finance, where the standard deviation is used as an indicator of the volatility of a stock.

How It Works

One of two different awk programs is used depending on whether the input is a list of numbers or a table with the frequency and the number on the same line.

Usage

```
stdev [-t] [FILE ...]
```

As with other scripts in this section, stdev can take its data from one or more files or from the standard input. The data can be in a list, or, if you use the -t option, it can be in the form of a table with the items in the first column and the frequency in the second.

The Script

```
progname=${0##*/}
table=0
precision=.2

## Parse command-line options
while getopts tp: var
do
  case $var in
     t) table=1 ;;
     p) precision=$OPTARG ;;
  esac
done
shift $(( $OPTIND - 1 ))

if [ $table -eq 0 ] ## Values input one per line
then
  awk '{
        tot += $1    ## Add value to total
        x[NR] = $1 ## Add value to array for later processing
      }

    END {
          mean = tot / NR ## Calculate arithmetical mean
          tot=0              ## Reset total
          for (num in x) {
              ## The difference between each number and the mean
              diff = x[num] - mean

              ## Square difference, multiply by the frequency, and add to total
              tot += diff * diff
          }
          ## Deviation is total divided by number of items
          printf "%" precision "f\n", sqrt( tot / NR )
      }' precision=$precision ${1+"$@"}
else ##
  awk '{
      num += $2
      tot += $1 * $2
      items += $2
      x[NR] = $1
      f[NR] = $2
      }
```

```
        END {
                mean = tot / num ## Calculate arithmetical mean
                tot=0           ## Reset total
                    for (num in x) {
                            ## The difference between each number and the mean
                            diff = x[num] - mean

                            ## Square difference, multiply by the frequency, and add to total
                            tot += diff * diff * f[num]
                    }
                    printf "%" precision "f\n", sqrt( tot / items )
                }' precision=$precision ${1+"$@"}
fi
```

Converting Between Unit Systems

Is 25° warm or cold? Is 1,000 meters too far to walk for a loaf of bread? Which is more, 500 grams or 1 pound? Will I get a speeding ticket if my speedometer says 100?

Chris grew up using imperial weights and measures in the U.K., the U.S., and Canada, and an adult living in Canada when the country changed to the metric system. Rather, it started to change, then it descended into chaos. The change has not been enforced since 1983, and there is now a mixture. At the supermarket, he buys meat by the kilogram and fruit and vegetables by the pound. He once bought a 4-foot by 8-foot sheet of plywood that was 19 mm thick.

While there may be more need for converting to and from metric units in Canada, it is still needed in the U.S. Most of the world uses the metric system, and the U.S. needs to interact with it.

5.14 conversion-funcs—Converting Metric Units

While most people know the common metric temperatures (0°C is 32°F, the freezing point of water, and 20°C is a comfortable room temperature), and they know that a kilogram is 2.2 pounds, it may be a stretch to know what 32°C is in Fahrenheit, or how many pounds are in 3.5 kilograms. Shell scripts can do the conversion calculations between metric and imperial measurement systems.

How It Works

Unix systems have traditionally included a utility called units. While it is a powerful program that can be extended by defining conversions in an external file, it is slow, and not easy to use in a script. Some versions can do only linear conversions, which excludes Fahrenheit to Celsius, and some Unix systems do not install it by default. There are some scripts for conversions that you could use frequently. For this chapter, there are even more.

Usage

```
CMD [UNITS]
_CMD UNITS
```

Like most of the previous functions in this chapter, these come in two flavors. The first is for interactive use, and will prompt for input if no argument is given. The second expects an argument, and stores the result in a variable, which is the name of the function (including the underscore) in uppercase.

There are 16 commands in the `conversion-funcs` script, which can be sourced in a shell initialization file (e.g., `$HOME/.profile`—see Chapter 1 for more information on shell initialization and sourcing files) for interactive use, or at the top of a script to make them available there:

- `f2c`: Degrees Fahrenheit to Celsius

- `f2k`: Degrees Fahrenheit to kelvins

- `c2f`: Degrees Celsius to Fahrenheit

- `k2f`: Kelvins to degrees Fahrenheit

- `m2km`: Miles to kilometers

- `km2m`: Kilometers to miles

- `y2m`: Yards to meters

- `m2y`: Meters to yards

- `i2cm`: Inches to centimeters

- `i2mm`: Inches to millimeters

- `cm2i`: Centimeters to inches

- `mm2i`: Millimeters to inches

- `lb2kg`: Pounds to kilograms

- `kg2lb`: Kilograms to pounds

- `oz2g`: Ounces to grams

- `g2oz`: Grams to ounces

These functions are also available through the `conversion` menu script that follows the functions.

The Script

First the `math-funcs` library is loaded, which in turn loads the `standard-funcs` library.

```
. math-funcs
```

Sixteen conversions make up the `conversion-funcs` script, each of which has two functions: one to do the calculation, and one to print the result. When used in a script, rather than interactively, the result need not be printed, and the script will get the result from the variable set in each function.

1. Convert Degrees Fahrenheit to Celsius

```
f2c()
{
    units="degrees Celsius"
    prompt="Degrees Fahrenheit" arg "$@"
    _f2c "$arg"
    printf "%s%s\n" "$_F2C" "${units:+ $units}"
}
```

```
_f2c()
{
    eval "`echo $1 |
            awk '{
              printf "_F2C=%" pr "f\n", ($1 - 32) * 0.555556
            }' pr=${precision:-.2}`"
}
```

2. Convert Degrees Fahrenheit to Kelvins

```
f2k()
{
    prompt="Degrees Fahrenheit" arg "$@"
    echo "$arg" |
            awk '{
              printf "%" pr "f\n", ($1 - 32) * 0.555556 + 273.15
            }' pr=${precision:-.2}
}
_f2k()
{
    eval "`echo $1 |
            awk '{
              printf "_F2K=%" pr "f\n", ($1 - 32) * 0.555556 + 273.15
            }' pr=${precision:-.2}`"
}
```

3. Convert Degrees Celsius to Fahrenheit

```
c2f()
{
    prompt="Degrees Celsius" arg "$@"
    echo "$arg" |
       awk '{
              printf "_C2F=%" pr "f\n", $1 * 1.8 + 32
            }' pr=${precision:-.2}
}

_c2f()
{
    eval "`echo "$1" |
            awk '{
              printf "_C2F=%" pr "f\n", $1 * 1.8 + 32
            }' pr=${precision:-.2}`"
}
```

4. Convert Kelvins to Degrees Fahrenheit

```
k2f()
{
    units="degrees Fahrenheit"
    prompt="Kelvins" arg "$@"
    echo "$arg" |
        awk '{
                printf "%" pr "f%s\n", ($1 - 273.15) * 1.8 + 32, units
            }' pr=${precision:-.2} units="${units:+ $units}"
}

_k2f()
{
    eval "`echo "$1" |
            awk '{
                printf "_K2F=%" pr "f\n", ($1 - 273.15) * 1.8 + 32
            }' pr=${precision:-.2}`"
}
```

5. Convert Miles to Kilometers

```
m2km()
{
    units=kilometers
    prompt=Miles arg "$@"
    _m2km "$arg"
    printf "%s%s\n" "$_M2KM" "${units:+ $units}"
}

_m2km()
{
    _fpmul "$1" 1.609344
    _M2KM=$_FPMUL
}
```

6. Convert Kilometers to Miles

```
km2m()
{
    units=miles
    prompt=Kilometers arg "$@"
    _fpmul "$arg" .62135
    printf "%s%s\n" "$_FPMUL" "${units:+ $units}"
}

_km2m()
{
    _fpmul "$1" .62135
    _KM2MILE=$_FPMUL
}
```

7. Convert Yards to Meters

```
y2m()
{
    units=meters
    prompt=Yards arg "$@"
    _y2m "$arg"
    printf "%s%s\n" "$_Y2M" "${units:+ $units}"
}

_y2m()
{
    _fpmul "$1" 0.914402
    _Y2M=$_FPMUL
}
```

8. Convert Meters to Yards

```
m2y()
{
    units=yards
    prompt=Meters arg "$@"
    _m2y "$arg"
    printf "%s%s\n" "$_M2Y" "${units:+ $units}"
}

_m2y()
{
    _fpmul "$1" 1.09361
    _M2Y=$_FPMUL
}
```

9. Convert Inches to Centimeters

```
i2cm()
{
    units=centimeters
    prompt=inches arg "$@"
    _i2cm "$arg"
    printf "%s%s\n" "$_I2CM" "${units:+ $units}"
}

_i2cm()
{
    _fpmul "$1" 2.54
    _I2CM=$_FPMUL
}
```

10. Convert Inches to Millimeters

```
i2mm()
{
    units=millimeters
    prompt=inches arg "$@"
    _i2mm "$arg"
    printf "%s%s\n" "$_I2MM" "${units:+ $units}"
}

_i2mm()
{
    _fpmul "$1" 25.4
    _I2MM=$_FPMUL
}
```

11. Convert Centimeters to Inches

```
cm2i()
{
    units=inches
    prompt=Millimeters arg "$@"
    _cm2i "$arg"
    printf "%s%s\n" "$_MM2I" "${units:+ $units}"
}

_cm2i()
{
    _fpmul "$1" .3937
    _CM2I=$_FPMUL
}
```

12. Convert Millimeters to Inches

```
mm2i()
{
    units=inches
    prompt=Millimeters arg "$@"
    _cm2i "$arg"
    printf "%s%s\n" "$_CM2I" "${units:+ $units}"
}

_mm2i()
{
    _fpmul "$1" .03937
    _MM2I=$_FPMUL
}
```

13. Convert Pounds to Kilograms

```
lb2kg()
{
    units=kilograms
    prompt=Pounds arg "$@"
    _lb2kg "$arg"
    printf "%s%s\n" "$_LB2KG" "${units:+ $units}"
}

_lb2kg()
{
    _fpmul "$1" .4545
    _LB2KG=$_FPMUL
}
```

14. Convert Kilograms to Pounds

```
kg2lb()
{
    units=pounds
    prompt=Kilograms arg "$@"
    _kg2lb "$arg"
    printf "%s%s\n" "$_KG2LB" "${units:+ $units}"
}

_kg2lb()
{
    _fpmul "$1" 2.2
    _KG2LB=$_FPMUL
}
```

15. Convert Ounces to Grams

```
oz2g()
{
    units=grams
    prompt=Ounces arg "$@"
    _oz2g "$arg"
    printf "%s%s\n" "$_OZ2G" "${units:+ $units}"
}

_oz2g()
{
    _fpmul "$1" 28.35
    _OZ2G=$_FPMUL
}
```

16. Convert Grams to Ounces

```
g2oz()
{
    units=ounces
    prompt=Grams arg "$@"
    _g2oz "$arg"
    printf "%s%s\n" "$_G2OZ" "${units:+ $units}"
}

_g2oz()
{
    _fpmul "$1" 0.0353
    _G2OZ=$_FPMUL
}
```

5.15 conversion—A Menu System for Metric Conversion

A menu system would make using the conversion functions easier, at least until one has memorized all the function names.

How It Works

The 16 commands are divided into 4 groups, with a menu for each group. A single keystroke invokes each menu item. The names of the functions are included in the menus to help users memorize them.

Usage

```
conversion
```

This script takes no options and requires no arguments. At the main menu, pressing a number from 1 to 4 will take you to the menu for the selected category of conversion. In each menu, one keystroke will bring up a prompt to enter the number you want converted. The answer will be printed, and the script will wait for another keystroke before returning to the menu.

In this sample run, the user selects weight conversions, then ounces to grams, and enters 2. The script prints the answer and prompts for a keypress before returning to the menu. Pressing 0 takes the user to the previous menu, and another 0 exits the script.

The characters in bold are the user's input, which do not actually appear when the script is run.

```
$ conversion

        ============================
            Conversion functions
        ============================


        0. Exit
        1. Lengths and distances
        2. Weights
        3. Temperature
```

```
        ==============================
        Select [0-3]: 2

        ===================================
                        Weights
        ===================================

          0. Exit
          1. lb2kg - pounds to kilograms
          2. kg2lb - kilograms to pounds
          3. oz2g - ounces to grams
          4. g2oz - grams to ounces


        ===================================

        Select [0-4]: 3

Ounces? 2
56.7 grams

<PRESS ANY KEY>

        ===================================
                        Weights
        ===================================

          0. Exit
          1. lb2kg - pounds to kilograms
          2. kg2lb - kilograms to pounds
          3. oz2g - ounces to grams
          4. g2oz - grams to ounces


        ===================================

        Select [0-4]: 0
        ==============================
            Conversion functions
        ==============================

          0. Exit
          1. Lengths and distances
          2. Weights
          3. Temperature


        ==============================

        Select [0-3]: 0
$
```

The Script

Four functions from standard-funcs are used in this menu program:

- menu1: Creates a simple menu system.

- get_key: Returns a key pressed by the user.

- press_any_key: Prompts the user to press any key.

- cleanup: Called from a trap, cleanup restores any terminal settings that have been changed.

The conversion script has a separate function for the main menu and for each submenu. More categories can be added easily.

```
progname=${0##*/}

## if this is the development version of the script (i.e. ends with "-sh"),
## use the development version of the function libraries
## (more on this appears in the Script Development System chapter)
case $progname in
    *sh) shx=-sh ;;
esac

trap cleanup EXIT

. conversion-funcs$shx
```

The Main Menu

```
main_menu()
{
    menu="
        ==============================
                Conversion functions
        ==============================

            0. Exit
            1. Lengths and distances
            2. Weights
            3. Temperature


        ==============================

        Select [0-3]: "

menu1 distances weights temperatures
}
```

The Lengths and Distances Menu

```
distances()
{
    menu="

           ===================================
                    Lengths and distances
           ===================================

            0. Exit
            1. m2km - miles to kilometers
            2. km2m - kilometers to miles
            3. y2m - yards to meters
            4. m2y - meters to yards
            5. i2cm - inches to centimeters
            6. cm2i - centimeters to inches
            7. i2cm - inches to millimeters
            8. cm2i - millimeters to inches


           ===================================

            Select [0-8]: "

        pause_after=1 menu1 m2km km2m y2m m2y i2cm cm2i i2mm mm2i
}
```

The Weights Menu

```
weights()
{
    menu="

           ===================================
                          Weights
           ===================================

            0. Exit
            1. lb2kg - pounds to kilograms
            2. kg2lb - kilograms to pounds
            3. oz2g - ounces to grams
            4. g2oz - grams to ounces


           ===================================

            Select [0-4]: "

        pause_after=1 menu1 lb2kg kg2lb oz2g g2oz

}
```

The Temperature Conversion Menu

```
temperatures()
{
    menu="

        =====================================
                    Temperatures
        =====================================

            0. Exit
            1. f2c - Fahrenheit to Celsius
            2. c2f - Celsius to Fahrenheit
            3. f2k - Fahrenheit to kelvin
            4. k2f - kelvins to degrees Fahrenheit


        =====================================

        Select [0-4]: "

    pause_after=1 menu1 f2c c2f f2k k2f
}

precision=.2
main_menu
printf "\n"
```

Summary

This chapter has barely scratched the surface of the numerical manipulations possible with shell scripts. There are more in other chapters, and no doubt you can think of many more, too.

Most of these scripts are very simple; a program doesn't have to be complicated to be useful. You can create a new metric conversion script if you know the formula, and anything can be found on the Internet. (You don't think we remembered them all, do you?)

CHAPTER 6

■ ■ ■

Loose Names Sink Scripts: Bringing Sanity to Filenames

The Naming of Files is a serious matter,

This isn't just one of your Usenet flames;

You may think at first it doesn't much matter

But I tell you, a file should have a SENSIBLE NAME.

(with apologies to T. S. Eliot)

What *is* a sensible name, and what can be done about pathological filenames? In this chapter, we describe alternatives for creating acceptable filenames and provide scripts for dealing with bad names. We also provide shell replacement functions for the basename and dirname commands.

What's in a Name?

A Unix filename may contain any character except NUL and the forward slash (/). A NUL (a character in which all bits are 0) cannot be part of a filename because the shell uses it internally to signal the end of a string of characters. The slash is reserved for separating directories in the path to a file. Apart from those two, any character may be used in a filename. This is not to say that all of the permissible characters *should* be used in filenames.

In the early (and not-so-early) days of Unix, most file manipulation was done at the command line or in a shell script. Syntactically, a filename is a word or token, and that's what the shell is designed to handle. Putting spaces in a filename makes no sense in that context. The same is true of a number of other characters that cause problems: apostrophes and asterisks, brackets and backslashes, to name a few. The worst is the newline (NL).

Characters such as spaces, asterisks, and newlines can break many (especially older) scripts. Whitespace characters, space and tab, can usually be accommodated fairly easily by quoting all variables containing filenames. They do cause problems in scripts that pipe a list of files.

We'll cd to an empty directory and create some files with spaces in their names (this uses brace expansion from bash; it's not available in all POSIX shells):

```
$ touch {qwe,rty,uio}\ {asd,fgh,jkl}
```

Then we'll list them, one to a line:

```
$ ls -1 *
qwe asd
qwe fgh
qwe jkl
rty asd
rty fgh
rty jkl
uio asd
uio fgh
uio jkl
```

Note that the use of a wildcard preserves the integrity of the filenames. This integrity is lost when the filenames are the output of another command; then, each word is treated separately:

```
$ printf "%s\n" * | wc -l
9
$ printf "%s\n" `ls *` | wc -l
18
$ ls | xargs printf "%s %s %s\n"
qwe asd qwe
fgh qwe jkl
rty asd rty
fgh rty jkl
uio asd uio
fgh uio jkl
```

Frequently, files are piped to another command that reads them line by line. If newlines are in the filenames, this method obviously fails.

POSIX Portable Filenames

The POSIX standard (strictly speaking, IEEE Std 1003.1-2001) defines a Portable Filename Character Set[1] that is guaranteed to be portable across POSIX systems. Modern Unix systems are largely POSIX compliant, and this character set, which comprises the 52 upper- and lowercase letters, the 10 digits, and the period, hyphen, and underscore, is safe on all such systems (as well as most older ones). Portable filenames may not begin with a hyphen.[2]

A portable filename will not run afoul of any shell scripts (well, there are ways, but they needn't concern us here).

OK Filenames

For your own use, you can get away with a larger character set. I define this set by the characters that are *not* allowed. These include the whitespace characters (NL, CR, tab, and space), asterisk, question mark, parentheses, square brackets, angle brackets, braces, apostrophe, double quotes, octothorpe (#), and pipe (|). You may wish to add more characters.

---

[1]http://www.opengroup.org/onlinepubs/000095399/basedefs/xbd_chap03.html#tag_03_276
[2]http://www.opengroup.org/onlinepubs/000095399/basedefs/xbd_chap04.html#tag_04_06

Functioning Filenames: The filename-funcs Library

The filename-funcs library sources the standard-vars and string-funcs files (from Chapters 1 and 3, respectively), sets variables that define the portable and OK character sets, and defines a number of functions for manipulating filenames.

```
## source the variable and function libraries
. standard-vars$shx
. string-funcs$shx

## define characters for portable and OK character sets
## pfname_chars is a list of acceptable characters
pfname_chars="a-zA-Z._0-9-"
## xfname_chars is a list of unacceptable characters
xfname_chars="][|#?><*${BKS}\$'\"${SPC}${NL}${TAB}${CR}${BS}${DEL}()"
```

Most functions in this file follow the convention used earlier of pairing the functions; one sets a variable, and the other calls the first one, then prints the variable.

The first two functions, basename and dirname, are shell implementations of the standard commands. They conform to the POSIX specification,[3] but are faster because they do not start a new process. While most of the functions can be used on their own, the last two, fix_filename and fix_pwd, are intended to be called by the fixfname command that follows.

6.1 basename—Extract the Last Element of a Pathname

The basename command extracts the last element, usually a filename, from a pathname. Optionally, it also removes a suffix from that element.

How It Works

In a POSIX shell, the basename command is rarely needed. Parameter expansion can extract the filename from a pathname:

```
$ pathname=/home/jayant/work/book/chapter05.doc
$ filename=${pathname##*/}
$ printf "%s\n" "$filename"
chapter05.doc
```

It can also remove a suffix:

```
$ printf "%s\n" "${filename%.doc}"
chapter05
```

This basename function adds full POSIX compliance to the parameter expansion; it strips trailing slashes before extracting the basename, and does not remove a suffix if nothing would be left. It is a full replacement for the external command, and scripts that use basename do not need to be modified.

---

[3]http://www.opengroup.org/onlinepubs/009695399/utilities/basename.html and http://www.opengroup.org/onlinepubs/009695399/utilities/dirname.html

Usage

```
_basename PATHNAME [SUFFIX] ## result is stored in $_BASENAME
basename PATHNAME [SUFFIX]  ## result is printed
```

If a variable contains the path to a file (e.g., script=/home/jayant/bin/wf-sh), the filename alone can be printed with basename:

```
$ basename $script
wf-sh
```

To print the filename without the -sh suffix, use this:

```
$ basename $script -sh
wf
```

If the path given to basename ends in one or more slashes, then the slashes are removed, and the last part of the remaining path is returned:

```
$ basename /usr/local/bin/
bin
```

The Script

The strip_trailing_slashes function is used by both basename and dirname.

```
strip_trailing_slashes()
{
    _STRIP=$1
    while :
    do
        case $_STRIP in
            ## If the last characer is a slash, remove it
            */) _STRIP=${_STRIP%/} ;;
            ## otherwise exit the loop (and function)
            *) break ;;
        esac
    done
}

_basename() ## extract the last element from a pathname
{
    fn_path=$1
    fn_suffix=$2
    case $fn_path in
        ## The spec says: "If string is a null string, it is
        ## unspecified whether the resulting string is '.' or a
        ## null string." This implementation returns a null string
        "") _BASENAME=; return ;;
        *)
```

```
            strip_trailing_slashes "$fn_path"
            case $_STRIP in
            "") fn_path="/" ;;
            *) fn_path=${_STRIP##*/} ;;
        esac
        ;;
    esac

    ## If a suffix was given, and it is the final portion of the file name (but not
    ## the whole name), then remove it.
    case $fn_path in
        $fn_suffix | "/" ) _BASENAME="$fn_path" ;;
        *) _BASENAME=${fn_path%$fn_suffix} ;;
    esac
}

basename()
{
    _basename "$@" &&
    printf "%s\n" "$_BASENAME"
}
```

6.2 dirname—Return All but the Last Element of a Pathname

Return all of a pathname except the part that would be returned by basename. In other words, print the directory that contains the last element of the pathname.

How It Works

The dirname function is a full, POSIX-compliant replacement for the external dirname command.

Usage

```
_dirname PATHNAME ## result is stored in $_DIRNAME
dirname PATHNAME ## result is printed
```

Like basename, dirname does not honor the POSIX standard of interpreting a pathname ending with a slash as if it ended with slash-dot (/.).[4] All trailing slashes are removed before the last element is removed:

```
$ dirname /home/chris/Chess/
/home/chris
```

The POSIX definition of dirname allows the implementation to define whether a pathname consisting of // returns one or two slashes. This implementation returns a single slash:

```
$ dirname //
/
```

---

[4]"A pathname that contains at least one non-slash character and that ends with one or more trailing slashes shall be resolved as if a single dot character ('.') were appended to the pathname." http://www.opengroup.org/online-pubs/009695399/basedefs/xbd_chap04.html#tag_04_11

The Script

```
_dirname()
{
    _DIRNAME=$1
    strip_trailing_slashes
    case $_DIRNAME in
        "") _DIRNAME='/'; return ;;
        */*) _DIRNAME="${_DIRNAME%/*}" ;;
        *) _DIRNAME='.'; return ;;
    esac
    strip_trailing_slashes
     _DIRNAME=${_DIRNAME:-/}
}

dirname()
{
    _dirname "$@" &&
    printf "%s\n" "$_DIRNAME"
}
```

6.3 is_pfname—Check for POSIX Portable Filename

Whether checking existing files or validating a user's entry, a method is needed to determine whether a filename conforms to the POSIX portable filename standard described at the beginning of this chapter.

How It Works

Use a case statement to check whether the filename contains anything other than characters from the portable character set. Successful completion (return code 0) indicates that the name contains only acceptable characters and that the filename does not begin with a hyphen. An empty filename will also fail the test.

Usage

```
is_pfname "FILENAME"
```

The return code can be tested explicitly, or the decision can be made directly on success or failure of the command:

```
## Test the return code
is_pfname "$FILENAME"
if [ $? -eq 0 ]
then
    printf "%s is acceptable\n" "$FILENAME"
else
    printf "%s needs to be fixed\n" "$FILENAME"
fi
## Test for success or failure
if is_pfname "$FILENAME"
```

```
then
    printf "%s is acceptable\n" "$FILENAME"
else
    printf "%s needs to be fixed\n" "$FILENAME"
fi
```

Names that conform to the POSIX portable filename standard include Chapter_1.html, half-way.txt, and 4711-ch06.doc. Unacceptable filenames include william&mary (the ampersand is not allowed) and -lewis_and_clark (a leading hyphen is forbidden).

The Script

```
is_pfname()
{
    pfname_test="[!$pfname_chars]" ## Pattern to use in the case statement
    case $1 in
        ## Test for empty filename, leading hyphen, or deprecated characters
        "" | -* | *$pfname_test*) return 1 ;;
    esac
}
```

6.4 is_OKfname—Check Whether a Filename Is Acceptable

Checking whether a filename conforms to the looser OK standard described at the beginning of the chapter is similar to checking for a POSIX portable filename. It must not accept an empty name, a name beginning with a hyphen, or one containing any character in the proscribed lists.

How It Works

A case statement, similar to the one in is_pfname, checks for all three conditions.

Usage

```
is_OKfname "FILENAME"
```

This function can be used in exactly the same way as is_pfname. Both functions can also be used in a loop to list all nonconforming files:

```
for file in *
do
is_OKfname || printf ":: %s\n" "$file"
done
```

The Script

```
is_OKfname()
{
    xfname_test="[$xfname_chars]" ## Pattern to use in the case statement
    case $1 in
        ## Test for empty filename, leading hyphen, or deprecated characters
        "" | -* | *$xfname_test*) return 1 ;;
    esac
}
```

6.5 pfname—Convert Nonportable Characters in Filename

The previous two functions checked whether a filename conformed to an acceptable character set. The next step is to convert a filename to a portable filename (or, as in the script following this one, an OK filename).

How It Works

The pfname function uses _gsub from the string-funcs library (described in Chapter 3) to change all nonportable characters to an acceptable character: by default, an underscore. Another character (or even a string of characters) may be used by assigning it to rpl_char. A leading hyphen is converted to an underscore.

Usage

```
_pfname "FILENAME" ## result is stored in $_PFNAME
pfname "FILENAME"  ## result is printed
```

If the filename is already portable, pfname will not change it:

```
$ FILE=qwerty.uiop
$ pfname "$FILE"
qwerty.uiop
```

On the other hand, an invalid character will be converted to an underscore:

```
$ pfname "qwe rty=uiop"
qwe_rty_uiop
```

This short script uses pfname to fix a filename if it is not portable:

```
is_pfname "$FILE" || {
_pfname "$FILE"
mv "$FILE" "$_PFNAME"
}
```

146

A character other than an underscore can be used as the replacement character:

```
$ FILE=qwe=+rty
$ rpl_char=X
$ pfname "$FILE"
qweXXrty
```

To allow more characters, add them to the pfname_chars variable:

```
$ pfname qwe+rty=asd
qwe_rty_asd
$ pfname_chars=${pfname_chars}+=
$ pfname qwe+rty=a*sd
qwe+rty=a_sd
```

Since the plus and equal signs were added to the list of acceptable characters, only the asterisk was changed.

The Script

```
_pfname()
{
    pfname_pat="[!$pfname_chars]" ## Pattern for case statement
    _gsub "$1" "$pfname_pat" "${rpl_char:-_}" ## Change unacceptable characters
    case $_GSUB in
        -*) _PFNAME=_${_GSUB#?} ;; ## Convert leading hyphen to underscore
        *) _PFNAME=$_GSUB ;;
    esac
}

pfname()
{
    _pfname "$@" &&
    printf "%s\n" "$_PFNAME"
}
```

6.6 OKfname—Make a Filename Acceptable

Remove problematic characters from a filename by using a more liberal set of characters than the POSIX portable character filename set.

How It Works

Unlike pfname, which changes everything not included in a set of acceptable characters, OKfname converts unacceptable characters to underscore (or another character or string).

Usage

```
_OKfname "FILENAME" ## result is stored in $_OKFNAME
OKfname "FILENAME"  ## result is printed
```

Usage of OKfname is the same as pfname, except that the variable xfname_chars contains characters that should *not* be allowed:

```
$ fname=qwe+rty=asd
$ OKfname "$fname"
qwe+rty=asd
```

By adding the equal sign to the xfname_chars variable, it too will be converted to an underscore.

```
$ xfname_chars=${xfname_chars}= OKfname "$fname"

qwe+rty_asd
```

The Script

```
_OKfname()
{
    xfname_pat="[$xfname_chars]"
    _gsub "$1" "$xfname_pat" "${rpl_char:-_}"
    case $_GSUB in
        -*) _OKFNAME=_${_GSUB#?} ;;
        *) _OKFNAME=$_GSUB ;;
    esac
}

OKfname()
{
    _OKfname "$@" &&
    printf "%s\n" "$_OKFNAME"
}
```

6.7 is_whitespc—Does the Filename Contain Whitespace Characters?

Whitespace characters are the most common problem in filenames, so it is useful to have a function to determine whether a filename contains a space, a tab, a newline, or a carriage return.

How It Works

Use case pattern matching to check for whitespace characters.

Usage

```
is_whitespace "FILENAME"
```

Whitespace is bad, so is_whitespc fails if any whitespace is in the filename.

The Script

```
is_whitespc()
{
    case $1 in
        *[$SPC$TAB$NL$CR]*) return 1 ;;
    esac
}
```

6.8 whitespc—Fix Filenames Containing Whitespace Characters

Whether it's because we might know that the only problem characters are spaces, or because the other nonconforming characters are not going to cause any problems, sometimes all you might want to do is to convert whitespace characters to underscores.

How It Works

The _gsub function from the string-funcs library in Chapter 3 comes to the rescue to change those pesky critters to POSIX-abiding filenames.

Usage

```
_whitespc "FILENAME" ## result is in $_WHITESPC
whitespc "FILENAME" ## result is printed
```

By default, spaces are changed to underscores:

```
$ whitespc "Eric the Red"
Eric_the_Red
```

To use a different replacement character, set the rpl_char variable to that character or string:

```
$ rpl_char=- whitespc "definitely not the opera"
definitely-not-the-opera
```

The Script

```
_whitespc() ## convert whitespace to underscores
{
    _gsub "$1" "[ ${TAB}${NL}${CR}]" "${rpl_char:-_}"
    case $_GSUB in
        -*) _WHITESPC=_${_GSUB#?} ;;
        *) _WHITESPC=$_GSUB ;;
    esac
}
```

```
whitespc()
{
    _whitespc "$@"
    printf "%s\n" "$_WHITESPC"
}
```

6.9 is_dir—Is This a Directory I See Before Me?

Before calling a command that takes one or more directories as arguments, you want to check whether */ expands to at least one directory. You cannot use test -d, because it only accepts a single " you can call with */ as an argument, and have it tell me whether the argument has expanded successfully.

How It Works

The -d operand to test (usually used as [ ]) expects only one argument, so test -d */ will fail if it expands to more than one directory. By putting the test in a function (it could also be an external command), the shell expands the argument, and the function sees a list of directories (if there are any). The script only needs to check the first argument.

Usage

```
is_dir PATTERN
```

The function will fail if the first argument when PATTERN expands is not a directory:

```
$ is_dir */ && some_command "$@" || echo "No directory" >&2
```

It also works if given a single argument:

```
$ is_dir /home/chris/grid.ps && echo YES || echo NO
```

The Script

```
is_dir() ## is the first argument a directory?
{
    test -d "$1"
}
```

Notes

The function was designed for use with */ or /path/to/dir/*/ as the calling pattern. It does not work with a pattern that may expand to a mixture of files and directories, unless a directory happens to be first. A function to indicate whether any of the arguments is a directory could be written like this:

```
any_dirs()
{
    for x
  do
    test -d "$x" && return
  done
  return 1
}
```

6.10 nodoublechar—Remove Duplicate Characters from a String

After removing pathological characters from a filename, often there will be two or more consecutive underscores. This command is needed to remove duplicate underscores from a filename or other string.

How It Works

The ubiquitous _gsub function converts two characters to one.

Usage

```
_nodoublechar "FILENAME" [CHAR] ## result is in $_NODOUBLECHAR
nodoublechar "FILENAME" [CHAR] ## result is printed
```

After converting a filename such as tea & coffee with pfname or OKfname, three consecutive underscores remain. This function reduces them to a single underscore:

```
$ nodoublechar "tea coffee"
tea_coffee
```

The Script

```
_nodoublechar() ## remove duplicate characters
{
    _NODOUBLECHAR=$1 ## The string to modify
    _char=${2:-_} ## The character (or string) to operate on
    while :
    do
      case $_NODOUBLECHAR in
        ## If there is a double instance of the string,
        ## reduce to a single instance
        *${_char}${_char}*) _gsub "$_NODOUBLECHAR" "${_char}${_char}" "${_char}"
                _NODOUBLECHAR=$_GSUB
                ;;
```

```
            *) break ;; ## All clear; exit the loop and function
        esac
    done
}

nodoublechar()
{
    _nodoublechar "$@" &&
    printf "%s\n" "$_NODOUBLECHAR"
}
```

6.11 new_filename—Change Filename to Desired Character Set

This script will convert a filename using one of the four defined functions:

- pfname: Convert all characters not in the POSIX portable filename character set to underscores.

- OKfname: Convert all unacceptable characters to underscores.

- whitespc: Convert all whitespace characters to underscores.

- nodoublechar: Reduce multiple underscores to a single underscore.

How It Works

Set the ff_cmd variable to the desired conversion function and call new_filename with the old filename as the argument. If ff_cmd is not set, it defaults to _pfname. Another character (or string) can be used in place of an underscore by redefining rpl_char.

Usage

```
_new_filename "FILENAME" ## result in $_NEW_FILENAME
new_filename "FILENAME" ## result is printed
```

This function is intended to be called by the function fix_pwd, described in the following section; see that function for its use. Normally, the conversion function would be called directly by a script; this is a mechanism for selecting and calling the correct function.

The Script

```
_new_filename()
{
    ${ff_cmd:=_pfname} "$1"
    case $ff_cmd in
        _pfname)  _NEW_FILENAME=$_PFNAME ;;
        _OKfname) _NEW_FILENAME=$_OKFNAME ;;
        _whitespc) _NEW_FILENAME=$_WHITESPC ;;
        _nodoublechar) _NEW_FILENAME=$_NODOUBLECHAR ;;
    esac
```

```
    [ $nodoublechar -eq 1 ] && {
        _nodoublechar "$_NEW_FILENAME" _
        _NEW_FILENAME=$_NODOUBLECHAR
    }
}

new_filename()
{
    _new_filename "$@"
    printf "%s\n" "$_NEW_FILENAME"
}
```

6.12 fix_pwd—Fix All the Filenames in the Current Directory

Check each file in the current directory and convert any that do not fit the prescribed character set.

How It Works

Several variables control the behavior of fix_pwd:

- verbose: If set to 1 or greater, print progress information.
- pattern: Change only those files whose names match the pattern contained in the variable; the default is all files if pattern is empty.
- f_only: Only modify names of files.
- d_only: Only modify names of directories.
- ff_cmd: Use the function contained in the variable to modify the filename (see fix_filename).

Usage

```
fix_pwd
```

The function is controlled entirely by the variables just listed and takes no arguments.

The Script

```
fix_pwd()
{
    ## Print name of directory in verbose mode
    [ ${verbose:=0} -ge 1 ] && printf ":: %s ::\n" "${PWD%/}/" >&2

    ## Loop through all files that match the pattern
    for file in ${pattern:-*}
    do
      [ -e "$file" ] || continue  ## should be unnecessary
```

```
## find file type
[ -f "$file" ] && f_type=f
[ -d "$file" ] && f_type=d

## only operate on regular files and directories
case $f_type$d_only$f_only in
    f0? | d?0) ;;
    *) continue ;;
esac

## check whether filename is OK, and modify if not
is${ff_cmd:=_pfname} "$file" || {
    _new_filename "$file"
    new_base=$_NEW_FILENAME
    n=1

    ## if $_NEW_FILENAME exists, append a number
    while [ -e "$_NEW_FILENAME" ]
    do

      _NEW_FILENAME=$new_base.$n
      [ $verbose -ge 1 ] && printf "%s\r" "$_NEW_FILENAME" >&2
      n=$(( $n + 1 ))
    done

    [ $verbose -ge 1 ] &&
            printf "%s -> %s " "$file" "$_NEW_FILENAME" >&2
    mv "./$file" "./$_NEW_FILENAME" && [ $verbose -ge 1 ] &&
            printf "OK\n" >&2 || printf "failed\n" >&2
  }
  done
}
```

6.13 fixfname—Convert Filenames to Sensible Names

Filenames containing spaces or tabs are annoying. Filenames beginning with a hyphen may be confused with command options. Filenames containing an apostrophe may be considered incomplete. Filenames containing a newline are an abomination. All of these, and more, can break scripts.

Unless there's a good reason not to (such as an application that expects to find badly named files), these filenames should be fixed. At the very least, all whitespace characters should be removed, perhaps converted to underscores. At the most, all filenames should conform to the POSIX portable filename standard. A reasonable compromise is to get rid of the most trouble- some characters, the OK character set.

How It Works

Here is a script that will convert all the filenames in a directory to your choice of POSIX, OK, or just whitespace-free. The unsavory characters are replaced by underscores (or another character of your choice). You can choose to squeeze multiple underscores to a single character.

You can convert the current directory, or you can descend a directory tree (excluding symbolic links). You can convert only directory names, or only filenames. You can limit the conversion to names that match a pattern.

When a converted filename matches an existing filename, a number is added to the end of the name. This number is incremented as necessary to make the filename unique.

Usage

`fixfname [OPTIONS] [DIRECTORY ...]`

Command-line options control the behavior of `fixfname`, including the type of conversion (by default, `fixfname` uses the POSIX standard):

- `-c C`: Use C to replace undesirable characters instead of an underscore.

- `-k`: Use the more liberal OK character set instead of POSIX.

- `-s`: Just convert the whitespace characters: space, tab, newline, and carriage return.

- `-u`: Replace double (or triple, or more) underscores with a single underscore. Do not perform any other conversion.

- `-d`: Convert directory names, but leave filenames alone. This does not affect recursion.

- `-f`: Change filenames; directory assistance is not required.

- `-p PAT`: Transform only those names that match PAT, using pathname expansion. Avoid using problematic characters (spaces, etc.) in PAT.

- `-U`: Convert multiple underscores, as with `-u`, but combined with another conversion.

- `-v`: Verbose mode; print (to standard error) the names of directories that are entered, and the old and new filenames when a conversion is made.

- `-R`: Descend directories recursively (but do not descend through symbolic links).

- `-V`: Print the version number of the script and exit.

With `fixfname`, you can operate on anything from a single file to an entire directory hierarchy. Here are a few examples.

To convert all spaces in the .jpg filenames in the current directory to underscores, use this:

`fixfname -sp "*.jpg"`

To convert all .ogg files in the current directory tree to portable filenames with all multiple underscores reduced to a single one, use this:

`fixfname -Rup "*.ogg"`

To change all files named `test@file.txt` in the current directory and all its subdirectories, use this:

`fixfname -Rvp 'test@file.txt'`

The Script

```
progname=${0##*/} ## this can usually replace `basename $0`

## While under development, my scripts have names ending with "-sh"
## These scripts call the development versions of function libraries
## whose names also end in -sh. (The script development system, which copies
## the script to the bin directory and removes the suffix, is presented in
## Chapter 20.)
case $progname in
    *-sh) shx=-sh ;;
    *) shx= ;;
esac

## filename-funcs[-sh] contains all the preceding functions
. filename-funcs$shx

## Set defaultsverbose=0
recurse=0         ## Do not descend into directories
ff_cmd=_pfname    ## Use POSIX filenames
rpl_char=_        ## Replace bad characters with underscore
pattern=*         ## All files in current directory
nodoublechar=0    ## Do not squeeze double underscores
f_only=0          ## Do not modify only directories
d_only=0          ## Do not modify only files
R_opt=            ## Clear options for recursive operation

## Parse command-line options
while getopts vRUVfdksuc:p: var
do
  case $var in
      c) rpl_char=$OPTARG ## replacement for underscore
         R_opt="$R_opt -c '$rpl_char'" ;;
      k) ff_cmd=_OKfname ## use OK filenames rather than portable ones
         R_opt="$R_opt -k" ;;
      s) ff_cmd=_whitespc ## just convert whitespace to underscores
         R_opt="$R_opt -s" ;;
      u) ff_cmd=_nodoublechar ## convert double underscores to single
         R_opt="$R_opt -u" ;;
      d) d_only=1 ## only process directories
         R_opt="$R_opt -d" ;;
      f) f_only=2 ## only process files
         R_opt="$R_opt -f" ;;
o     p) pattern=$OPTARG ## only change names matching $pattern
         R_opt="$R_opt -p '$pattern'" ;;
      U) nodoublechar=1 ## convert __[...] to _ (with other fixes)
         R_opt="$R_opt -U"
         ;;
      v) verbose=$(( $verbose + 1 )) ## print progress reports
         R_opt="$R_opt -v"
         ;;
```

```
      R) recurse=1 ;; ## descend directories recursively
      V) printf "$progname: %s\n" $version; exit ;;
  esac
done
shift $(( $OPTIND - 1 ))

## If there is a directory on the command line.....
if [ -d "$1" ]
then
  for dir ## ...enter it and any other directories in turn
  do
    ( [ -L "${dir%/}" ] && continue ## do not descend symlinked directories
      cd "$dir" || continue ## Skip to next if dir not cd-able
      fix_pwd ## Do it
      [ $recurse -eq 1 ] && is_dir ./*/ && eval "\"$0\"" -R $R_opt ./*/"
    )
  done
else
  fix_pwd
  [ $recurse -eq 1 ] && is_dir ./*/ && eval "\"$0\"" -R $R_opt ./*/"
fi
```

Summary

I hope you have no doubt about my feelings regarding badly formed filenames. If shell scripts were never used, it wouldn't matter. But despite the popularity of languages such as Perl and Python, it is exceedingly unlikely that shell scripts will ever disappear entirely. They are a natural complement to the command line.

You may have realized that, despite my ranting over @!$#%^*& filenames (I've run out of polite things to call them), You have a chapter full of scripts that can process any file- names you can come up with. It is possible to do it, but a lot of scripting techniques are ruled out because of them. If you need to write shell scripts that work on spaced-out filenames, remember two things:

1. Populate variables with the results of filename expansion (wildcards), not the output of commands such as cat or ls.

2. Enclose the variables in quotes when you use them: "$filename" not $filename.

CHAPTER 7

■ ■ ■

Treading a Righteous PATH

The PATH variable is a colon-separated list of directories that your shell will search for a command. It usually includes /bin, /usr/bin, and /usr/local/bin. If you are root, it will also include /sbin and /usr/sbin. There may be other directories, and there may even be a dot, which puts your current directory in the PATH. For example, a typical user's $PATH looks like this:

/usr/bin:/bin:/usr/local/bin:/usr/games:/usr/X11R6/bin:/home/chris/bin

Whenever you enter a command without a full path (e.g., ls instead of /bin/ls), the shell searches the directories listed in your PATH variable for the command. If all the directories you need are not included, commands will not be found. If the current directory is included, especially near the front, there are security risks. If spurious and duplicate directories are included, the search for commands may be infinitesimally slower; it's not really a problem, but why not keep things neat and tidy?

In this chapter, you have a library of functions for manipulating your PATH variable: to add and delete directories, to check that all entries are valid, and to display your PATH in a more readable form. If you source path-funcs, and run checkpath in your .profile, you can view your PATH with path and manipulate it with addpath and rmpath, avoiding any potential problems.

The path-funcs Library

You can use the functions in this library to keep your PATH variable in good shape by adding and removing directories, ensuring that all its elements are, in fact, directories, and that the current directory is not among them.

7.1 path—Display a User's PATH

For 15 years, the computer Chris used was an Amiga; it had a path command. When called without any arguments, it would print your command path one directory per line—a format that is more legible than a single colon-separated line, which may break a directory in two if the PATH is longer than a screen width. If there were one or more arguments, it would add those arguments to the command path. He missed that command, so he wrote a Unix version.

How It Works

Since PATH is a colon-separated list, it can be split by assigning a colon to the internal field separator, IFS. A single printf statement prints each directory on a separate line. If one or more directories is given as an argument, the PATH is not printed and the addpath function (introduced later in this chapter) is used to append them to the PATH variable.

Usage

```
path [DIR ...]
```

My PATH contains two subdirectories of my $HOME directory, as well as the sbin directories usually reserved for the root user:

```
$ path
/bin
/usr/bin
/usr/X11R6/bin
/usr/local/bin
/home/chris/bin
/home/chris/scripts
/usr/local/kde/bin
/sbin
/usr/sbin
/usr/local/sbin
```

The Script

```
path()
{
    if [ -n "$*" ]; then
        addpath "$@" || return
    else
        ( ## Use a subshell so IFS is not changed in the main shell
          IFS=:
          printf "%s\n" ${PATH}
        )
    fi
}
```

7.2 unslash—Remove Extraneous Slashes

The functions in this chapter that alter the $PATH (checkpath, addpath, and rmpath) compare directory names, so they need to have a standardized format. This means removing trailing slashes and collapsing double slashes to single slashes.

How It Works

Trailing slashes are easily removed with parameter expansion. Double slashes are changed to single slashes with _gsub, from Chapter 3's string-funcs library. If the library has not been loaded, unslash will source the string-funcs file.

Usage

```
_unslash "pathname"      ## result in $_UNSLASH
unslash "pathname"       ## result is printed
```

Like many of the functions in this book, unslash is paired with an underscore function.

```
$ unslash /usr//bin//////
/usr/bin
$ _unslash //x//y//
$ printf "%s\n" "$_UNSLASH"
/x/y
```

The Script

```
_unslash()
{
    _UNSLASH=$1
    while :
    do
     case $_UNSLASH in
         ## remove trailing slashes
         */) _UNSLASH=${_UNSLASH%/} ;;


         ## change // to /
         *//*) type _gsub >/dev/null 2>&1 || . string-funcs
             _gsub "$_UNSLASH" "//" "/"
             _UNSLASH=$_GSUB
             ;;

         *) break ;;
     esac
    done
}

unslash()
{
    _unslash "$@" && printf "%s\n" "$_UNSLASH"
}
```

7.3 checkpath—Clean Up the PATH Variable

Along the route from login to command prompt, many scripts are sourced. Some of them add directories to the PATH variable. They rarely check whether the directory is already in the PATH, and sometimes they put the current directory in the PATH. In some, this is deliberate; in others, it's the result of careless scripting.

One Linux distribution arrived at the prompt with this PATH:

```
/usr//bin:/bin:/usr/bin::/usr/local/bin:/usr/X11R6/bin:/usr/games:/home/me/bin:
```

The double inclusion of /usr/bin (in two different forms) is not a serious problem, just a minor inefficiency. However, another directory is implicitly included twice. Empty fields, created in this case by :: and the final colon, are interpreted as the current directory. It's not as serious at the end of the PATH; anywhere else, it represents a potentially dangerous security hole.

Any empty element (a leading or trailing colon or two successive colons) or a period in your PATH will be interpreted as the current directory. For security reasons, putting the current directory in one's PATH is not recommended. If the current directory is ahead of /bin in your PATH, and

a rogue program with the same name as a standard command (ls, for example) is in your current directory, it would be executed, and it could damage your files or your system. It is a good idea to clean up your PATH in your .profile.

How It Works

By first standardizing the format of the directories in $PATH (with unslash), checkpath can easily find duplicates. The current directory, represented explicitly by a dot or implicitly by an empty field, will not be included.

Usage

```
checkpath [-v]
```

In verbose mode (-v), checkpath prints information about the items it deletes; otherwise, it does its job silently.

```
$ PATH=/usr//bin::/bin:/usr/bin/:
$ checkpath -v
checkpath: removing /usr/bin (already in PATH)
$ path
/usr/bin
/bin
```

The Script

```
checkpath()
{
    verbose=0
    OPTIND=1
    while getopts  v var
    do
      case "$var" in
            v) verbose=1 ;;
      esac
    done

  ## assign the directories in PATH to the positional parameters
  oldIFS=$IFS
  IFS=":"
  set -- $PATH
  IFS=$oldIFS
  newPATH=
```

```
for p   ## Loop through directories in $PATH (now set as positional parameters)
do
case $p in
    ""|.) continue ;; ## do not allow current directory in PATH
esac
if [ -d "$p" ] ## Is it actually a directory?
then
  _unslash "$p"    ## Remove multiple slashes
  p=$_UNSLASH
  case :$newPATH: in
      *:"$p":*) [ $verbose -ge 1 ] &&
          echo "checkpath: removing $p (already in PATH)" >&2
          ;;
      *) newPATH=${newPATH:+$newPATH:}$p ;; ## Add directory
  esac
else
  [ $verbose -ge 1 ] &&
      echo "checkpath: $p is not a directory; removing it from PATH" >&2
fi
done
PATH=$newPATH
}
```

7.4 addpath—Add Directories to the PATH Variable

When you add a directory to the PATH variable, you want to be sure that the directory is not already there and that it is, in fact, a directory. If you have a directory of alternative commands, you will want to add it to the beginning instead of the end of PATH so that they are used in place of the standard versions.

How It Works

The addpath function checks that each argument is a directory, and that the directory is not already in the PATH. If the argument passes the tests, it is added to the end of PATH. The -i option tells addpath to insert directories at the beginning of PATH instead of appending them.

Usage

```
addpath [-iq] DIR ...
```

One or more directories may be specified on the command line:

```
$ PATH=/bin:/usr/bin
$ addpath /usr/local/bin $HOME/bin
$ path
/bin
/usr/bin
/usr/local/bin
/home/chris/bin
```

The -i option tells addpath to place the directory at the beginning of PATH rather than the end, and the -q option suppresses the printing of error messages:

```
$ addpath -i /usr/games /chess /bin
addpath: /chess is not a directory
addpath: /bin already in path
$ addpath -q /bin    ## no output
$ path
/usr/games
/bin
/usr/bin
/usr/local/bin
/home/chris/bin
```

For duplicate detection to work properly, the PATH should be standardized with checkpath before running this function. Ideally, this will already have been done as part of the shell's start-up scripts.

The Script

```
addpath()

{
    ## Set defaults
    prefix=0    ## Do not insert at beginning of PATH
    quiet=0     ## Do print information on bad directories

    ## Parse command-line options
    OPTIND=1
    while getopts iq var
    do
     case "$var" in
        i) prefix=1 ;;
        q) quiet=1 ;;
     esac
    done
    shift $(( $OPTIND - 1 ))

    for p  ## Loop through directories on the command line
    do
     _unslash "$p"     ## remove double slashes
     p=$_UNSLASH
     case :$PATH: in
        *:$p:*) [ $quiet -eq 0 ] && echo "addpath: $p already in path" >&2
                continue  ## Skip directories already in PATH
            ;;
     esac
     if [ -d "$p" ]
     then
         if [ $prefix -eq 1 ]
         then
             PATH="$p:$PATH"
```

```
        else
            PATH="$PATH:$p"
        fi
    else
        [ $quiet -eq 0 ] && echo "addpath: $p is not a directory" >&2
    fi
done
}
```

7.5 rmpath—Remove One or More Directories from $PATH

You might sometimes want to add a directory to the PATH, then decide later that you don't need it anymore. Removing it by hand can be tedious. This is a job for a shell script.

How It Works

When the directory to be removed is at the beginning or end of PATH, parameter expansion can remove it easily. When it's in the middle, the _sub function from the string-funcs library (see Chapter 3) is used.

Usage

```
rmpath DIR ...
```

The components of the PATH should be standardized with checkpath before using rmpath.

The Script

```
rmpath() # remove directory or directories from $PATH
{

    for p in "$@"
    do
      _unslash "$p"
       p=$_UNSLASH
       case $PATH in                    ## Look for directory....
           "$p":*) PATH=${PATH#$p:} ;; ## at beginning of PATH
           *:"$p") PATH=${PATH%:$p} ;; ## at end of PATH
           *:"$p":*) type _sub >/dev/null 2>&1 || . string-funcs
                    _sub "$PATH" ":$p:" ":" ## in the middle
                    PATH=$_SUB ;;
    esac
done
}
```

Summary

PATH is one of the most important variables in a shell environment, but it can be awkward to do anything other than add a directory to it. If the current directory is added to the PATH, whether deliberately or accidentally, there are security issues. If an error is made in typing the name of a directory, commands may not be found, or the wrong commands may be executed.

The functions in this chapter provide a safe way to add and remove directories from the PATH, and validate existing entries.

CHAPTER 8

■ ■ ■

The Dating Game

The Y2K bug is all but forgotten, and the Unix 2038 bug should be a non-issue (unless you are still using software that was compiled more than 30 years earlier).[1] Date-calculating software in use today should be good to the year 9999, and perhaps beyond. Unless, that is, adjustments have been made to the calendar to accommodate the couple of days discrepancy that will have crept in by then.

Although the uproar reached a peak in the months before January 1, 2000, the Y2K problem had been felt for many years. There were programs that had to deal with people born before 1900 and others (or even the same people) who would live into the twenty-first century. Two digits was inadequate. Some software worked around the problem by adding 1900 when the two digits exceeded a certain threshold (say, 30), and adding 2000 when it was less. That still didn't work if you were dealing both with people born before 1930 and people who could live until after 2030.

For no good reason, programmers continued to enter and store a year as two digits. There was a quip making the rounds on the Internet in the late 1990s saying, "Trust programmers to shorten the year 2000 to Y2K; that's what caused the problem in the first place." Well, no, it's not. The Y2K bug was caused by dates being stored with only the last two digits of the year. Information was lost by doing that; no information is lost in the abbreviation Y2K.

New Year's Eve 1999 slid into New Year's Day 2000 with hardly a ripple. Was that because the Y2K problem had been overstated, or because a sterling job had been done in fixing all extant software? I think it was a bit of both. I occasionally see dates in this century displayed as 12/12/14, because the year is stored in two digits; and a lot of systems were upgraded unnecessarily because of uncertainty about the bug.

When working on a system that has very little memory or storage space, cramming information into the smallest space possible makes sense. I did it on 8-bit machines, but with today's computers, space is so cheap, and compression so efficient, that there's no excuse for using two- digit years any more (small, embedded systems might be an exception, but even then, there should be better ways of saving space).

This chapter gives you more than a dozen functions for manipulating and formatting dates. With them you can convert a date in almost any format to an ISO standard date (e.g., "28 February 2005" or "feb 28 2005" to 2005-02-28). You can calculate how many days late your creditors are, or whether any given date is a valid date. You can find the day of the week on which you were born, or how many days old you are. You can find yesterday's date, tomorrow's date, or the date 666 days from now. You can store consistent ISO dates and quickly display them in a user- friendly format. And you can use these functions to build many more date commands that I didn't have room for.

---

[1] On Unix, the system time is stored as seconds since the epoch (1 January 1970) in a 32-bit integer. The maximum capacity of such an integer will be reached on 19 January 2038. This will be (and already is being) solved by using a 64-bit integer, whether on a 64-bit computer with a native integer of that size, or with the field being defined as a 64-bit integer on a 32-bit computer. For a more complete discussion, see *The Year 2038 Problem* by Roger M. Wilcox at `http://pw2.netcom.com/~rogermw/Y2038.html`.

The date-funcs Library

The scripts in this chapter never use anything but the full year, whether as input or storage. The only shortcut taken is that they are limited to the Gregorian calendar. Since most of the world had switched from the Julian calendar by the end of 1752, there is little practical consequence.

8.1 split_date—Divide a Date into Day, Month, and Year

Dates often arrive in a program in a format such as the International Standard (ISO 8601), 2005-03-01, or the common usage of 3/7/2004 (or the unspeakable 4/5/06). For most programming purposes, this needs to be translated into either three separate variables or a single integer (which requires the three values for its calculation). A script must be able to split the date and assign its components to the correct variables (is 3/7/2004 the 3rd of July or the 7th of March?). The conversion to an integer comes later in the chapter.

How It Works

Using a customized field separator, IFS, split-date breaks the date into three parts and assigns each part to a variable specified on the command line. Leading zeroes are stripped, so the results can be used in arithmetic expressions.

Usage

```
split_date "DATE" [VAR1 [VAR2 [VAR3]]]
```

The elements of the date may be separated by whitespace, or a hyphen, period or slash. If the date contains whitespace, it must be quoted on the command line:

```
$ format="  Day: %s\nMonth: %s\n Year: %s\n"
$ split_date "May 5 1977" month day year
$ printf "$format" "$day" "$month" "$year"
  Day: 5
Month: May
 Year: 1977
```

If no variables are specified on the command line, defaults are used, assigning the first part to SD_YEAR, the second to SD_MONTH, and the third to SD_DAY:

```
$ split_date "1949-09-29"
$ printf "$format" "$SD_DAY" "$SD_MONTH" "$SD_YEAR"
  Day: 29
Month: 9
 Year: 1949
```

The split_date function makes no assumptions about the validity of the components; the only change it makes to its input is that it removes a leading zero, if there is one, so that the resulting number can be used in arithmetic expressions.

The Script

```
split_date()
{
  ## Assign defaults when no variable names are given on the command line
    sd_1=${2:-SD_YEAR}
    sd_2=${3:-SD_MONTH}
    sd_3=${4:-SD_DAY}

    oldIFS=$IFS               ## save current value of field separator
    IFS='-/. $TAB$NL'         ## new value allows date to be supplied in other formats
    set -- $1                 ## place the date into the positional parameters
    IFS=$oldIFS               ## restore IFS
    [ $# -lt 3 ] && return 1  ## The date must have 3 fields

    ## Remove leading zeroes and assign to variables
    eval "$sd_1=\"${1#0}\"" $sd_2=\"${2#0}\"" $sd_3=\"${3#0}\""
}
```

8.2 is_leap_year—Is There an Extra Day This Year?

Some date calculations need to know whether there are 365 or 366 days in any given year, or whether February has 28 or 29 days.

How It Works

A leap year is a year divisible by 4 but not by 100 unless it is also divisible by 400. This calculation can be done easily in a POSIX shell, but there is a faster method that works even in a Bourne shell.

Usage

```
is_leap_year [YEAR]
```

If no year is given, is_leap_year uses date to get the current year. The result may be derived from the return code or from the _IS_LEAP_YEAR variable:

```
$ is_leap_year && echo yes || echo no ## assuming the current year is 2005
no
$ is_leap_year 2004
$ echo $_IS_LEAP_YEAR
1
$ is_leap_year 2003
$ echo $_IS_LEAP_YEAR
0
```

The Script

Leap years can be determined from the last two, three, or four digits of the number. For example, a year ending in 04 or 08 is always a leap year. Pattern matching reduces the number of possibilities to six, making a look-up table (that works in any Bourne-type shell) the most efficient method.

```
is_leap_year() { ## USAGE: is_leap_year [year]
    ily_year=${1:-$(date +%Y)}
    case $ily_year in
        *0[48] |\
        *[2468][048] |\
        *[13579][26] |\
        *[13579][26]0|\
        *[2468][048]00 |\
        *[13579][26]00 ) _IS_LEAP_YEAR=1
                        return 0 ;;
        *) _IS_LEAP_YEAR=0
            return 1 ;;
    esac
}
```

Notes

Although slower than the preceding script, the canonical method of checking for a leap year would have been a perfectly acceptable script in this book:

```
is_leap_year() {
    ily_year=${1:-`date +%Y`}
    [ $(( $ily_year % 400)) -eq 0 -o \
        \( $(( $ily_year % 4)) -eq 0 -a $(( $ily_year % 100)) -ne 0 \) ] && {
        _IS_LEAP_YEAR=1
        return 0
    } || {
        _IS_LEAP_YEAR=0
        return 1
    }
}
```

8.3 days_in_month—How Many Days Hath September?

One method of determining whether a date is valid uses the number of days in the month. If the day entered is higher than the number of days in the month, the program should reject that date.

How It Works

A simple look-up table will give the number of days in any month except February. For February, the year is also necessary.

Usage

```
_days_in_month [month [year]]  ## result in _DAYS_IN_MONTH
days_in_month [month [year]]   ## result is printed
```

If no month is entered on the command line, date_vars, from the standard-funcs library in Chapter 1, is used to get the current month and year. If the month is February and no year is given, date is used to get the current year.

```
$ days_in_month    ## it is now February 2005
28
$ days_in_month 2 2004
29
```

The Script

```
_days_in_month()
{
    if [ -n "$1" ]  ## If there's a command-line argument...
    then
      dim_m=$1          ## $1 is the month
      dim_y=$2          ## $2 is the year
    else                ## Otherwise use the current date
      date_vars         ## set date variables (from standard-funcs)
      dim_y=$YEAR
      dim_m=$MONTH
    fi
    case ${dim_m#0} in
        ## For all months except February,
        ## a simple look-up table is all that's needed
        9|4|6|11) _DAYS_IN_MONTH=30 ;; ## 30 days hath September...
        1|3|5|7|8|10|12) _DAYS_IN_MONTH=31 ;;

        ## For February, the year is needed in order to check
        ## whether it is a leap year
        2) is_leap_year ${dim_y:-`date +%Y`} &&
            _DAYS_IN_MONTH=29 || _DAYS_IN_MONTH=28 ;;
        *) return 5 ;;
    esac
}

days_in_month()
{
    _days_in_month $@ && printf %s\n $_DAYS_IN_MONTH
}
```

8.4 Julian Dates

What date will it be 45 days from now? How many days are there until my rent is due? How many days overdue is payment for that invoice I sent? How many days until Christmas? The easy way to calculate dates such as these is to convert them to integers; the dates can then be manipulated by simple addition and subtraction.

How It Works

The Julian Date system used by astronomers was invented by Joseph Scaliger in 1583 and named for his father, Julius Caesar Scaliger, not the Roman emperor (though I expect the connection contributed to the choice of name). The Julian Date is the number of days since noon on January 1, -4712, i.e., January 1, 4713 BC. The time of day is represented by a decimal fraction. Since the Julian day starts at noon, .5 is midnight, and .75 is 6:00 a.m.

For our purposes, we want the day number to refer to the calendar day, from midnight to midnight, so we use the Julian Day (JD) number at noon, which has a time component of 0. There are various formulas for calculating the JD number; this book uses one that was posted to the comp.unix.shell newsgroup by Tapani Tarvainen.

Usage

```
date2julian [YEAR-MONTH-DAY]
julian2date JulianDayNumber
```

The conversion functions to and from a Julian Day are mirror images. The first takes an ISO date (YYYY-MM-DD), day, month, and year, and converts them to a single JD integer. The reverse function, julian2date, converts the JD number to an ISO date.

```
$ date2julian 1974-10-18
2442339
$ julian2date 2441711
1973-01-28
```

Both these functions are paired with underscore versions (_date2julian and _julian2date) that just set a variable, but do not print it.

If date2julian has no argument, the current day is used; julian2date requires an argument.

The Script

```
_date2julian()
{
   ## If there's no date on the command line, use today's date
   case $1 in
       "") date_vars ## From standard-funcs, Chapter 1
           set -- $TODAY
           ;;
   esac
```

```
    ## Break the date into year, month and day
    split_date "$1" d2j_year d2j_month d2j_day || return 2

    ## Since leap years add a day at the end of February,
    ## calculations are done from 1 March 0000 (a fictional year)
    d2j_tmpmonth=$((12 * $d2j_year + $d2j_month - 3))

    ## If it is not yet March, the year is changed to the previous year
    d2j_tmpyear=$(( $d2j_tmpmonth / 12))

    ## The number of days from 1 March 0000 is calculated
    ## and the number of days from 1 Jan. 4713BC is added
    _DATE2JULIAN=$((
        (734 * $d2j_tmpmonth + 15) / 24 - 2 * $d2j_tmpyear + $d2j_tmpyear/4
          - $d2j_tmpyear/100 + $d2j_tmpyear/400 + $d2j_day + 1721119 ))
}

date2julian()
{
    _date2julian "$1" && printf "%s\n" "$_DATE2JULIAN"
}

# ISO date from JD number
_julian2date()
{
    ## Check for numeric argument
    case $1 in
        ""|*[!0-9]*) return 1 ;;
    esac

    ## To avoid using decimal fractions, the script uses multiples.
    ## Rather than use 365.25 days per year, 1461 is the number of days
    ## in 4 years; similarly, 146097 is the number of days in 400 years
    j2d_tmpday=$(( $1 - 1721119 ))
    j2d_centuries=$(( (4 * $j2d_tmpday - 1) / 146097))
    j2d_tmpday=$(( $j2d_tmpday + $j2d_centuries - $j2d_centuries/4))
    j2d_year=$(( (4 * $j2d_tmpday - 1) / 1461))
    j2d_tmpday=$(( $j2d_tmpday - (1461 * $j2d_year) / 4))
    j2d_month=$(( (10 * $j2d_tmpday - 5) / 306))
    j2d_day=$(( $j2d_tmpday - (306 * $j2d_month + 5) / 10))
    j2d_month=$(( $j2d_month + 2))
    j2d_year=$(( $j2d_year + $j2d_month/12))
    j2d_month=$(( $j2d_month % 12 + 1))

    ## pad day and month with zeros if necessary
    case $j2d_day in ?) j2d_day=0$j2d_day;; esac
    case $j2d_month in ?) j2d_month=0$j2d_month;; esac

    _JULIAN2DATE=$j2d_year-$j2d_month-$j2d_day
}
```

```
julian2date()
{
    _julian2date "$1" && printf "%s\n" "$_JULIAN2DATE"
}
```

8.5 dateshift—Add or Subtract a Number of Days

The date2julian script lets me convert a date to an integer. Now you need to put that to use and get
yesterday's date, or the date one week ago.

How It Works

By encapsulating the conversion to Julian Day, the arithmetic, and the conversion back to ISO date in the
dateshift function, a single command can return the date at any offset from any given date.

Usage

```
dateshift [YYYY-MM-DD] OFFSET
```

If a date (in ISO format) is not entered on the command line, today's date is used. Therefore, to retrieve
yesterday's date:

```
$ dateshift -1 ## at the time of writing the first Edition, it is October 15, 2004
2004-10-14
```

When is Twelfth Night?

```
$ dateshift 2004-12-25 +12
2005-01-06
```

The Script

```
_dateshift()
{
    case $# in
        ## If there is only 1 argument, it is the offset
        ## so use today's date
        0|1) ds_offset=${1:-0}
            date_vars
            ds_date=$TODAY
            ;;
        ## ...otherwise the first argument is the date
        ) ds_date=$1
          ds_offset=$2
          ;;
    esac
    while :
    do
```

```
        case $ds_offset in
            0*|+*) ds_offset=${ds_offset#?} ;; ## Remove leading zeros or plus signs
            -*) break ;;                        ## Negative value is OK; exit the loop
            "") ds_offset=0; break ;;           ## Empty offset equals 0; exit loop
            *[!0-9]*) return 1 ;;               ## Contains non-digit; return with error
            *) break ;;                         ## Let's assume it's OK and continue
        esac
    done
    ## Convert to Julian Day
    _date2julian "$ds_date"
    ## Add offset and convert back to ISO date
    _julian2date $(( $_DATE2JULIAN + $ds_offset ))
    ## Store result
    _DATESHIFT=$_JULIAN2DATE
}

dateshift()
{
    _dateshift "$@" && printf "%s\n" "$_DATESHIFT"
}
```

Notes

It is convenient to have separate commands for the commonly used calculations:

```
_yesterday()
{
    _date2julian "$1"
    _julian2date $(( $_DATE2JULIAN - 1 ))
    _YESTERDAY=$_JULIAN2DATE
}

_tomorrow()
{
    _date2julian "$1"
    _julian2date $(( $_DATE2JULIAN + 1 ))
    _TOMORROW=$_JULIAN2DATE
}
```

8.6 diffdate—Find the Number of Days Between Two Dates

How many days do you have until the next deadline? How many days are between my birthday and Christmas?

How It Works

This is another encapsulation of conversion and arithmetic, using two dates.

Usage

```
diffdate YYYY-MM-DD [YYYY-MM-DD]
```

If only one date is given, the current date is used as the first date:

```
$ diffdate 2004-12-25 ## today is October 15, 2004
71
```

If the second date is earlier than the first, the result will be negative:

```
$ diffdate 2005-03-22 1998-10-18
-2347
```

The Script

This script simply converts the two dates (or one date and today's date) and subtracts one from the other.

```
_diffdate()
{
    case $# in
        ## If there's only one argument, use today's date
        1) _date2julian $1
           dd2=$_DATE2JULIAN
           _date2julian
           dd1=$_DATE2JULIAN
           ;;
        2) _date2julian "$1"
           dd1=$_DATE2JULIAN
           _date2julian "$2"
           dd2=$_DATE2JULIAN
           ;;
    esac
    _DIFFDATE=$(( $dd2 - $dd1 ))
}
diffdate()
{
    _diffdate "$@" && printf "%s\n" "$_DIFFDATE"
}
```

8.7 day_of_week—Find the Day of the Week for Any Date

You need to know whether a certain date is a business day, or whether it is on the weekend.

How It Works

This is another use for the Julian Day. If you add 1 to the JD and divide by 7, the remainder is the day of the week, counting from Sunday as 0. A look-up table converts the number to a name.

Usage

```
day_of_week [YYYY-MM-DD]
dayname N
```

To find which day of the week Christmas is on, use this:

```
$ day_of_week 2005-12-25
0
```

Christmas Day, 2005 falls on a Sunday. To convert the number to the name of the day, dayname uses a simple look-up table:

```
$ dayname 0
Sunday
```

The dayname function will also complete the name of the day if you give it an abbreviation:

```
$ dayname wed
Wednesday
```

If day_of_week is called without an argument, it uses the current day's date.

The Script

```
_day_of_week()
{
    _date2julian "$1"
    _DAY_OF_WEEK=$(( ($_DATE2JULIAN + 1) % 7 ))
}

day_of_week()
{
    _day_of_week "$1" && printf "%s\n" "$_DAY_OF_WEEK"
}

## Dayname accepts either 0 or 7 for Sunday, 2-6 for the other days
## or checks against the first three letters, in upper or lower case
_dayname()
{
    case ${1} in
        0|7|[Ss][Uu][Nn]*) _DAYNAME=Sunday ;;
        1|[Mm][Oo][nN]*) _DAYNAME=Monday ;;
        2|[Tt][Uu][Ee]*) _DAYNAME=Tuesday ;;
        3|[Ww][Ee][Dd]*) _DAYNAME=Wednesday ;;
        4|[Tt][Hh][Uu]*) _DAYNAME=Thursday ;;
        5|[Ff][Rr][Ii]*) _DAYNAME=Friday ;;
        6|[Ss][Aa][Tt]*) _DAYNAME=Saturday ;;
        *) return 5 ;; ## No match; return an error
    esac
}
```

```
dayname()
{
    _dayname "$@" && printf "%s\n" "$_DAYNAME"
}
```

8.8 display_date—Show a Date in Text Format

The ISO date format is great for computers, but it's not as easy for people to read. We need a way to display dates in a more user-friendly way.

How It Works

Look-up tables convert the day of the week and the month to their respective names. The user can supply different strings to vary the format used.

Usage

```
display_date [-f FMT] [YYYY-MM-DD]
```

If no format is supplied, the default is used:

```
$ display_date 2005-02-14
Wednesday, 14 February 2005
```

There are only four format strings defined at the moment (WMdy, dMy, Mdy, and WdMy), but you can easily add more. Here are examples of all four formats:

```
$ for fmt in WMdy dMy Mdy WdMy
> do
>    date=$(( $RANDOM % 100 + 1950 ))-$(( $RANDOM % 12 ))-$(( $RANDOM % 28 ))
>    display_date -f "$fmt" "$date"
> done
Thursday, July 12, 1998
14 November 1964
January 21, 2009
Monday, 18 January 2018
```

The Script

```
display_date()
{
    dd_fmt=WdMy ## Default format

    ## Parse command-line options for format string
    OPTIND=1
    while getopts f: var
    do
```

```
    case $var in
        f) dd_fmt=$OPTARG ;;
    esac
done
shift $(( $OPTIND - 1 ))

## If there is no date supplied, use today's date
case $1 in
    "") date_vars ## Function from standard-funcs in Chapter 1
        set -- $TODAY
        ;;
esac

split_date "$1" dd_year dd_month dd_day || return 2

## Look up long names for day and month
_day_of_week "$1"
_dayname $_DAY_OF_WEEK
_monthname $dd_month

## Print date according to format supplied
case $dd_fmt in
    WMdy) printf "%s, %s %d, %d\n" "$_DAYNAME" "$_MONTHNAME" \
                "$dd_day" "$dd_year" ;;
    dMy)  printf "%d %s %d\n" "$dd_day" "$_MONTHNAME" "$dd_year" ;;
    Mdy)  printf "%s %d, %d\n" "$_MONTHNAME" "$dd_day" "$dd_year" ;;
    WdMy|*) printf "%s, %d %s %d\n" "$_DAYNAME" "$dd_day" \
                "$_MONTHNAME" "$dd_year" ;;
esac
}

## Set the month number from 1- or 2-digit number, or the name
_monthnum()
{
    case ${1#0} in
        1|[Jj][aA][nN]*) _MONTHNUM=1 ;;
        2|[Ff][Ee][Bb]*) _MONTHNUM=2 ;;
        3|[Mm][Aa][Rr]*) _MONTHNUM=3 ;;
        4|[Aa][Pp][Rr]*) _MONTHNUM=4 ;;
        5|[Mm][Aa][Yy]*) _MONTHNUM=5 ;;
        6|[Jj][Uu][Nn]*) _MONTHNUM=6 ;;
        7|[Jj][Uu][Ll]*) _MONTHNUM=7 ;;
        8|[Aa][Uu][Gg]*) _MONTHNUM=8 ;;
        9|[Ss][Ee][Pp]*) _MONTHNUM=9 ;;
        10|[Oo][Cc][Tt]*) _MONTHNUM=10 ;;
        11|[Nn][Oo][Vv]*) _MONTHNUM=11 ;;
        12|[Dd][Ee][Cc]*) _MONTHNUM=12 ;;
        *) return 5 ;;
    esac
}
```

```
monthnum()
{
    _monthnum "$@" && printf "%s\n" "$_MONTHNUM"
}

## Set the month name from 1- or 2-digit number, or the name
_monthname()
{
    case ${1#0} in
        1|[Jj][aA][nN]) _MONTHNAME=January ;;
        2|[Ff][Ee][Bb]) _MONTHNAME=February ;;
        3|[Mm][Aa][Rr]) _MONTHNAME=March ;;
        4|[Aa][Pp][Rr]) _MONTHNAME=April ;;
        5|[Mm][Aa][Yy]) _MONTHNAME=May ;;
        6|[Jj][Uu][Nn]) _MONTHNAME=June ;;
        7|[Jj][Uu][Ll]) _MONTHNAME=July ;;
        8|[Aa][Uu][Gg]) _MONTHNAME=August ;;
        9|[Ss][Ee][Pp]) _MONTHNAME=September ;;
       10|[Oo][Cc][Tt]) _MONTHNAME=October ;;
       11|[Nn][Oo][Vv]) _MONTHNAME=November ;;
       12|[Dd][Ee][Cc]) _MONTHNAME=December ;;
        *) return 5 ;;
    esac
}

monthname()
{
    _monthname "$@" && printf "%s\n" "${_MONTHNAME}"
}
```

8.9 parse_date—Decipher Various Forms of Date String

Dates come in many different formats, some straightforward, some ambiguous. Some are easy to parse, others are not. Some put the month before the date, some put it after. Some use numbers for the month, some use the name of the month. Some separate the components with spaces, some with slashes. Out of these many formats, is there a way to extract a coherent date?

How It Works

Designed to give the widest possible latitude in date entry, parse_date can be told to expect a specific format, or it can chew on the input and, with a bit of luck, spit out a valid ISO date. The three options tell parse_date to interpret the fields as YMD, DMY, or MDY. If no option is given, the script will attempt to figure out what is meant.

Usage

```
parse_date [-eiu] DATE
```

The options set the order that parse_date assigns the fields: -e uses day-month-year, -u uses month-day-year, and -i uses year-month-day (think English, US, and International).

The month may be entered as a number from 1 to 12, or as the name of the month; the fields may be separated by whitespace, periods, hyphens, or slashes. The result is printed as an ISO date, year-month-day:

```
$ parse_date -e 12.4.2001
2001-04-12
$ parse_date -u 12.4.2001
2001-12-04
$ parse_date 12.apr.2001
2001-04-12
```

Invalid dates are caught, and an error is returned:

```
$ parse_date -u 2004-12-10; echo $?
2
$ parse_date -i 12.4.2001; echo $?
2
```

There are a few shortcuts. Today, yesterday, and tomorrow can be used instead of the actual dates; these can be represented by a period, hyphen, and plus sign, respectively:

```
$ parse_date .
2004-10-15
$ parse_date +
2004-10-16
$ parse_date -
2004-10-14
```

A date 30 days from now may be entered as +30; one week ago can be entered as -7:

```
$ parse_date +30
2004-11-14
$ parse_date -7
2004-10-08
```

Ambiguous dates return an error (but an option can remove the ambiguity):

```
$ parse_date 2.3.2001 || echo ambigous >&2
ambigous
$ parse_date -e 2.3.2001 || echo ambigous
2001-03-02
$ parse_date -u 2.3.2001 || echo ambigous
2001-02-03
```

The Script

```
_parse_date()
{
    ## Clear variables
    _PARSE_DATE=
    pd_DMY=
    pd_day=
```

```
    pd_month=
    pd_year=

    ## If no date is supplied, read one from the standard input
    case $1 in
        "") [ -t 0 ] && printf "Date: " >&2 ## Prompt only if connected to a terminal
            read pd_date
            set -- $pd_date
            ;;
    esac

    ## Accept yesterday, today and tomorrow as valid dates
    case $1 in
        yes*|-)
            _yesterday && _PARSE_DATE=$_YESTERDAY
            return
            ;;
        tom*|+)
            _tomorrow && _PARSE_DATE=$_TOMORROW
            return
            ;;
        today|.)
            date_vars && _PARSE_DATE=$TODAY
            return
            ;;
        today*|\
        .[-+1-9]* |\
        [-+][1-9]* )
            pd_=${1#today}
            pd_=${pd_#[-+]}
            _dateshift $pd_ && _PARSE_DATE=$_DATESHIFT
            return
            ;;
    esac

    ## Parse command-line options for date format
    OPTIND=1
    while getopts eiu var
    do
      case $var in
        e) pd_DMY=dmy ;;
        i) pd_DMY=ymd ;;
        u) pd_DMY=mdy ;;
      esac
    done
    shift $(( $OPTIND - 1 ))

    ## Split date into the positional parameters
    oldIFS=$IFS
    IFS='/-.
$TAB$NL'
```

```
        set -- $*
        IFS=$oldIFS

        ## If date is incomplete, use today's information to complete it
        if [ $# -lt 3 ]
        then
          date_vars
          case $# in
              1) set -- $1 $MONTH $YEAR ;;
              2) set -- $1 $2 $YEAR ;;
          esac
        fi

        case $pd_DMY in
            ## Interpret date according to format if one has been defined
          dmy) pd_day=${1#0}; pd_month=${2#0}; pd_year=$3 ;;
          mdy) pd_day=${2#0}; pd_month=${1#0}; pd_year=$3 ;;
          ymd) pd_day=${3#0}; pd_month=${2#0}; pd_year=$1 ;;

            ## Otherwise make an educated guess
          *) case $1--$2-$3 in
                [0-9][0-9][0-9][0-9]*-*)
                            pd_year=$1
                            pd_month=$2
                            pd_day=$3
                            ;;
                *--[0-9][0-9][0-9][0-9]*-*) ## strange place
                            pd_year=$2
                            _parse_dm $1 $3
                            ;;
                *-[0-9][0-9][0-9][0-9]*)
                            pd_year=$3
                            _parse_dm $1 $2
                            ;;
                *) return 5 ;;
            esac

            ;;
        esac

        ## If necessary, convert month name to number
        case $pd_month in
            [JjFfMmAaSsOoNnDd]*) _monthnum "$pd_month" || return 4
                                pd_month=$_MONTHNUM
                                ;;
            *[!0-9]*) return 3 ;;
        esac

        ## Quick check to eliminate invalid day or month
        [ "${pd_month:-99}" -gt 12 -o "${pd_day:-99}" -gt 31 ] && return 2
```

```
    ## Check for valid date, and pad day and month if necessary
    _days_in_month $pd_month $pd_year
    case $pd_day in ?) pd_day=0$pd_day;; esac
    case $pd_month in ?) pd_month=0$pd_month;; esac
    [ ${pd_day#0} -le $_DAYS_IN_MONTH ] &&
                _PARSE_DATE="$pd_year-$pd_month-$pd_day"
}

parse_date()
{
    _parse_date "$@" && printf "%s\n" "$_PARSE_DATE"
}

## Called by _parse_date to determine which argument is the month
## and which is the day
_parse_dm()
{
    ## function requires 2 arguments; more will be ignored
    [ $# -lt 2 ] && return 1
    ## if either argument begins with the first letter of a month
    ## it's a month; the other argument is the day
    case $1 in
        [JjFfMmAaSsOoNnDd]*)
        pd_month=$1
        pd_day=$2
        return
        ;;
esac
case $2 in
    [JjFfMmAaSsOoNnDd]*)
    pd_month=$2
    pd_day=$1
    return
    ;;
esac

## return error if either arg contains non-numbers
case $1$2 in *[!0-9]*) return 2;; esac

## if either argument is greater than 12, it is the day
if [ $1 -gt 12 ]
then
  pd_day=$1
  pd_month=$2
elif [ ${2:-0} -gt 12 ]
then
  pd_day=$2
  pd_month=$1
```

```
  else
    pd_day=$1
    pd_month=$2
    return 1 ## ambiguous
  fi
}
```

8.10 valid_date—Where Was I on November 31st?

When you already have a well-formed date, parse_date is overkill for verification. A simpler script will suffice.

How It Works

If you convert a date to a Julian Day, then convert it back, the values will not be the same if the date is not valid:

```
$ julian2date $(date2julian 2004-12-32)
2005-01-01
```

This function does just that, and fails if the dates do not match.

Usage

```
valid_date YEAR-MONTH-DAY
```

There are only 30 days in April, so April 31 will not be valid:

```
$ valid_date 2005-04-31 && echo OK || echo Invalid date
Invalid date
$ valid_date 2005-04-30 && echo OK || echo Invalid date
OK
```

The Script

```
valid_date()
{
    _date2julian "$1" || return 8
    _julian2date $_DATE2JULIAN || return 7
    [ $_JULIAN2DATE = $1 ]
}
```

Summary

Many of the functions presented here can be achieved with the GNU version of the date command. Others, such as parse_date, have more flexibility. These functions will often be faster than date, but not always by much. They do speed up script writing by tucking many details away behind the scenes.

Many more date functions could be included, some that haven't yet been separated into their own functions because they are small additions to scripts already here, and they can easily be entered in-line with the rest of a script. Some are here because they could be used a lot, or because they answer some newsgroup FAQs.

An example that fits into both categories is yesterday. You could have a cron job that runs every night at midnight and archives certain files. You might want to date them with the preceding day's date. Having a one-word command made the script easier to write, and the result easier to read.

I have thought about writing a script that would accept a formatting string for printing the date, a display_date on steroids, but it would be far more work to write than it warrants. You can use GNU date when you need that facility.

■ ■ ■

## CHAPTER 9

Good Housekeeping: Monitoring and Tidying Up File Systems

Whether you are the system administrator or just a user, whether you have your own box or an account on a remote machine, sooner or later you will need to do some clean-up work. You will want to remove duplicate files and clean out empty files. Symbolic links are sometimes left hanging when a file is removed, so you would probably like to delete those. And, of course, you will want to keep an eye on your hard drives' levels of usage.

9.1 dfcmp—Notify User of Major Changes in Disk Usage

Unix systems do not take kindly to running out of disk space. I have seen a computer reduced to a jabbering idiot when there was no room left on the hard drive to write a message to a log file. This generated an error, which the system tried to write to a log file. Since there was no space on the /var/log partition, the system generated an error that it tried to write to a log file. There was no space on the partition, so the system generated an error, which it tried to write to a log file. The partition was full, so . . .

As other processes tried to write to a log file, more and more errors were generated. The machine slowed to a crawl while spewing hundreds (or maybe thousands) of error messages per second to the console. The computer quickly became unusable.

I needed something to warn me when drives were getting full, or when there was any major change in disk usage.

How It Works

Every night, a crontab entry runs dfcmp, which uses the df command to save the current state of the drives (as a percentage of space used) to a file. This file is compared to the previous day's file, as well as the previous week's and previous month's files. If the difference exceeds 10 percentage points, a report is sent. If the space used is greater than 90%, only a 1% change is needed to set off the alarm.

The amount of change needed to generate a warning can be adjusted by a configuration file or by command-line options.

Usage

```
dfcmp [-d NN][-h NN][-p NN][-f][-c CFG]
```

The d, h, and p options set the percentages of difference required before a report is generated, and the point at which the amount used changes. To receive a report if the difference is greater than 5%, and when it exceeds 2% when the file system is more than 80% full:

```
dfcmp -d5 -h2 -p80
```

The -c option tells dfcmp to use a configuration file other than the default, $HOME/.config/dfcmp.cfg.

The Script

To find the date one month ago, the _last_month function assumes that date_vars has been called, and the current date is therefore in $_DAY, $_MONTH, and $_YEAR.

```
_last_month()
{
    lm_day=0$_DAY
    lm_month=$_MONTH
    lm_year=$YEAR
    case $_MONTH in
        ## If it's January, use December of the previous year
        1) lm_year=$(( $lm_year - 1 ))
           lm_month=12
           ;;
        ## otherwise just subtract one from the month
        *) lm_year=$YEAR
           lm_month=0$(( $lm_month - 1 ))
           ;;
    esac

    ## Check that the day is no greater than the days in last month
    ## and set to last day of the month if it is
    if [ "${lm_day#0}" -gt 28 ]
    then
      _days_in_month $lm_month $lm_year
      [ "${lm_day#0}" -gt "$_DAYS_IN_MONTH" ] && lm_day=$_DAYS_IN_MONTH
    fi
    _LAST_MONTH=$lm_year-${lm_month#${lm_month%??}}-${lm_day#${lm_day%??}}
}
```

To compare two df_ files and print major differences, the cmp_df function uses the Unix join command to merge the two files on the first field. Each line then contains a file-system mount point and its percentage used from each file. If the difference is greater than the configured threshold, the information is printed.

```
cmp_df()
{
    [ -f "$1" ] && [ -f "$2" ] &&
    join -t "$TAB" $1 $2 |
```

```
    while read fs today yesterday
    do
      notify=0
      [ $today -eq $yesterday ] && continue

      diff=$(( $today - $yesterday ))
      if [ $today -ge $high_point ]
      then
        [ ${diff#-} -ge $high_diff ] && notify=1
      elif [ ${diff#-} -ge $min_diff ]
      then
        notify=1
      fi
      if [ $notify -gt 0 ]
      then
        printf "%20s %9d%% %7d%% (%d)\n" $fs $today $yesterday $diff
      fi
    done
}

progname=${0##*/} ## Extract the name of the script
case $progname in
    -sh) shx=-sh ;;
    *) shx= ;;
esac


. date-funcs$shx

df_dir=/var/log/df
[ -d "$df_dir" ] || mkdir "$df_dir" ||
die 5 "Could not create directory, $df_dir"

## Defaults, may be overridden by config file or options
min_diff=10        ## level of change needed to generate report
high_diff=1        ## level of change to report when disk is nearly full
high_point=90      ## level at which $high_diff is used instead of $min_diff
configfile=$HOME/.config/dfcmp.cfg ## default config file
mkfile=0           ## do not re-create today's file if it already exists

## Parse command-line options
while getopts fc:d:h:p: var
do
  case $var in
      c) configfile=$OPTARG ;;
      d) min_diff=$OPTARG ;;
      h) high_diff=$OPTARG ;;
      p) high_point=$OPTARG ;;
      f) mkfile=1 ;; ## force creation of today's file
  esac
done
shift $(( $OPTIND - 1 ))
```

```
## check for config file, and source it if it exists
[ -f "$configfile" ] && . "$configfile"

## set today's date variables
date_vars

## set file names
df_file=$df_dir/df_$TODAY
_yesterday $TODAY
df_yesterfile=$df_dir/df_$_YESTERDAY        ## yesterday
_dateshift $TODAY -7 || die 2
df_lastweekfile=$df_dir/df_$_DATESHIFT      ## last week
_last_month || die 2
df_lastmonthfile=$df_dir/df_$_LAST_MONTH   ## last month

## create today's file if it doesn't exist (or if -f is selected)
[ -f "$df_file" ] || mkfile=1
[ $mkfile -eq 1 ] &&
  df | { read ## discard header
      while read fs b u a pc m
      do

        case $fs in
            ## skip samba and NFS mounts, proc, etc.
            //*|*:*) continue ;;
            */*) ;; ## regular file system
            *) continue ;; ## unknown; skip it
        esac

        ## when line is split due to long filesystem name, read next line
        case $b in "") read b u a pc m ;; esac
        printf "%s\t%d\n" $m "${pc%\%}"
      done
  } | sort > "$df_file"

## Compare today's file with each of the three old files
set YESTERDAY "1 WEEK AGO" "1 MONTH AGO"
for file in $df_yesterfile $df_lastweekfile $df_lastmonthfile
do
  result=`cmp_df $df_file $file`
  if [ -n "$result" ]
  then
    printf "%20s %10s %10s %s\n" FILESYSTEM TODAY "$1" DIFF
    printf "%s\n" "$result"
  fi
  shift
done
```

9.2 symfix—Remove Broken Symbolic Links

Because symbolic links refer to files by name, they can be broken by the removal of the file they point to. Broken links don't really cause any problems, but they can make a directory look untidy. Unless you want to keep a broken link as a reminder to create its target (or, perhaps, watch for the creation of the target), why not get rid of them?

How It Works

Using a long listing (ls -l) piped through grep ^l, the symlinked files and their targets are extracted. If the target doesn't exist, the link is removed.

Usage

```
symfix [OPTIONS] [FILE ...|DIR ...]
```

By default, symfix removes all the broken links in the current directory. If the first argument is a directory, all arguments are assumed to be directories; each one is entered in turn, and all broken links are removed. Otherwise, any arguments are taken as filenames, and any that are broken links will be removed.

Three options are accepted by symfix: -i, -v, and -R (interactive, verbose, and recursive, respectively). In interactive mode, the user is prompted and may delete or leave each broken link. Verbose mode prints the names of all directories it enters, and all links removed. Recursive mode deletes all broken links in the directories listed on the command line and all their descendants; if no directories are on the command line, broken links are removed from the current directory and the entire tree beneath it. In recursive mode, a file pattern is only effective on the current directory, and only if no directories are given.

The Script

The fix_pwd function processes broken symlinks in the current directory, prompting the user when in interactive mode.

```
fix_pwd()
{
    ls -l "$@" | grep "^l" |
    while read -r perms links owner group size month day time file x link
    do
      link=${file#* -\> }
      file=${file% -\> *}
      [ -e "$link" ] || {
          if [ $interactive -ge 1 ]
          then
            printf "Remove %s (%s) (Y/n/q)? " "$file" "$link"
            get_key < /dev/tty
            printf "\n"
            case $_KEY in
                y|Y|"") ok=1 ;;
                q|Q) break ;;
                *) ok=0 ;;
```

```
            esac
        fi
        [ $verbose -ge 1 ] &&
         printf "Broken link: '%s'; removing %s\n" "$link" "$file" >&2
        [ "$ok" -eq 1 ] && rm "$file"
    }
  done
}

progname=${0##*/} ## extract name of script

## Default settings
interactive=0
recurse=0
verbose=0
R_opt=
ok=1
opts=ivR

. standard-funcs ## load functions

## Parse command-line options
while getopts $opts var
do
  case $var in
      i) interactive=1
         R_opt="$R_opt -i" ;;
      R) recurse=1 ;;
      v) verbose=$(( $verbose + 1 ))
         R_opt="$R_opt -v" ;;
  esac
done
shift $(( $OPTIND - 1 ))

    ####### is_dir function is in standard-funcs #######
## If a directory is given on the command line, enter it
## (or loop through each of them, if there is more than one)
## In recursive mode, is_dir is called to check
## whether there are any subdirectories in the current directoryif [ -d "$1" ]
then
  for dir
  do
    (
    [ -L "$dir" ] && continue ## do not descend symlinked directories
    cd "$dir" || continue
    [ $verbose -ge 1 ] && printf "Directory: %s\n" "$PWD"
    fix_pwd
    [ $recurse -eq 1 ] && is_dir ./*/ && eval "$0 -R $R_opt ./*/"
    )
  done
```

```
else
  fix_pwd "$@"
  [ $recurse -eq 1 ] && is_dir ./*/ && eval "$0 -R $R_opt ./*/"
  : ## return successfully even if [ $recurse -eq 1 ] fails
fi
```

9.3 sym2file—Converts Symbolic Links to Regular Files

As I write this book, I have a separate directory for each chapter. In each, I have symbolic links to that chapter's scripts, which I keep in my main scripts directory. When I finish the draft of a chapter, I want to keep each script as I used it in the chapter, and not have it change whenever I tinker with the script. To do that, I needed to convert each symlink to a regular file.

How It Works

As with symfix, the output of ls -l is parsed to extract the file and its target; the file is removed, and the target is copied into its place.

Usage

```
sym2file [OPTION] [FILE ...]
```

With the interactive option, -i, sym2file prompts before doing the conversion. With the verbose option, all operations are echoed to the screen.

Note that although the script examines the BASH_VERSION variable, it does not require bash to run. If the file is being executed by bash (version 2 or later) a more efficient get_key function is used.

The Script

Rather than use the generic get_key function from standard-funcs (see Chapter 1), the capability of bash's built-in read command to return after a specified number of characters is used instead of stty and dd—if a capable version of bash is executing the script.

```
case $BASH_VERSION in
    [2-9]* | [1-9][0-9]*) ## bash 2 or later
        get_key()
        {
            read -sn1 -u0 ${1:-_KEY}
        }
        ;;
    *) [ -t 0 ] && _STTY=`stty -g`
        get_key()
        {
            [ -t 0 ] && stty -echo -icanon
            _KEY=`dd bs=1 count=1 2>/dev/null </dev/tty`
            [ -n "$1" ] && eval "$1=\"\$_KEY\""
```

```
              [ -t 0 ] && stty "$_STTY"
              [ -n "$_KEY" ]
        }
      ;;
esac

progname=${0##*/} ## Extract name of script

## Defaults
interactive=0
verbose=0

## Parse command-line options
opts=iv
while getopts $opts var
do
  case $var in
      i) interactive=1 ;;
      v) verbose=$(( $verbose + 1 )) ;;
  esac
done
shift $(( $OPTIND - 1 ))

##
ls -l "$@" | grep "^l" |
  while read perms links owner group size month day time file
  do
    link=${file#* -\> }
    file=${file% -\> *}

    ## If the link does not point to a file, skip it
    [ -f "$link" ] || {
        [ $verbose -ge 1 ] &&
            printf "'%s' is not a file; skipping\n" "$link" >&2
        continue
    }
    ok=1

## In interactive mode, prompt the user for a decision
if [ $interactive -ge 1 ]
then
  printf "Copy %s to %s (Y/n/q)? " "$link" "$file"
  get_key </dev/tty
  printf "\n"
  case $_KEY in
      y|Y|"") ok=1 ;;
      q|Q) break ;;
      *) ok=0 ;;
  esac
fi
```

```
## In batch mode, or when the user has given the green light,
## delete the symlink and copy the file into its place.
if [ $ok -ge 1 ]
then
  rm "$file" && [ $verbose -ge 1 ] && printf "Deleted: %s\n" "$file"
  cp -p "$link" "$file" && [ $verbose -ge 1 ] &&
                    printf " Copied: '%s' -> '%s'\n" "$link" "$file" ||
                    touch "$file"
  fi
done
```

9.4 zrm—Remove Empty Files

Sometimes, empty files exist for a reason, perhaps to change a program's behavior by the existence or nonexistence of the file. Usually, however, they are not wanted; they have been created accidentally or in error, and you will want to delete them.

How It Works

Rather than getting a file's size by parsing the output of ls -l, we can use the test command (which is a synonym for [ ]). It has the -s operator that returns true if the file exists and is not empty. A second test ensures that the file actually exists before trying to remove it.

Usage

```
zrm [OPTION] [FILE ...]
```

The three options to zrm, -f, -i, and -v, are passed directly to rm as options to do the following: force removal without prompting the user when the file is not writable (but the directory ownership and permissions allow it), prompt the user before removing a file, and explain what is being done. The -v option is not available on all versions of rm.

The Script

```
## Parse command-line options
opts=
while getopts fiv var
do
  case $var in
    f) opts="$opts -f" ;;
    i) opts="$opts -i" ;;
    v) opts="$opts -v" ;;
  esac
done
shift $(( $OPTIND - 1 ))

## If no files are specified on the command line,
## check all files in the current directory
[ $# -eq 0 ] && set -- *
```

```
## Examine each file, and delete it if empty
for f
do
  [ -s "$f" ] && continue ## file exists, but is not empty
  [ -f "$f" ] && rm ${opts:--f} "$f"
done
```

9.5 undup—Remove Duplicate Files

They may be backup copies, they may be the same file downloaded under different names, but sooner or later you will wind up with a directory containing duplicate files. Unless they are linked, they represent space that can be freed. Doing it by hand is a tedious chore; can the duplicates be removed with a script?

How It Works

The files are sorted by size, using the output of ls -l; when two successive files are the same size, they are compared (using cmp). If the files are identical, the user is prompted with information about the files and given the options of deleting either copy, symlinking one to the other, or doing nothing.

Usage

```
undup [-z] [DIR]
```

If no directory is given, the current directory is searched. When a duplicate pair is found, information is displayed, and the user is asked to press a number from 1 to 5:

```
$ undup .
```

```
1. Delete Minder.htm
2. Delete Minder.html
3. Make 'Minder.htm' a symlink to 'Minder.html'
4. Make 'Minder.html' a symlink to 'Minder.htm'
5. Ignore

ASCII English text: 5240 bytes: _
```

Press 1, and Minder.htm will be deleted; press 2, and Minder.html is gone; press 3 or 4, and a symbolic link will be created; press 5, and you will proceed to the next duplicate, if any.

The -z option uses zrm to clean out empty files before looking for duplicates.

The Script

The eq_query function takes two filenames as arguments and asks the user whether to delete one or the other, turn one into a symbolic link (to retain both names, but reduce the space used), or to ignore the duplication.

```
eq_query()
{
    [ $# -ne 2 ] && return 5
    eq_1=$1
    eq_2=$2
```

```
    filetype=`file $eq_1`
    printf "\n"
    printf "\t%d. Delete %s\n" 1 "$eq_1" 2 "$eq_2"
    printf "\t%s\n" "3. Make '$eq_1' a symlink to '$eq_2'" \
                    "4. Make '$eq_2' a symlink to '$eq_1'" \
                    "5. Ignore"

    printf "\n\t%s: %d bytes: " "${filetype#*: }" $size
    get_key < /dev/tty
    printf "\n"
    case $_KEY in
        1) rm "$eq_1" && printf "\n\tRemoved $eq_1\n\n" ;;
        2) rm "$eq_2" && printf "\n\tRemoved $eq_2\n\n" ;;
        3) ln -sf "$eq_2" "$eq_1" && { printf "\n"; ls -l "$eq_1"; } ;;
        4) ln -sf "$eq_1" "$eq_2" && { printf "\n"; ls -l "$eq_2"; } ;;
        q) break 3 ;;
        *) return 0 ;;
    esac
    _EQ_QUERY=$_KEY
}
```

Files in the current directory are sorted by size, and files that are the same size are examined by cmp; if the files are identical, eq_query is called to ask the user to determine disposition of the files.

```
rm_dups()
{
    ls -l "$@" | sort -k5n | {
        read -r perms_ links_ owner_ group_ size_ month_ day_ time_ file_
        while read -r perms links owner group size month day time file
        do
            [ ${verbose:-0} -ge 1 ] && printf "%10s %s\n" $size "$file" >&2
            [ -f "$file" ] || continue
            [ ${size:--0} -eq ${size_:--1} ] &&
                cmp $file $file_ >/dev/null && {
                [ ${verbose:-0} -ge 1 ] && printf "%10s %s\n" $size_ "$file_" >&2
                eq_query $file $file_
            }
            case $_EQ_QUERY in
                1|3) continue ;;
            esac
            size_=$size
            file_=$file
        done
    }
}
```

The main program loops through the list of directories on the command line (using the current directory if there are none), and calls rm_dups for each one.

```
. standard-funcs ## Load the standard functions
zrm=0
TMOUT=60
```

```
## Parse command-line options
opts=zv
while getopts $opts opt
do
  case $opt in
      v) verbose=$(( ${verbose:-0} + 1 )) ;;
      z) zrm=1 ;;
  esac                    .
done
shift $(( $OPTIND - 1 ))

## Reset tty on exit
trap cleanup EXIT

set -- "${@:-.}"
for dir
do
  (
      cd "${dir:-.}" || continue
      : ${PWD:=`pwd`}
      [ $zrm -ge 1 ] && zrm *
      rm_dups
  )
done
```

9.6 lsr—List the Most Recent (or Oldest) Files in a Directory

I often want to view the most recent files in a directory. It may be my download directory because I don't remember the name of that file I just pulled off the Web, or it may be because I have forgotten the name I used for the script I wrote a few hours ago (don't laugh; it happens).

How It Works

Laziness is the mother of invention, and that is certainly the case with lsr. Listing the ten most recently modified files in a directory is as easy as this:

```
ls -lt $HOME/dld | head
```

To get the ten oldest is only one letter more:

```
ls -lrt $HOME/dld | head
```

To cut that down to the five newest files adds more characters:

```
ls -lt $HOME/dld | head -5
```

Now that's long enough to justify a script, isn't it?

Usage

```
lsr [OPTIONS] [FILE ...]
```

By default, lsr lists the ten most recently modified files. The -n option allows the user to select any number of files:

```
$ lsr -n3 /usr/local/bin/*
-r-xr-xr-x 1 chris chris    1444 Nov 2 17:41 /usr/local/bin/sym2file
-rwxr-xr-x 1 chris chris    4158 Nov 2 12:36 /usr/local/bin/standard-funcs
-r-xr-xr-x 1 chris chris    1926 Nov 2 12:29 /usr/local/bin/rand-funcs
```

The -o option tells the script to show the oldest files:

```
$ lsr -on3 /usr/bin
-rwxr-xr-x 1 root root    741588 Dec 12 2000 plain-gmc
-rwxr-xr-x 1 root root    750432 Dec 12 2000 gmc
-rwxr-xr-x 1 root root      1939 Jan 10 2003 newsgroups
```

The -a option includes dot files:

```
$ lsr -an3 ~
drwx------ 4 chris chris  8192 Nov 2 23:34 mail
-rw------- 1 chris chris 44035 Nov 2 23:33 .jnewsrc-nin.as
drwxr-xr-x 3 chris chris 16384 Nov 2 23:31 scripts
```

When listing files at the command line, I always want a long listing, but I may want just the names when piping the result to another program. The short option, -s, gives me that:

```
$ lsr -asn4 ~
scripts
.
.followup
.bash_history
```

The Script

```
num=10     ## Default to ten most recent files
short=0    ## Use long listing by default
## Parse command-line options
opts=an:o:s
while getopts $opts opt
do
  case $opt in
     a) ls_opts="$ls_opts -a" ;;
     n) num=$OPTARG ;;
     o) ls_opts="$ls_opts -r" ;;
     s) short=1 ;;
  esac
done
shift $(( $OPTIND - 1 ))
```

```
## Add -t to ls options and -l if not using short mode
case $short in
      1) ls_opts="$ls_opts -t" ;;
      *) ls_opts="$ls_opts -l -t" ;;
esac
ls $ls_opts "$@" | {
      ## If the first line is "total ...", it is removed
      read -r line
      case $line in
          total*) ;;
          *) printf "%s\n" "$line" ;;
      esac
      cat
} | head -$num
```

Summary

The scripts in this chapter run the gamut from totally interactive (undup) to fully automated (dfcmp). Somewhere in between, symfix, sym2file, and zrm can do their work unhindered, or can prompt the user for confirmation of each action. Though designed for use at the command line, lsr needs no interaction, and can be used in scripts.

This is typical of a file management system, of which these scripts would be only a small part. Some tasks can be automated, but you will always want to control some things yourself. In addition to these, and the file-aging scripts in Chapter 14, you will probably need a good file manager. Some people swear by Midnight Commander (mc), others by Konqueror. My favorite is gentoo, which was based on the Amiga file manager, Directory Opus. Many applications also have interactive file managers: lynx, emacs, pine, and others.

In addition, you will probably need to write some more scripts to deal with your own particular situation.

CHAPTER 10

■ ■ ■

Screenplay: The screen–funcs Library

Data Entry on terminal screens involved positioning the cursor on the screen at various places, displaying pieces of information in bold or reverse text. The usual method of positioning the cursor and setting attributes such as bold and reverse involves tput, a Unix utility that outputs screen codes for the particular terminal or terminal emulation you are using. Even with processors running at multigigahertz speeds, calling an external command multiple times can produce a noticeable delay.

For a certain project, Chris took the easy way out and placed the cursor-positioning codes for terminals in a printat function, and the printing attributes (bold, reverse, underline) in variables. He rationalized this by assuring himself that, as this was a specialized script, it would never be run anywhere else.

Naturally, a year later his client replaced the system, and the new terminals did not understand the same codes. So he set out to replace the old codes with the new, and it took almost no time at all. The old codes were in functions in a single file; the changeover was less than an hour's work. (Actually, there were a few renegade lines of code in other files that took a little longer to ferret out, but that was a minor problem). This is a perfect example of how changes that can break your code.

Because there are many different types of terminal (the termcap file that defines the codes can contain entries for hundreds of terminals), tput is often used to produce the correct screen codes for positioning the cursor and setting or removing bold, underline, or other attributes. On terminals that support color, tput can generate the codes for setting the background and foreground colors.

Unfortunately, tput has problems (besides the time it takes as an external command). First, some systems do not have it. These are rare nowadays, but not unknown. Second, two different sets of commands are accepted by tput. Most versions only accept one set or the other. Both of the following commands place the cursor at the fifth column on the third row:

```
tput cup 2 4
tput cm 4 2
```

The first command works on a GNU/Linux system, the second on a computer running FreeBSD. For tput commands to work correctly on all systems, you would have to test which version was present, and use different commands depending on the result. Then there are those systems without any version of tput.

The vast majority of terminals and terminal emulations use the American National Standards Institute (ANSI) set of codes. These were first implemented on the DEC vt100 terminal in 1978, and are often referred to as *vt100* codes. Communications programs such as hyperterminal and putty use these codes, or have options to use them, in what is often called vt100 emulation. The functions in this chapter all use the ANSI standard codes, which will work in any terminal having vt100 emulation.

The `screen-funcs` library first sources `standard-funcs` from Chapter 1 and the `screen-vars` file:

```
. standard-funcs
. screen-vars
```

10.1 screen-vars—Variables for Screen Manipulation

After playing around with ANSI screen codes over the last 2-3 decades, one might not still remember them all. Many of us don't even remember all the ones used frequently. Luckily, the computer's memory is better, and you can let it do the work.

How It Works

A good way was to use constants or variables with understandable names. These could be placed together in one file to be used on top of every script that might need them.

Usage

These variables are used mostly in the functions defined in `screen-funcs`, but they can be used directly in a script or at the command line (after sourcing `screen-vars`). For example, to clear the screen without using an external command, there is $CLS:

```
printf "$CLS"
```

To print a bar across the screen, plug the reverse attribute into $set_attr:

```
printf "\n$set_attr%${COLUMNS}.${COLUMNS}s\n" $reverse
```

To draw the same bar with words in it is just a matter of printing a carriage return (so that the cursor stays on the same line) and then the text:

```
{
  printf "\n$set_attr%${COLUMNS}.${COLUMNS}s\r" $reverse
  printf " * * * %s * * * \n" "Stars of the ANSI screen"
}
```

The $cu_row_col variable, like $set_attr and others, can be used as the format string in a `printf` statement to place the cursor anywhere on the screen; for example, the top left corner:

```
printf "$cu_row_col" 1 1
```

For anything more complex (and even for positioning the cursor), It is recommend using the functions, rather than the variables. That way, when you run into a nonstandard terminal, all you need change are the functions (the format for the variables might not be the same).

The Script

```
. standard-vars ## load standard variables ($NL, $ESC, etc. from Chapter 1)

## attributes: printf "$set_attr" $bold
      bold= 1
       dim= 2  ## may not be supported
 underline= 4
     blink= 5  ## may not be supported
   reverse= 7
    hidden= 8  ## may not be supported

## screen codes
CSI=$ESC[            ## Control Sequence Introducer
 NA=${CSI}0m         ## Reset attributes to the default
CLS=${CSI}H${CSI}2J  ## Clear the screen
cle=$ESC[K           ## Clear to end of line

## cursor movement
cu_row_col="${CSI}%d;%dH"      ## position cursor by row and column
      cu_up=${CSI}%dA          ## mv cursor up N lines
    cu_down=${CSI}%dB          ## mv cursor down N lines
      cu_d1=${CSI}1B           ## mv cursor down 1 line
   cu_right=${CSI}%dC          ## mv cursor right N columns
    cu_left=${CSI}%dD          ## mv cursor left N columns
    cu_save=${ESC}7            ## save cursor position
 cu_restore=${ESC}8            ## restore cursor to last saved position
     cu_vis="${CSI}?12l${CSI}?25h"    ## visible cursor
   cu_invis="${CSI}?25l"              ## invisible cursor
      cu_NL=$cu_restore$cu_d1$cu_save  ## move to next line

## set attributes
set_attr=${CSI}%sm   ## set printing attribute
set_bold=${CSI}1m    ## equiv: printf "$set_attr" $bold
  set_ul=${CSI}4m    ## equiv: printf "$set_attr" $underline
 set_rev=${CSI}7m    ## equiv: printf "$set_attr" $reverse

## unset attributes
unset_bold=${CSI}22m
  unset_ul=${CSI}24m
 unset_rev=${CSI}27m

## colors (precede by 3 for foreground, 4 for background)
  black=0
    red=1
  green=2
 yellow=3
   blue=4
```

```
magenta=5
   cyan=6
  white=7
     fg=3
     bg=4

## set colors
  set_bg="${CSI}4%dm"      ## e.g.: printf "$set_bg" $red
  set_fg="${CSI}3%dm"      ## e.g.: printf "$set_fg" $yellow
set_fgbg="${CSI}3%d;4%dm" ## e.g.: printf "$set_fgbg" $yellow $red
```

10.2 set_attr—Set Screen-Printing Attributes

When dealing with a character-based terminal, the ways of changing text appearance are limited. The ANSI modes for terminals are bright, dim, underscore, blink, reverse, and hidden. If you are lucky, your terminal will not support the blink attribute (*"We don't need no blinkin' text!"*), but you will want bold and reverse.

How It Works

The $set_attr variable contains a format string that is used as a format string for printf.

Usage

```
set_attr [ATTRIBUTE[;ATTRIBUTE]]
```

The blink, dim, and hidden attributes may not be implemented on your terminal. They are included in screen-vars for completeness. I do not recommend using them.

Multiple attributes can be specified in a single call (note the 0 to turn off any attributes currently in effect before setting new values):

```
set_attr 0 $bold $underline
```

Colors may also be set with set_attr, but there are functions for that which are easier to use (see set_fg, set_bg, and set_fgbg later in this chapter).

The Script

```
set_attr()
{
    for _attr in "${@:-0}"
    do
      case $_attr in
      ## if argument is negative, remove the attribute
          -"$bold") printf "$set_attr" "22" ;; ## 21 may not work
          -[0-9]*) printf "$set_attr" "2${_attr#-}" ;;
          ## positive number; add an attribute
          [0-9]*|"") printf "$set_attr" "${1:-0}" ;;
      esac
    done
}
```

10.3 set_fg, set_bg, set_fgbg—Set Colors for Printing to the Screen

The vast majority of users nowadays will be running the shell in a color environment, whether it is the Linux console or an telnet/ssh window. This allows more attractive displays from shell scripts. To ease the use of color, these functions set the foreground and background colors.

How It Works

Defined in screen-vars at the beginning of this chapter, the printf format strings set_fg, set_bg, and set_fgbg are the basis for these three functions.

Usage

```
set_fg [0-7]          ## set the foreground (printing) color
set_bg [0-7]          ## set the background color
set_fgbg [0-7] [0-7] ## set the foreground and background colors
```

Though the arguments are all a single digit from 0 to 7, there is no need to remember which number represents which color; that's already done for you with the color definitions in screen-vars. You can just use the color variables:

```
set_fg $red
set_bg $white
set_fgbg $blue $yellow
```

These settings affect subsequent text, not colors already displayed. An argument of -1 in any position sets all colors and attributes to the default. Any other argument returns an error.

These functions may be used anywhere set_attr is used in this or future chapters.

The Script

```
## set the foreground color
set_fg()
{
    case $1 in
        [0-7]) printf "$set_fg" "$1" ;;
        -1|"") printf "$NA" ;;
        *) return 5 ;;
    esac
}

## set the background color
set_bg()
{
    case $1 in
        [0-7]) printf "$set_bg" "$1" ;;
        -1|"") printf "$NA" ;;
        *) return 5 ;;
    esac
}
```

```
## set both foreground and background colors
set_fgbg()
{
    case $1$2 in
        [0-7][0-7]) printf "$set_fgbg" "$1" "$2" ;;
        *-1*|"") printf "$NA" ;;
        *) return 5 ;;
    esac
}
```

10.4 cls—Clear the Screen

When using the full screen (or window) for script output, one usually starts with a clean slate. The clear command will do this, but it is an external command; is there a way to do it just using the shell?

How It Works

Since clear prints your terminal's code for clearing the screen (or enough blank lines to clear it if there is no such code), its output can be captured in a variable and printed to the screen when needed. The ANSI code to clear the screen is set in screen-vars, but it can be deleted, and the cls function will use the correct code for your terminal, setting the variable at the same time.

Usage

cls

There are no arguments nor options to this simple function.

The Script

If $CLS is not defined, this function will use the output of clear, assigning it to $CLS as well as printing the result. Normally, $CLS will have been defined; clear is a fall-back (that will be called no more than once) in case screen-vars has not been sourced.

```
cls()
{
    printf "${CLS:=$(clear)}"
}
```

Notes

One evening, while playing in a pub trivia league, it occurred to Chris that the cls function could be enhanced. (Don't ask why it came to him during a set of questions on medieval history!) He was in the middle of writing this chapter at the time, so he jotted it down on a scrap of paper. It adds the capability of changing the colors and other attributes of the screen as well as clearing it.

It uses three functions that are defined earlier in this chapter: set_attr, set_bg, and set_fgbg. When called without any arguments, its behavior is exactly the same as the simpler version. When there is one argument, that value is used to set the background color. With two arguments, the first defines the foreground color, the second the background color. With more than two arguments, all remaining values are used to set attributes such as bold, underline, and reverse. The first two arguments must be digits in the range 0 to 7, representing the eight colors available in the ANSI system.

```
cls() {
    case $# in
        0) ;;
        1) set_bg $1 ;;
        2) set_fgbg $2 $1 ;;
        *) set_fgbg $2 $1
            shift 2
            set_attr "$@"
            ;;
    esac
    printf "${CLS:=$(clear)}"
}
```

10.5 printat—Position Cursor by Row and Column

You can use two methods to send the output of a script to a terminal screen. The traditional method uses the terminal as if it were a printer or teletypewriter (which is the origin of the abbreviation tty for the screen or terminal). In this mode, as each line is printed, the paper, or screen image, is scrolled up. Old lines fall to the floor, or disappear off the top of the screen. It's simple, and it is more than adequate for many applications.

The second method is the subject of most of this chapter; it treats the screen as a blackboard or canvas, and prints to specific points on its surface. It overprints previously written sections, using spaces to erase when necesssary. It may print text in columns or at specific locations on the screen. The terminal becomes a random-access, rather than serial, device. A command to place the cursor at any chosen point on the screen is needed to implement this method.

How It Works

Most terminals and terminal emulations use an escape sequence to position the cursor. The standard ANSI sequence is ESC[<ROW>;<COL>m. This string has been converted to the printf format string cu_row_col (see screen-vars earlier in this chapter). The printat function uses its command-line arguments and this variable to place the cursor at the requested coordinates.

Usage

```
printat [row [column [string]]]
```

If either the row or column argument is missing or is an empty string, a 1 is used, representing the top row or the leftmost column. If string is present, it is printed at the specified location without a terminating linefeed. (In this mode of screen printing, linefeeds are never used, as they could cause the screen to scroll, ruining its formatting.)

Besides using printat directly, its output can be stored in a variable and used many times, saving on computational time. For example, to display information one record at a time from /etc/passwd, use this script:

```
. screen-funcs ## load variables and functions

form=$( ## store empty form in a variable
  printat 2 1 " User Name: "
  printat 2 30 "UID: "
  printat 2 40 "GID: "
  printat 3 1 "    Full name: "
  printat 4 1 "Home Directory: "
  printat 5 1 "         Shell: "
)

print_form() ## print $form with fields filled in
{

    cls
    set_attr 0 ## turn off bold, reverse, etc.
    printf "%s" "$form"
    set_attr $bold
    printat 2 17 "$id"
    printat 2 35 "$uid"
    printat 2 45 "$gid"
    printat 3 17 "$name"
    printat 4 17 "$home"
    printat 5 17 "$shell"
}

## loop through the lines in /etc/passwd
while IFS=: read -r id x uid gid name home shell
do
  print_form
  set_attr $reverse
  printat 12 1 " <PRESS ANY KEY TO CONTINUE> $CR"

  ## standard input is redirected, so read keyboard from /dev/tty
  get_key x < /dev/tty
  case $x in q) break;; esac
done < /etc/passwd
printf "$cle"
set_attr 0
```

Figure 10-1 shows the resulting output.

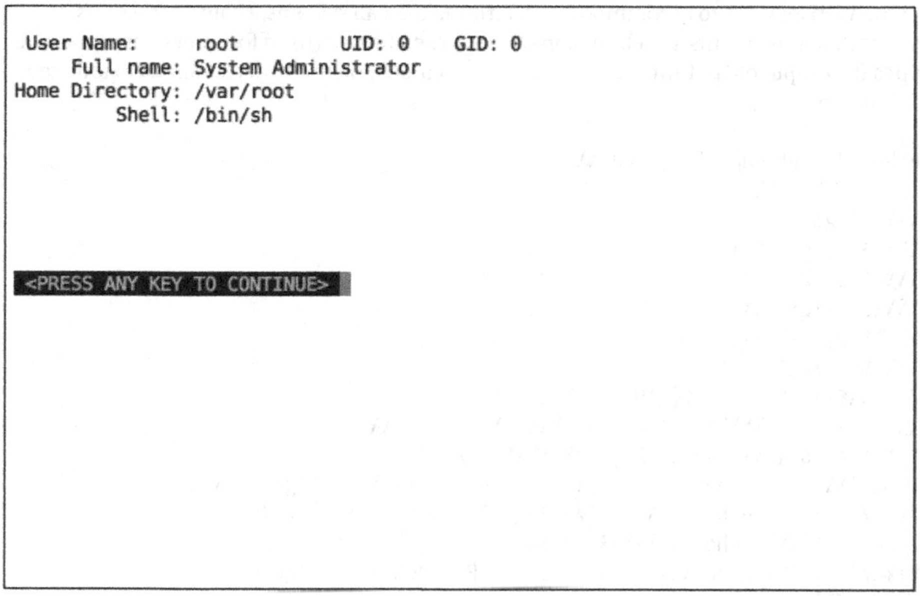

```
 User Name:      root           UID: 0   GID: 0
     Full name: System Administrator
Home Directory: /var/root
         Shell: /bin/sh




<PRESS ANY KEY TO CONTINUE>
```

Figure 10-1. *One record from the password file*

The Script

```
printat()
{
    printf "$cu_row_col" ${1:-1} ${2:-1}

    ## remove the first two arguments
    case ${2+X} in
      X) shift 2 ;;
    esac

    ## print any remaining arguments
    case "$*" in
      *?*) printf "%s" "$*" ;;
    esac
}
```

Notes

If not using an ANSI terminal (the VT100 emulation common to most terminal programs understands the ANSI codes), you need to know the correct command for your terminal. If your system has tput, one of tput cup Y X, tput cm Y X, or tput cm X Y, will position the cursor at column X on row Y (counting from 0,0 as the top left corner; printat and the terminal codes count from 1,1). Your TERM variable will determine the string required. If you don't have tput, you must look up the correct string in your terminal's manual or termcap or terminfo file.

While searching the Web for ways to accommodate all terminals on all systems, I came across this snippet. It's from a script that implements a shell version of the curses library (used for screen manipulation in C programs). It pipes the output of tput through sed to create a cursorpositioning command customized for whatever terminal you are using.

```
eval CMD_MOVE=\`echo \"`tput cup`\" \| sed \\\
-e \"s/%p1%d/\\\\\${1}/g\" \\\
-e \"s/%p2%d/\\\\\${2}/g\" \\\
-e \"s/%p1%02d/\\\\\${1}/g\" \\\
-e \"s/%p2%02d/\\\\\${2}/g\" \\\
-e \"s/%p1%03d/\\\\\${1}/g\" \\\
-e \"s/%p2%03d/\\\\\${2}/g\" \\\
-e \"s/%p1%03d/\\\\\${1}/g\" \\\
-e \"s/%d\\\;%dH/\\\\\${1}\\\;\\\\\${2}H/g\" \\\
-e \"s/%p1%c/'\\\\\\\\`echo \\\\\\\${1} P | dc\\\\\\\\`'/g\" \\\
-e \"s/%p2%c/'\\\\\\\\`echo \\\\\\\${2} P | dc\\\\\\\\`'/g\" \\\
-e \"s/%p1%\' \'%+%c/'\\\\\\\\\`echo \\\\\\\${1} 32 + P | dc\\\\\\\\`'/g\" \\\
-e \"s/%p2%\' \'%+%c/'\\\\\\\\\`echo \\\\\\\${2} 32 + P | dc\\\\\\\\`'/g\" \\\
-e \"s/%p1%\'@\'%+%c/'\\\\\\\\\`echo \\\\\\\${1} 100 + P | dc\\\\\\\\`'/g\" \\\
-e \"s/%p2%\'@\'%+%c/'\\\\\\\\\`echo \\\\\\\${2} 100 + P | dc\\\\\\\\`'/g\" \\\
-e \"s/%i//g\;s/%n//g\"\`
```

When run in a standard ANSI terminal, this produces the equivalent of the $cu_row_col variable I introduced in screen-vars. But the phrase "molasses in January" leaped into my head when I realized what it produced for a Wyse 60 terminal: a command substitution string that makes two calls to the (external) dc command to do the arithmetic **every** time it is used. I could make this snippet considerably faster (in shells with a built-in printf) by using the chr function from Chapter 3, but it still wouldn't work on systems that use cm instead of cup as the tput attribute. They generate an error, not a format string, when cm has no arguments.

Here is a version for a popular terminal, the Wyse 60:

```
printat()
{
    printf "\e="
    chr -n $(( 32 + ${1:-1} )) $(( 32 + ${2:-1} ))
    case ${2+X} in
        X) shift 2 ;;
    esac
    case "$*" in
        *?*) printf "%s" "$*" ;;
    esac
}
```

10.6 put_block_at—Print Lines in a Column Anywhere on the Screen

You want to print blocks of information at different locations on the screen; for example, a list at column 65 on row 1 and subsequent rows, and another at column 10 on row 9 and below. You could prefer not to have to call printat for each line.

How It Works

Three variables defined in screen-vars, $cu_save, $cu_d1 and $cu_restore are combined in $cu_NL, which restores a previously saved cursor position, moves the cursor down one line, and saves the cursor position. When $cu_NL is used at the end of a printf format string instead of $NL, each argument is printed immediately below the previous one, instead of a—t the beginning of the next line.

Usage

```
put_block ARG1 ...
put_block_at ROW COL ARG1 ...
```

The arguments to put_block are printed, one to a line, aligned beneath the first character of the first line.

```
$ cls; printat 1 25; put_block The quick brown fox
                        The
                        quick
                        brown
                        fox
```

The second function, put_block_at, incorporates printat, so this will give the same output as the previous command line:

```
$ cls; put_block_at 1 25 The quick brown fox
```

Here is an example of building a more complex screen using printat and put_block_at. First, lists are stored in three variables:

```
{
 q=$(cut -d: -f1 /etc/passwd)
 w=$(cut -d: -f7 /etc/passwd | sort -u)
 e=$(grep -v '^#' /etc/shells)
```

Then we source the screen-funcs library (which loads screen-vars), turn off the cursor, clear the screen, and print the lists at different places:

```
. screen-funcs-sh
cls
bar==============================================
printf "$cu_invis"
put_block_at 1 65 $q
put_block_at 9 10 $w
put_block_at 9 30 $e
```

211

```
printat 3 40 "List of users ==>"
printat 8 1
printf "%63.63s" "$bar$bar$bar"
printat 7 10 "Shells used"
printat 7 30 "Shells allowed"
sleep 5
printat $LINES 1 "$cu_vis"
}
```

The result looks something like this:

```
                                                            root
                                                            daemon
                                        List of users ==>   bin
                                                            sys
                                                            sync
                                                            games
          Shells used          Shells allowed man
================================================================ lp
          /bin/bash            /bin/ash                     mail
          /bin/false           /bin/bash                    news
          /bin/sh              /bin/csh                     uucp
          /bin/sync            /bin/sh                      proxy
                               /usr/bin/es                  www-data
                               /usr/bin/ksh                 backup
                               /bin/ksh                     list
                               /usr/bin/rc                  irc
                               /usr/bin/tcsh                gnats
                               /bin/tcsh                    nobody
                               /usr/bin/zsh                 messagebus
                               /bin/sash                    postfix
                               /bin/zsh                     cfaj
                               /usr/bin/esh                 fetchmail
                               /bin/dash                    hal
                               /usr/bin/screen              dictd
```

The Script—

```
put_block()
{
    printf "$cu_save" ## save cursor location
    printf "%s$cu_NL" "$@"
}

put_block_at()
{

    printat $1 $2 "$cu_save"
    shift 2
    printf "%s$cu_NL" "$@"
}
```

10.7 get_size—Set LINES and COLUMNS Variables

To draw to the screen, we need to know how big it is. The bash shell automatically initializes the variables $LINES and $COLUMNS, but other shells are not so cooperative.

How It Works

Both stty and tput can print the size of the screen, but I have found stty size to be more consistent across different systems than tput lines and tput cols; stty size is usually faster, though not enough to sway the decision. Neither command is required by the POSIX specifications to give the desired information, but all implementations I've seen do.

Usage

```
get_size
```

If, for some reason, stty size does not produce the expected output, defaults of 80 columns and 24 lines are used. These are the traditional values for a character terminal.

The Script

```
get_size()

{
    set -- $(stty size 2>/dev/null)
    COLUMNS=${2:-80}
    LINES=${1:-24}
    export COLUMNS LINES
}
```

10.8 max_length—Find the Length of the Longest Argument

The output of the put_block functions may collide with and overwrite text already on the screen, making it illegible. For example, if I run these two commands:

```
put_block_at 1 10 Jonathon Christopher Emilio
put_block_at 1 10 Sue John Bob
```

I'll end up with nonsense on the screen:

```
Sueathon
Johnstopher
Boblio
```

The print_block function that follows needs to know the length of the longest item in the list so it can erase any text already on the screen.

How It Works

Unfortunately, there is no choice but to cycle through all the items, keeping track of the longest. POSIX shell parameter expansion is used to obtain the number of characters in each argument.

Usage

```
_max_length [ARG ...] ## store result in $_MAX_LENGTH
max_length [ARG ...]  ## print result
```

As with many other functions in this book, max_length is paired with an underscore function, _max_length, for efficiency. If no arguments are given, _MAX_LENGTH will contain 0; no error is generated.

The Script

```
_max_length()
{
    ## initialize _MAX_LENGTH with the length of the first argument
    _MAX_LENGTH=${#1}
    [ $# -eq 0 ] && return ## if no arguments, just return
    shift    ## remove the first argument
    for var  ## cycle through the remaining args
    do
      [ "${#var}" -gt "$_MAX_LENGTH" ] && _MAX_LENGTH=${#var}
    done
}

max_length()
{
    _max_length "$@"
    printf "%s\n" $_MAX_LENGTH
}
```

10.9 print_block_at—Print a Block of Lines Anywhere on the Screen

On an empty screen, put_block is an adequate method of printing a list. When the screen is full, the output may be jumbled with existing text. To make reading easier, I would like to erase all the characters in a rectangle to contain the list.

How It Works

After finding the length of the longest item in the list by using _max_length, a width specification is used with printf to pad the lines. A line is added before and after the list, and a space is printed before and after each padded item.

Usage

```
print_block ARG1 ...
print_block_at ROW COL ARG1 ...
```

The usage of print_block is identical to that of put_block, but the result is quite different if text is already on the screen.

```
. string-funcs; . screen-funcs         ## load libraries
cls                                     ## clear the screen
_repeat 'BBBBBBB' ${COLUMNS}0           ## build string 10 lines long
printf "%s" "$_REPEAT"                  ## print long string
sleep 1                                 ## take a nap
box=$(print_block The quick brown fox)  ## store block in variable
printat 2 66 "$box"                     ## print near right of screen
set_attr $bold                          ## turn on bold printing
printat 3 16 "$box"                     ## print near left of screen
```

With all the nasty details hidden away in the function library, this short script produces this:

```
BBBBBBBBBBBBBBBBBBBBBBBBBBBBBBBBBBBBBBBBBBBBBBBBBBBBBBBBBBBBBBBBBBBBBBBBBBBBBBBBB
BBBBBBBBBBBBBBBBBBBBBBBBBBBBBBBBBBBBBBBBBBBBBBBBBBBBBBBBBBBBBBBBBBBBBBBB   BBBBBBBB
BBBBBBBBBBBBBBB         BBBBBBBBBBBBBBBBBBBBBBBBBBBBBBBBBBBBBBBBBBBB The   BBBBBBBB
BBBBBBBBBBBBBBB The     BBBBBBBBBBBBBBBBBBBBBBBBBBBBBBBBBBBBBBBBBBBB quick BBBBBBBB
BBBBBBBBBBBBBBB quick BBBBBBBBBBBBBBBBBBBBBBBBBBBBBBBBBBBBBBBBBBBBBBB brown BBBBBBBB
BBBBBBBBBBBBBBB brown BBBBBBBBBBBBBBBBBBBBBBBBBBBBBBBBBBBBBBBBBBBBBBB fox   BBBBBBBB
BBBBBBBBBBBBBBB fox     BBBBBBBBBBBBBBBBBBBBBBBBBBBBBBBBBBBBBBBBBBBBB     BBBBBBBB
BBBBBBBBBBBBBBB         BBBBBBBBBBBBBBBBBBBBBBBBBBBBBBBBBBBBBBBBBBBBBBBBBBBBBBBBBBBBB
BBBBBBBBBBBBBBBBBBBBBBBBBBBBBBBBBBBBBBBBBBBBBBBBBBBBBBBBBBBBBBBBBBBBBBBBBBBBBBBBB
BBBBBBBBBBBBBBBBBBBBBBBBBBBBBBBBBBBBBBBBBBBBBBBBBBBBBBBBBBBBBBBBBBBBBBBBBBBBBBBBB
```

The Script

```
print_block_at()
{
    printat $1 $2 "$cu_save"
    ## _BLOCK_PARMS stores values for clearing the area later
    _BLOCK_PARMS="$1 $2"
    shift 2
    print_block "$@"
}

print_block()
{
    _max_length "$@"
    [ $_MAX_LENGTH -gt $(( $COLUMNS - 2 )) ] &&
        pb_w=$(( $COLUMNS - 2 )) || pb_w=$_MAX_LENGTH
```

```
    ## printf re-uses its format string until
    ## all the arguments are printed
    printf " %-${pb_w#-}.${pb_w#-}s $cu_NL" " " "$@" " "

    ## store paramters for use with the clear_area_at function
    _BLOCK_PARMS="$_BLOCK_PARMS $(( $_MAX_LENGTH + 2 )) $(( $# + 2 ))"
}
```

10.10 vbar, hbar—Print a Vertical or Horizontal Bar

The graphical possibilities with shell scripts are limited, but horizontal and vertical bars are well within its capabilities. What's needed are functions to make drawing them easy.

How It Works

With printf's width specification, any number of characters of a string can be printed. With a loop and the $cu_NL variable to restore the cursor position and move to the same column in the next line, a bar can be repeated as many times as necessary. The bar can be the width of a single character or as wide as the screen.

Usage

```
vbar HEIGHT [WIDTH [STRING]]
hbar [WIDTH [STRING]]
```

By default, both commands will draw invisible bars. To make them visible, either an atttribute must be set (reverse, or a color different from the background), or a string must be specified. The default width is one character.

To print a vertical bar down the middle of the screen:

```
cls                     ## clear the screen
set_attr $reverse       ## set reverse printing
vbar $(( $COLUMNS / 2 )) ## print bar
```

To print a horizontal bar across the middle of the screen:

```
cls
printat $(( $LINES / 2 )) 1 ## position cursor
set_attr $reverse          ## set reverse printing
hbar $COLUMNS              ## print bar
```

To print a vertical red bar (only on a color terminal, of course) 10 characters wide and 20 lines deep:

```
set_attr $bg$red ## set background red
vbar 20 10       ## draw the bar
```

The Script

```
vbar()
{
    printf "$cu_save" ## save cursor position

    ## If a string is given, repeat it until it is long enough to
    ## fill the width of the bar
    case $3 in
        ?*) vb_char=$3
            while [ ${#vb_char} -lt ${2:-1} ]
            do
              vb_char=$vb_char$vb_char$vb_char
            done
            ;;
        *) vb_char=" " ;;
    esac
    ## A loop starts with vbar_ set to 0, and increments it until
    ## the specified number of lines have been printed.
    vbar_=0
    while [ $vbar_ -lt ${1:-$LINES} ]
    do
      printf "%${2:-1}.${2:-1}s$cu_NL" "$vb_char"
      vbar_=$(( $vbar_ + 1 ))
    done
}

## A horizontal bar is a vertical bar one line deep.
hbar()
{
    vbar 1 ${1:-$COLUMNS} "$2"
}
```

10.11 center—Center a String on N Columns

A title sometimes looks better when centered on the screen or in a box. The calculations needed to do the positioning are not complicated, and are easily within the capabilities of the POSIX shell.

How It Works

Using parameter expansion to get the length of the string to be printed, this is added to the width in which it is to be centered, and the total is halved. Then printf is used to position the string flush right across that many characters.

Usage

```
center [-NUM] string
```

When NUM is not supplied, center prints its non-option arguments across the width of the screen, as defined by the $COLUMNS variable. No linefeed is printed.

```
center This line is centered across the entire screen ; printf "\n"
center And this is centered beneath it                 ; printf "\n\n"
center -40 Centered in 40 columns                      ; printf "\n"
center -40 Also in 40 columns                          ; printf "\n\n"
center -60 Centered in 60 columns                      ; printf "\n"
center -60 Once again in 60 columns                    ; printf "\n\n"
```

This script produces:

```
            This line is centered across the entire screen
                    And this is centered beneath it


          Centered in 40 columns
            Also in 40 columns


                    Centered in 60 columns
                  Once again in 60 columns
```

If the string exceeds the allotted space, it will be truncated:

```
$ { center -30 Now is the time                    ; printf "\n"
center -30 for all good men to come to the aid of ; printf "\n"
center -30 the party                              ; printf "\n"
}
```

```
        Now is the time
for all good men to come to the ai
          the party
```

The Script

```
center() {
    case $1 in
        -[0-9]*) c_cols=${1#-}
                shift
                ;;
        *) c_cols=${COLUMNS:-78} ;;
    esac
    string="$*"
    c_len=$(( ( $c_cols - ${#string} ) / 2 + ${#string}))
    printf "%${c_len}.${c_len}s" "$*"
}
```

10.12 flush_right—Align String with the Right Margin

Though not used as often as center, I do sometimes want to print text against the right margin of the screen or a column.

How It Works

When a width is supplied to a format specification in a printf format string, by default it prints its argument aligned at the right-hand side of the width. This makes the flush_right function a snap to write.

Usage

```
flush_right [-NUM] string
```

As with center, if NUM is not supplied, the entire width of the screen is used as the canvas.

```
flush_right This line is flush right across the entire screen; printf "\n"
flush_right At the right of the screen                        ; printf "\n\n"
flush_right -40 Flush right across 40 columns                 ; printf "\n"
flush_right -40 The same again                                ; printf "\n\n"
flush_right -60 Flush right across 60 columns                 ; printf "\n"
flush_right -60 Once more with 60 columns                     ; printf "\n\n"
```

If any string had been longer than its allotted space, it would have been truncated, but these all fit:

```
This line is flush right across the entire screen
                At the right of the screen

Flush right across 40 columns
          The same again

Flush right across 60 columns
  Once more with 60 columns
```

The Script

```
flush_right() {
    case $1 in
        -[0-9]*) fr_cols=${1#-}
                 shift
                 ;;
        *) fr_cols=${COLUMNS:-78} ;;
    esac
    printf "%${fr_cols}.${fr_cols}s" "$*"
}
```

10.13 ruler—Draw a Ruler Across the Width and Height of the Window

When designing a screen or checking the output of a script, it often helps to have a reference for the numbering of rows and columns.

How It Works

The horizontal ruler uses `printf` to truncate the numbering at the edge of the screen, and a loop to count the lines down the side.

Usage

```
ruler
```

This is a simple function with no options and no arguments. The output is shown in Figure 10-2.

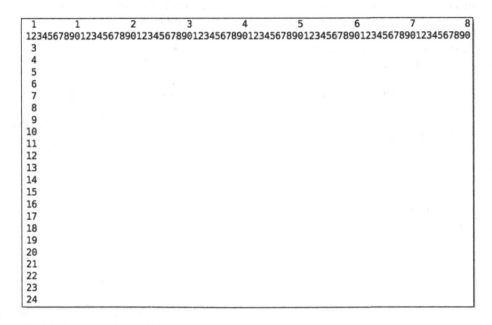

Figure 10-2. *The* `ruler` *function's output displayed in a window*

The Script

```
ruler()
{
    printat 1 1

    ## build tens and units strings to print across the top of the screen
    tens="          1         2         3         4         5         6         7"
    tens="$tens          8         9         0"
    tens=$tens$tens$tens
    printf "%${COLUMNS:=80}.${COLUMNS:=80}s\n" "$tens"
    vruler
    printat 2 1
    one2ten=1234567890
    while [ ${#one2ten} -lt $COLUMNS ]
    do
       one2ten=$one2ten$one2ten$one2ten
    done
    printf "%-${COLUMNS}.${COLUMNS}s\n" "$one2ten"
}

vruler()
{
    n=$(( ${bar_line:-1} ))
    printat 1 1 "$cu_save"
    while [ $n -le $LINES ]
    do
       printf "%2s$cu_NL" $n
       n=$(( $n + 1 ))
    done
}
```

10.14 box_block, box_block_at—Print Text Surrounded by a Box

To draw attention to a block of text, it sometimes helps to draw a box around it. I want to be able to control the colors of the box and the background and text colors inside it.

How It Works

Two variables are used to set the attributes, including colors, for the outline and the interior. A technique similar to that used in print_block is used to print the box.

Usage

```
bx_border=$(...)bx_body=$(...)
box_block_at COL ROW [STRING ...]
box_block [STRING ...]
```

The two variables, bx_border and bx_body, must be set to strings that control the colors and attributes for the box and its interior. These are usually the output of set_attr and set_fgbg. Usually, set_attr 0 should be used first to clear any existing settings. For example, this sets the box to blue and prints the text in bold red on a yellow background:

```
bx_border=$(set_attr 0; set_bg $blue)
bx_body=$(set_attr 0 $bold; set_fgbg $red $yellow)
box_block_at 3 3 Trooping the colors
```

Figure 10-3 shows the output.

Figure 10-3. *A boxed message printed using box_block_at*

The location and size of the resulting box is stored in $_BLOCK_PARMS, which can be used as the argument to clear_block_at, which is presented in the next section of this chapter.

The Script

```
box_block_at()
{
    printat $1 $2
    _BLOCK_PARMS="$1 $2"
    shift 2
    box_block "$@"
}

box_block()
{

  _max_length "$@"
  [ $_MAX_LENGTH -gt $(( $COLUMNS - 4 )) ] &&
      pb_w=$(( $COLUMNS - 4 )) || pb_w=$_MAX_LENGTH
```

```
## use the maximum length of the arguments for width specification
pb_w1=$pb_w.$pb_w
pb_w=$(( $pb_w + 2 )).$(( $pb_w + 2 ))

## print the top line using the $bx_border attributes
printf "$cu_save$bx_border"
printf " %-${pb_w}s $cu_NL" " "

## printf re-uses its format string till all the arguments are printed
printf "$bx_border $bx_body %-${pb_w}s $bx_border $cu_NL" " " "$@" " "
printf "$bx_border %-${pb_w}s $bx_body$cu_NL" " "

## store parameters for use with clear_area_at
 _BLOCK_PARMS="$_BLOCK_PARMS $(( $_MAX_LENGTH + 4 )) $(( $# + 4 ))"
}
```

10.15 clear_area, clear_area_at—Clear an Area of the Screen

When using the screen as a blackboard, I frequently need to erase an area to reuse for new or different information. I need to be able to specify the location and size of the area, and set the background color.

How It Works

As in several other functions in this chapter, the background color is set before the function is called. The function loops the desired number of times, printing spaces to the width specified.

Usage

```
clear_area WIDTH HEIGHT
clear_area_at ROW COL WIDTH HEIGHT
```

The print_block_at and box_block_at functions store their parameters in $_BLOCK_PARMS. This variable can be used as the argument to the clear_area_at function.

```
cls
set_fgbg $green $white
print_block_at 2 33 "Diving into Python" \
        "Practical Subversion" "Shell Scripting Recipes"
sleep 2
set_attr
clear_area_at $_BLOCK_PARMS
```

If you make another call to print_block_at or box_block_at before you call clear_area_at, you will need to save the values in $_BLOCK_PARMS to another variable, because it will be over- written:

```
print_block_at 22 33 12 34 Please clean the board
block=$_BLOCK_PARMS
sleep 2 ## do other stuff
clear_area_at $block
```

The Script

```
clear_area()
{
    printf "$cu_save"                   ## save cursor position
    n=0                                 ## set counter
    while [ $n -le $2 ]                 ## loop till counter ...
    do                                  ## reaches the value of $2
      printf "%${1}.${1}s$cu_NL" " "    ## print spaces to WIDTH
      n=$(( $n + 1 ))                   ## increment counter
    done
}

clear_area_at()
{
    printat $1 $2    ## position cursor
    clear_area $3 $4 ## clear the area
}
```

10.16 box_area, box_area_at—Draw a Box Around an Area

Sometimes I want to clear an area on the screen and put a box around it, clearing an area of the screen so that I can place information in it at a later time, perhaps in repsonse to user input or the completion of another task. Figure 10-4 shows the result.

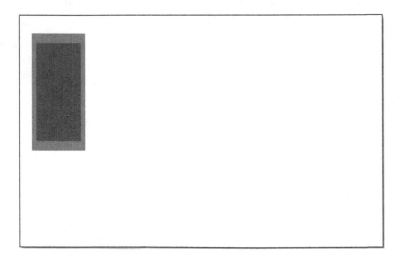

Figure 10-4. *An area cleared and boxed*

How It Works

As with some of the other tasks in this chapter, there are two functions for drawing a box around an arbitrary area: one that performs a task at the current cursor position, and another that moves to a certain position before doing its thing. Unlike the previous functions, these use different techniques.

Since box_area_at knows its location (the first two arguments), it can return to that point to draw the inner box. On the other hand, box_area doesn't have that information, and to save and restore the position would be more complicated. It therefore proceeds on a one-way journey from top to bottom.

Usage

```
bx_border=$(...) bx_body=$(...)
box_area WIDTH HEIGHT
box_area_at ROW COL WIDTH HEIGHT
```

As with box_block, the box_area functions take their colors and attributes from the bx_border and bx_body variables.

```
cls
bx_border=$(set_attr 0; set_bg $yellow)
bx_body=$(set_attr 0 $bold; set_fgbg $blue $magenta)
box_area_at 3 3 12 12
```

The Script

```
box_area_at()
{
    ## set the border style
    printf "$bx_border"

    ## clear the whole area with the border color
    clear_area_at $1 $2 $3 $(( $4 - 1 ))

    ## return to the top left corner,
    ## one square down and one to the right
    printat $(( $1 + 1 )) $(( $2 + 1 ))

    ## set the interior style
    printf "$bx_body"

    ## clear a smaller area with the body color
    clear_area $(( $3 - 2 )) $(( $4 - 3 ))
}
box_area()
{
    printf "$bx_border$cu_save"

    ## print the top line with the border values
    printf "%${1}.${1}s$cu_NL" " "
```

```
  ## create a string to contain the border for each line
  ba_border="$bx_border $bx_body"

  ## calculate the width of the inside area
  ba_w=$(( $1 - 2 ))

  ## loop until we reach the bottom line
  ba_=2
  while [ $ba_ -lt $2 ]
  do
    ## print the border left and right on each line
    printf "$ba_border%${ba_w}.${ba_w}s$ba_border$cu_NL"
    ba_=$(( $ba_ + 1 ))
  done

  ## print the bottom line of the box
  printf "$bx_border$cu_save"
  printf "%${1}.${1}s$cu_NL" " "
}
```

10.17 screen-demo—Saving and Redisplaying Areas of the Screen

A useful technique is to save the results in variables so that boxes can be redrawn over later ones. This demonstration script prints three boxes with text, and then moves them back and forth in front of each other:

How It Works

The output of three calls to box_block_at are stored in variables. This includes the cursor-positioning codes, so the blocks appear at the same location on the screen when they are printed. See Figure 10-5 for the result.

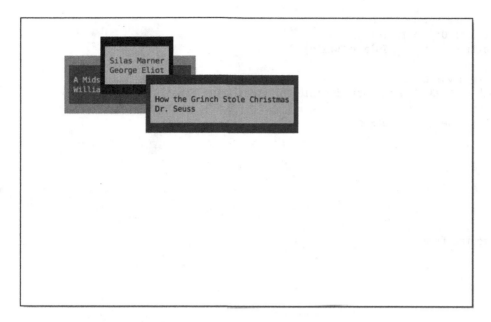

Figure 10-5. *The screen-demo script at work*

Usage

```
screen-demo
```

The Script

```
screen-funcs          ## load the libraries
cls $cyan $cyan       ## clear the screen (with alternate version of cls)
printf "$cu_invis"    ## hide the cursor

## set attributes and colors for box 1
bx_border=$(set_attr 0; set_bg $yellow)
bx_body=$(set_attr 0 $bold; set_fgbg $white $red)

## print box 1 to a variable
box1=$(box_block_at 5 10 "A Midsummer Night's Dream" \
    "William Shakespeare")

## set attributes and colors for box 2
bx_border=$(set_attr 0; set_bg $black)
bx_body=$(set_attr 0 $reverse $bold; set_fgbg $red $white)
-
## print box 2 to a variable
box2=$(box_block_at 3 18 "Silas Marner" "George Eliot")
```

```
## set attributes and colors for box 3
bx_border=$(set_attr 0; set_bg $blue)
bx_body=$(set_attr 0; set_fgbg $black $white)

## print box 3 to a variable
box3=$(box_block_at 7 28 "How the Grinch Stole Christmas" "Dr. Seuss")

## print all three overlapping boxes
printf "$box1"
printf "$box2"
printf "$box3

## take a nap
sleep 1

## move boxes to the front
printf "$box1"
sleep 1
printf "$box3"
sleep 1
printf "$box2"
sleep 1
printf "$box1"
sleep 1
printf "$box3"

# restore cursor and move down a few lines
printf "$cu_vis\n\n\n\n"
```

Summary

Unlike most functions in this book, those presented in this chapter have little application at the command line; they are designed almost exclusively for use in other scripts. They are useful in interactive scripts such as games or data entry forms. They can be used for presentations (put a series of "slides" in a bash array, and move through them, forward or backward, with a keypress) or menus. They are not as fancy as GUI applications, but can be used to create impressive displays in very little time.

■ ■ ■

## CHAPTER 11

Aging, Archiving, and Deleting Files

Files grow. It's a fact of life. There are log files in /var/log (they may be in /var/adm, or somewhere else, depending on your system). In my mail directory I have saved-messages, and sent-mail, and files for the various mailing lists I'm on. In my Chess directory, fics.pgn stores every game of chess I play online. Files in my News directory swell with my Usenet posts.

Most modern Unix systems offer a log rotation program that can be configured to suit many of your needs. Files can be rotated daily, weekly, monthly, or whenever they reach a certain size. They can be compressed or not, as you wish. Traditionally, log rotation files have been numbered, with the most recent always having a suffix of .0, the next oldest having .1, and so on. When a new rotation was performed, the files all had to be renamed. The one with the highest number would be deleted.

My e-mail client, by default, renames saved-messages and sent-mail files at the beginning of every month. It uses filenames with a three-letter abbreviation for the month. My e-mail client sorts them chronologically, but the standard Unix utilities do not.

I prefer file aging to rotation, by renaming the file with a datestamp in the international format; messages would become messages_2004-11-27 or messages_2004-11-27_23.12.39, or any other date format I choose. Files aged once a month only need the year and the month, fics_2004-09. With this method, the files never need further renaming. A system needs to be installed to move or delete files as they get old, but that's simpler, and more flexible, than having to rename every file in the rotation every time. This can be done either by removing files after they reach a certain age, or by keeping only the newest files; scripts for both methods are presented after the script to create date-stamped files.

11.1 date-file—Add a Datestamp to a Filename

I want certain e-mail files moved at the beginning of each month, with the year and month appended to the name. My Usenet posts, which are separated by newsgroup, should be moved when they get too big (for me, too big is 100,000 bytes, for you it may be 10 kilobytes or 1 gigabyte; it needs to be configurable). I want my online chess file renamed every month. Log files need to be renamed every month or every week, and some every day.

How It Works

The simplest solution of all was for my chess file, fics.pgn. The script that loads xboard (a graphical chessboard that connects to http://www.freechess.org or other sites) specifies the file in which games are to be saved. We can modify that script to include the date in the filename with fics_`date +%Y-%m`.pgn instead of fics.pgn. Problem solved. Wouldn't it be nice if all programs created their log files that way?

Well, it turns out that my e-mail client (pine) now has an option to use a YYYY-MM format for its pruned files (it wasn't there the last time I looked!). Perhaps I don't need this script after all? No such luck; there are too many other places where I do.

My original plan for this script was short and sweet:

```
mv "$file" "${file}_$(date +%Y-%m-%d)"
```

If we wanted to be able to change the date format, we can add an option. We know that myfile_2004-11-26.c would look better than myfile.c_2004-11-26, so we can add an option to put the date before the extension. The script grew until it had all the features necessary (and a few that just felt good) for pruning any file that grows over a period of time.

Usage

```
date-file [OPTIONS] FILE ...
```

By default, date-file adds a date in the format .YYYY-MM-DD to the end of each filename supplied on the command line. If the filename is -, filenames are read from the standard input. The options can change everything from the format of the date to the location of the file's final resting place.

- -c: Create a new, empty file (because some logging utilities write to a log file only when it already exists).

- -d DIR: Move file to directory DIR. If the directory doesn't exist, date-file will try to create it. If it is unsuccessful, it will exit with an error.

- -D: Include time and date in the new filename by using the format string _%Y-%m-%d_%H.%M.%S.

- -f FMT: Use FMT as the date format string instead of .%Y-%m%d.

- -h CMD: Execute the command CMD after moving the file. If a program keeps its log file open, it could continue to write to the old file. Sending the HUP signal causes it to reload its configuration files and close any files it has open. On my Mandrakelinux system, for example, logrotate uses /usr/bin/killall -HUP syslogd to tell syslogd to close the old log file and use the new one.

- -s: Insert the date before the final suffix.

- -S SUFF: Insert the date before the suffix, SUFF, if it matches the end of the filename.

- -v: Verbose mode; print the old and new names for each file.

- -z: Compress the file with gzip.

- -Z CMD: Compress the file with CMD, (bzip2, for example).

Here are a few samples, first with the default date format and using gzip -v to compress the resulting file:

```
$ date-file -Z 'gzip -v' yule.log
yule.log_2004-11-26: 80.0% -- replaced with yule.log_2004-11-26.gz
```

With the date format string, _%a, the abbreviated day of the week is used instead of the full date, the -c option tells datefile to create another file of the same name, and -v puts it in verbose mode so we can see the results:

```
$ date-file -c -v -f _%a easter.ogg
"easter.ogg"             -> "easter.ogg_Fri"
```

With -s, the date is inserted before the .gif suffix, and -d logs moves the file into the logs directory:

```
$ date-file -vsd logs xmas.gif
"xmas.gif"               -> "logs/xmas_2004-12-25.gif"
```

The Script

```
## The change of name is done by the mv_file function.
## USAGE: mv_file PATH/TO/FILE
mv_file()
{
    ## if the file in $1 does not exist, return an error
    [ -f "$1" ] || return 5

    if [ $pre_suffix -eq 0 ]
    then
      ## By default, date-file adds the date to the end of the name
      newname=$1$DATE
    else
      ## If pre_suffix has been set to anything other than 0,
      ## the date is inserted before the suffix
      basename=${1%$suffix}        ## get filename without suffix
      postfix=${1#$basename}       ## get the suffix alone
      newname=$basename$DATE$postfix ## place the date between them
    fi

    ## If a destination directory has been given, the new name is
    ## the destination directory followed by a slash and the
    ## filename without any old path
    [ -n "$dest" ] && newname=$dest/${newname##*/}

    ## If in verbose mode, print the old and new filenames
    if [ $verbose -ge 1 ]
    then
      printf "\"%-25s -> \"%s\"\n" "$1\"" "$newname" >&2
    fi
    ## Move the file to its new name or location
    mv "$1" "$newname"

    ## If the option is selected, create a new, empty file
    ## in place of the old one
    [ $create -eq 1 ] && touch "$1"
```

```
    ## If the application that writes to the log file keeps the
    ## file open, send it a signal with the script in $hup.
    [ -n "$hup" ] && eval "$hup"

    ## Compress if selected
    [ -n "$gzip" ] && $gzip "$newname"
        return 0
}

## All these defaults may be overridden by command-line options
pre_suffix=0    ## do not place DATE before suffix
suffix=".*"     ## used if pre_suffix is set to 1
dfmt=_%Y-%m-%d  ## default date format: _YYYY-MM-DD
verbose=0       ## verbose mode off
dest=           ## destination directory
create=0        ## do not re-create (empty) file
gzip=           ## do not use compression
hup=            ## command to interrupt program writing to file

## Parse command-line options
opts=cd:Df:h:o:sS:vzZ:
while getopts $opts opt
do
  case $opt in
      c) create=1 ;;                    ## Create new, empty file
      d) [ -d "$OPTARG" ] ||            ## Move files to different dir
         mkdir "$OPTARG" ||            ## create if necessary
         exit 5                         ## return error if not possible
         dest=${OPTARG%/} ;;           ## remove trailing slash
      D) dfmt=_%Y-%m-%d_%H.%M.%S ;;     ## use time as well as date
      f) dfmt=$OPTARG ;;                ## use supplied date format
      h) hup=$OPTARG ;;                 ## command to run after mv
      s) pre_suffix=1 ;;                ## place date before suffix
      S) suffix=$OPTARG                 ## place date before specified
         pre_suffix=1 ;;               ## suffix
      v) verbose=$(( $verbose + 1 )) ;; ## verbose mode
      z) gzip=gzip ;;                   ## compress file with gzip
      Z) gzip=$OPTARG ;;                ## compress file with supplied cmd
      *) exit 5 ;;                      ## exit on invalid option
  esac
done
shift $(( $OPTIND - 1 )) ## Remove options from command line

## Store the date in $DATE
eval $(date "+DATE=$dfmt ")

## Loop through files on the command line
for file
do
  case $file in
      -) ## If a $file is "-", read filenames from standard input
```

```
        while IFS= read -r file
        do
          mv_file "$file"
        done
        ;;
    *) mv_file "$file" ;;
  esac
done
```

Notes

When aging a file on the first of the month, normally in the small hours of the morning, we want the date to reflect the previous month, which is when it was generated. We could consider adding a date offset option. That would be easy with the GNU or *BSD version of `date`, but complicated with a generic `date` command.

We can age the monthly files shortly after midnight on the first of each month, so we generate the date with a time zone that is one hour earlier. Chris is in the eastern time zone, which is five hours behind Coordinated Universal Time (UTC). By setting the TZ variable to an earlier time zone (Central), We can use yesterday's (i.e., last month's) date:

```
TZ=CST6CDT date-file FILENAME
```

11.2 rmold—Remove Old Files

Many of us have several directories where files collect until we can get around to cleaning them out. They are mostly temporary files, downloads, and aged files created with the `date-file` script. Downloaded files are usually tarballs or other packages that are not needed after their contents have been extracted. Vast areas of my hard drives fill up with old and unneeded files. When the drives fill up, we need to do something about them. We need a script to clear out old files.

How It Works

Being the consummate pack rat, I hate to get rid of anything unless I am sure I will never need it again under any circumstances no matter how unlikely, and then I have to think twice. The only way these files will ever be cleaned out (short of the disk being full) is if I make it easy to remove old files, or else automate the process. The `rmold` script can remove the old files without human intervention.

The script reads the list of directories to be pruned from a file specified on the command line or, by default, from `$HOME/.config/rmold.dirs`. The default is to remove files that are more than 30 days old, but each directory can have a longer or shorter period assigned to it, and the default can be changed by a command-line option.

Usage

```
rmold [OPTIONS]
```

The list of directories to be pruned is placed in `$HOME/.config/rmold.dirs`; this file location can be changed with the `-c` option. (Several scripts in this book keep their configuration files in `$HOME/.config`, creating it if necessary. If the directory does not exist, go ahead and `mkdir` it.) The file contains a list of directories, one to a line, with an optional age (in days) following a space, comma, or tab.

The default age for files (when not specified in the rmold.dirs file) is set with -d. If you are not sure about deleting your files, the -i option puts rm into interactive mode, and it will ask for your approval before removing any files:

```
$ rmold -i
rm: remove regular file `/home/chris/tmp/sh-utils-2.0/man/chroot.1'? y
rm: remove regular file `/home/chris/tmp/sh-utils-2.0/man/date.1'? y
rm: remove regular file `/home/chris/tmp/sh-utils-2.0/man/dirname.1'? n
```

With -m DEST, a destination directory can be given, and the files will be moved to that directory rather than be deleted. The final option, -v, works only with the GNU versions of rm and mv, as others do not have a verbose mode:

```
$ rmold -v
removed `/home/chris/tmp/sh-utils-2.0/man/echo.1'
removed `/home/chris/tmp/sh-utils-2.0/man/env.1'
removed `/home/chris/tmp/sh-utils-2.0/man/false.1'
```

If an empty filename is given with the -c option, the script will read the directories from the standard input. If that is a terminal, the user will be prompted to enter a directory and age:

```
$ rmold -vc ''
                Name of directory: ~/tmp/xx
 Delete files older than (days): 22
removed `/home/chris/tmp/xx/zzqw31055'
removed `/home/chris/tmp/xx/zzer21252'
removed `/home/chris/tmp/xx/zzty27584'
```

If stdin is not a terminal, the input will be expected in the same format as the rmold.dirs file (directory name with optional age in days separated by a space, tab, or comma):

```
$ echo ~/tmp/xx 33 | rmold-sh -vc ''
removed `/home/chris/tmp/xx/zzqw22088'
removed `/home/chris/tmp/xx/zzer4828'
removed `/home/chris/tmp/xx/zzty26562'
```

The Script

```
## Default values that can be changed with command-line options
days=30                          ## age in days
dir_file=$HOME/.config/rmold.dirs ## file containing list of dirs
rm_opts=                         ## options to rm

## Parse command-line options
opts=c:d:im:v
while getopts $opts opt
do
  case $opt in
      c) dir_file=$OPTARG ;;
      d) days=$OPTARG ;;
      i) rm_opts="$rm_opts -i" ;;
```

```
      m) move=1        ## move files instead of deleteing them
         dest=$OPTARG ## directory to place files in

         ## create $dest if it doesn't exist,
         ## and exit with an error if it cannot be created
         [ -d "$dest" ] || mkdir "$dest" || exit 5
         ;;
      v) rm_opts="$rm_opts -v" ;;
  esac
done
shift $(( $OPTIND - 1 ))

## if $dir_file contains a filename, check that it exists,
case $dir_file in
    -|"") dir_file= ;;
    *) [ -f "$dir_file" ] || exit 5 ;;
esac

## if $dir_file exists, use it
if [ -n "$dir_file" ]
then
  cat "$dir_file"

## otherwise, if stdin is a terminal, prompt user for directory
elif [ -t 0 ]
then
  printf "                 Name of directory: " >&2
  read dir
  eval "dir=$dir"
  [ -d "$dir" ] || exit 5
  printf " Delete files older than (days): " >&2
  read d
  printf "%s %d\n" "$dir" "$d"
else ## stdin is not a terminal, so pass input through unchanged
  cat
fi |
 while IFS=' ,' read dir days_ x
 do
   case $dir in
       "") break ;; ## skip blank lines
       \#*) ;;       ## skip comments
       *) ## last access time (-atime) is used rather than last
          ## modification time
          [ $move -eq 0 ] &&
           find "$dir" -atime +${days_:-$days} -type f \
                   -exec rm $rm_opts {} \; </dev/tty ||
           find "$dir" -atime +${days_:-$days} -type f \
                   -exec mv $rm_opts {} "$dest" \; </dev/tty
          ;;
   esac
done
```

11.3 keepnewest—Remove All but the Newest or Oldest Files

In the alt.linux newsgroup, Bernhard Kastner asked how to delete all the files in a directory except for the four most recently modified. Kastner answered the question himself a little later, after reading the sed manual:

```
rm `ls -t * | sed -e 1,4d`
```

For the file aging system, we have the rmold script, which deletes files based on age. For some directories, or some files in some directories, keeping a specific number works better. To fit into my scheme of things, the script would have to be able to move rather than delete files, and be able to keep a quantity other than four files.

How It Works

By breaking Kastner's script into two parts, and using variables instead of hard-coding the number, flexibility is added. The first part of the resulting script builds a list of filenames, the second part operates on them. Command-line options are used to adjust the number of files and their disposition. As a bonus, there is an option to keep the oldest rather than the newest files.

Usage

```
keepnewest [OPTIONS] [FILE...]
```

Without any options or other arguments, keepnewest deletes all but the four most recent files in the current directory. If a list of files is specified, usually done in the form of a pattern such as sent-mail*, all files matching the pattern, except the four most recent, will be deleted. To change the number of files kept, use the -n option:

```
keepnewest -n 13
```

To move the files rather than delete them, specify a destination directory with -d:

```
keepnewest -d old-files
```

To move the files and compress them with gzip, use -c and specify a directory:

```
keepnewest -cd old-files
```

A different compression command may be given as the argument to -C:

```
keepnewest -d old-files -C bzip2
```

The -o option keeps the oldest rather than the newest files. To keep the 12 oldest files beginning with a and move all the others (that begin with a) to the $HOME/a-old directory and compress them with gzip, use this:

```
keepnewest -d ~/a-old -n12 -o -c a*
```

The Script

```
## default values
n=4          ## number of files to keep
dest=        ## if a directory is specified, move the files
compress=    ## compress files that have been moved
old=         ## if set to -r, keep oldest files

## Usually, NL (newline) is defined by sourcing standard-vars,
## but since only one variable is needed, I have put the definition
## in-line
NL='
'

## parse command-line options
opts=cC:d:n:o
while getopts $opts opt
do
  case $opt in
      c) compress=gzip ;;  ## use the default command, gzip
      C) compress=${OPTARG:-bzip2}
         ## If the command (without options) doesn't exist,
          ## exit with error code 6
         type ${compress%% *} >/dev/null || exit 6
         ;;
      d) dest=$OPTARG
         [ -d "$dest" ] || ## check that the directory exists
          mkdir "$dest" || ## if it doesn't, create it
               exit 5     ## if that fails, exit with an error
         ;;
      n) case $OPTARG in
             ## exit with error if OPTARG contains
             ## anything other than a positive integer
             *[!0-9]*) exit 4 ;;
         esac
         n=$OPTARG
         ;;
      o) old=-r ;; ## keep oldest files, not newest
  esac
done
shift $(( $OPTIND - 1 ))

## We assume that an error has been made if no files are to be
## kept, since a script is not necessary for that (rm is enough)
## If you want the option to remove all files, comment out the
## following line.
[ $n -eq 0 ] && exit 5

## Store the list of files in a variable.
filelist=`ls $old -t "$@" | sed -e "1,${n}d"`
```

```
## By setting the internal field separator to a newline, spaces in
## $filelist will be treated as part of the filename, not as a
## space between diffrerent names
## Note: this script will fail if any filenames contain a newline
## character (they shouldn't).
IFS=$NL

case $dest in
  "") ## no destination directory is given, so delete the files
     rm $filelist ;;
  *) ## move files to another directory
     mv $filelist "$dest"

     ## if $compress is defined, cd to the destination directory
     ## and compress each file
     [ -z "$compress" ] || (
         cd "$dest" || exit 3
         for file in $filelist
         do
           $compress ${file##*/}
         done
     ) || exit
     ;;
esac
```

Summary

The scripts in this chapter are the building blocks of a file-aging system. While these commands can be used manually, their value increases when they are combined in a script tailored to your needs.

CHAPTER 12

■ ■ ■

Covering All Your Databases

A database is simply a collection of information. The information is usually divided into records that may be simple or complex. There may be a handful of records, or a few dozen. Or there may be thousands or millions of records.

Each record in a database may be a single word, or it may comprise a number of fields. These fields may be self-contained data, or they may be keys to another database. A record may be one or more lines in a file, or an entire file by itself.

The /etc/passwd file on a Unix system is a database containing one record for each user. Each record contains seven fields, separated by colons. A typical entry for root is

```
root:x:0:0:root:/root:/bin/sh
```

The word-finder and anagram scripts in Chapter 4 use a database of more than a hundred thousand words, each word being a record, and a Compounds file with three tab-separated fields on each line (a phrase with spaces removed, the original phrase, and the word lengths).

In Chapter 17, the general ledger (GL) entry script, gle, stores transactions in a file that is part of a relational database; some of the fields contain keys that can be looked up in other tables. A client may be entered in the GL as *sun*; this key can be looked up (using the lookup script, for example) in a table of clients to get the full name of the company, the address, phone number, or any other information it contains. Transactions are charged to accounts represented by abbreviations that can be looked up in the chart of accounts; *AR* can be looked up to reveal *Accounts Receivable*.

Even a membership database with thousands of records, such as the one Chris wrote for the Toronto Free-Net, works well with all programs written in shell scripts. A single record from the database looks like this (but all on one line, not four):

```
bq833:bBFRa3et3rOzM:43833:25:Fred Arnold:/homes/d02/33/bq833:
/usr/local/FreePort/bin/BBmenu:691 Don Bowie Avenue:Apt. 1:Toronto:Ontario:
Canada: :1949-09-29:2005-10-09:416-555-7940:farnold@xyz.invalid:416-555-7490: :
English:Lawless: :416-555-9407:20:1995-07-14:2005-01-20_17_16_24
```

The onscreen output is shown in Figure 12-1.

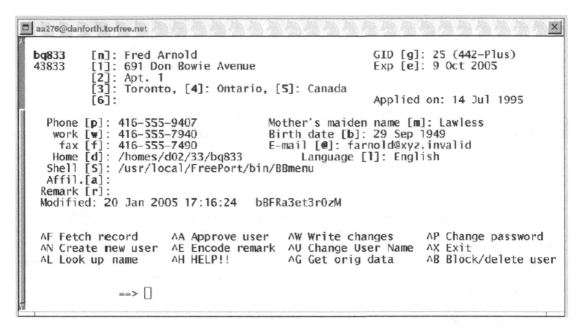

Figure 12-1. *The Toronto Free-Net membership database screen*

For complicated, interrelated databases where entry may be done by more than one person, and where transactions must pass the ACID[1] test, a full database management system should be used (`PostgreSQL` is a prominent open source example). The majority or personal databases do not require anything close to that complexity, and can be maintained with a few shell scripts.

The scripts in this chapter work with single-line records. Some use a delimiter to separate fields (often a tab or a comma); others use a free-form record without any defined fields.

12.1 lookup—Find the Corresponding Value for a Key

In the general ledger system, abbreviations are used to refer to clients, suppliers, and account types. The full information for each client is a record in another file. You would need a command to look up the abbreviation and retrieve the client's full name. The client file could look like this (though it actually contains more fields—and clients), with fields separated by tildes:

```
sun~The Toronto Sun~333 King Street East~Toronto~Ontario~416-555-1234
gt~Good Times~25 Sheppard Avenue West~North York~Ontario~416-555-2468
```

Since we will be using the result in a script, we need the field extracted from the record.

---

[1]Atomicity, Consistency, Isolation, and Durability. See `http://en.wikipedia.org/wiki/ACID`.

How It Works

If the abbreviation is always in the first field, and the full name is always in the second field, a very simple script is all you need (this one assumes a tab-delimited format; the $TAB variable contains a tab character, something we usually set by sourcing standard-vars from Chapter 1):

```
lookup() { grep "^$1$TAB" "$2" | cut -f2; }
```

■ **Note**   if you have jumped chapters or are trying out this command directly, simply set the variable TAB to the separator, the tilde in this example.

This can be called with the abbreviation to look up and the name of the file it is in:

```
$ lookup sun $HOME/clients
The Toronto Sun
```

The flexibility of the script can be enhanced by using awk with command-line options to specify fields for the key or the value to be retrieved, and to set the delimiter.

Usage

```
lookup [OPTIONS] KEY FILE
```

There are three options, all of which take an argument:

- -f: Sets the field delimiter
- -k: Sets the number of the field which contains the look-up key
- -v: Specifies which field to return

If you wanted to look up a user's home directory, the sixth field in the colon-delimited file, /etc/passwd, you could do this:

```
$ lookup -f: -v6 chris /etc/passwd
/home/chris
```

When we use lookup in a script, we have the names of the fields as variables; for example, when working with /etc/passwd, make these assignments:

```
_user=1
_passwd=2
_uid=3
_gid=4
_fullname=5
_homedir=6
_shell=7
```

Then, to find a user's full name, the variable can be used instead of the number:

```
$ lookup -v $_fullname -f: chris /etc/passwd
Chris F.A. Johnson
```

Since lookup is used primarily in scripts, the result is likely to be placed in a variable. For example, this will find *michael*'s shell:

```
shell=$(lookup -v $_shell -f: michael /etc/passwd)
```

To find out where the first partition of your second hard drive is mounted, the default values (the key in the first field and the value in the second) can be used to get the information from /etc/fstab:

```
$ lookup /dev/hdb1 /etc/fstab
/usr
```

The Script

```
## default field numbers may be changed by command-line options
key=1    ## field to use as the key
val=2    ## field containing desired value
F=       ## use default field separator
## parse command-line options
while getopts k:f:v: opt
do
  case $opt in
      f) F=$OPTARG ;;
      k) key=$OPTARG ;;
      v) val=$OPTARG ;;
  esac
done
shift $(( $OPTIND - 1 ))

str=$1     ## string to look up
shift      ## remove look-up string from positional parameters

## if $F is empty, the field separator is not changed
awk ${F:+-F "$F"} '$key == str { print $val }
   ' key=$key val=$val str="$str" "$@"
```

shdb-funcs: Shell Database Function Library

When you need a database, such as for bookkeeping or membership records, we could write it from scratch. Usually, their requirements are different so we can reuse very little code. There are, however, a number of functions that many could find useful when dealing with databases. These functions are collected in shdb-funcs and are designed for flexibility. They make use of shell arrays and other features of bash.

The first task is to load the standard-funcs library from Chapter 1, which in turn loads standard-vars.

```
. standard-funcs
```

12.2 load_db—Import Database into Shell Array

Moving back and forth among the records in a database is made much easier by having them all in memory.

How It Works

By setting the internal field separator, IFS, to a newline, the entire database file can be read into memory in a single statement, and each line assigned to one element in an array. The local keyword limits the scope of the variable to the function and its children.

Usage

```
load_db FILE
```

There's nothing complicated about this function, and if it weren't necessary to reset IFS, we could have used in-line code rather than a separate function. The entire database is stored in the ${db[]} array.

The Script

```
load_db()
{
    local IFS=$NL      ## Set IFS locally to a newline
    local shdb=$1      ## The first positional parameter is the file
    db=( `< "$shdb"` ) ## Slurp!
}
```

Notes

If you have a database with lines commented out, remove those lines from the file before slurping it into the array. This version of load_db will eliminate any line that begins with $NB (by default, #), ignoring any leading spaces or tabs:

```
load_db()
{
    local IFS=$NL      ## Set IFS locally to a newline
    local shdb=$1      ## The first positional parameter is the file
    local NB=${NB:-#}  ## NB contains the comment character
    db=( `grep -v "^[ $TAB]*$NB" "$shdb"` ) ## Slurp!
}
```

12.3 split_record—Split a Record into Fields

Many Unix configuration files are, in fact, databases. In most cases, they have one record to a line. The fields may be delimited by one or more whitespace characters (e.g., /etc/fstab), a colon (e.g., /etc/passwd, as shown in Figure 12-2), or some other character. The file system can be viewed as a hierarchical database with fields separated by slashes.

243

Figure 12-2. The first 22 records in my /etc/passwd

How It Works

By setting the IFS variable to the delimiter, the record is split and stored in a shell array.

Usage

```
split_record RECORD
```

By default, fields are separated by one or more whitespace characters, space and tab. This can be changed by setting the variable DELIM. In the password file, the delimiter is a colon. Here the entry for root is extracted from /etc/passwd with grep and split into an array:

```
$ DELIM=: split_record $(grep ^root: /etc/passwd)
$ printf "%s\n" "${record_vals[@]}"
root
x
0
0
root
/root
/bin/bash
```

The fields in /etc/fstab are separated by whitespace characters. Here, sed pulls the first line from the file, and that is used as the argument to split_record:

```
$ split_record $(sed -n 1p /etc/fstab)
$ printf "%s\n" "${record_vals[@]}"
/dev/hda1
/
ext3
defaults
1
1
```

The Script

```
split_record()
{
    local IFS=${DELIM:- $TAB} ## if DELIM not set, uses space and TAB
    local opts=$-             ## save shell option flags
    set -f                    ## disable pathname globbing
    record_vals=( $* )        ## store arguments in array

    ## reset globbing only if it was originally set
    case $opts in
      *f*) ;;
      *) set +f ;;
    esac
}
```

12.4 csv_split—Extract Fields from CSV Records

One common data interchange format uses comma-separated values (CSVs). Most spreadsheet programs can import and export CSV files. My credit unions allows me to download my account history in a CSV format. We can download stock quotes from finance.yahoo.com or currency exchange rates from the European Central Bank in CSV format.

There are variations in the format, but basically, the fields are separated by commas, and non-numeric fields are enclosed in quotation marks. In this way, text fields can contain commas or quotation marks. Splitting these records into their fields is more complicated than with a simple character-delimited record.

How It Works

Rather than splitting the record in a single step, as in split_record, it is necessary to loop through the record one field at a time, removing quotes when they enclose a field.

Usage

```
csv_split "RECORD"
```

The RECORD must be a single argument:

```
$ q='123,"Steinbeck, John","The Grapes of Wrath",1939,328'
$ csv_split "$q"
$ pr1 "${record_vals[@]}"
123
Steinbeck, John
The Grapes of Wrath
1939
328
```

Text fields may contain quotation marks and commas, but should not contain a double quote followed by a comma.

The Script

```
csv_split() {
    csv_vnum=0                 ## field number
    csv_record=${1%"${CR}"}    ## remove carriage return, if any
    unset record_vals          ## we need a pristine (global) array

    ## remove each field from the record and store in record_vals[]
    ## when all the records are stored, $csv_record will be empty
    while [ -n "$csv_record" ]
    do
      case $csv_record in
      ## if $csv_record starts with a quotation mark,
      ## extract up to '",' or end of record
      \"*) csv_right=${csv_record#*\",}
           csv_value=${csv_record%%\",*}
           record_vals[$csv_vnum]=${csv_value#\"}
           ;;
      ## otherwise extract to the next comma
      *) record_vals[$csv_vnum]=${csv_record%%,*}
        csv_right=${csv_record#*,}
        ;;
      esac

    csv_record=${csv_right}       ## the remains of the record

    ## If what remains is the same as the record before the previous
    ## field was extracted, it is the last field, so store it and exit
    ## the loop
    if [ "$csv_record" = "$csv_last" ]
    then
      csv_record=${csv_record#\"}
      record_vals[$csv_vnum]=${csv_record%\"}
      break
    fi
    csv_last=$csv_record
    csv_vnum=$(( $csv_vnum + 1 ))
  done
}
```

12.5 put_record—Assemble a Database Record from an Array

Once a record has been split into its constituent fields, and one or more of those fields has been modified (or a new record has been created), it needs to be reassembled into a record for putting back in the ${db[]} array, which will be written back to a file.

How It Works

Each field is printed using printf, followed by the delimiter, and stored in a variable. The final, trailing delimiter is removed. If the delimiter is a space or a tab, it may be necessary to use a placeholder for empty fields, since many utilities (including split_record) will interpret multiple consecutive whitespace characters as a single delimiter.

Usage

```
_put_record [-n C] "${ARRAY[@]}"   ## store record in $_PUT_RECORD
put_record [-n C] "${ARRAY[@]}"    ## print the record
```

The first form of the function stores the record in a variable, and the second prints the record. If the -n option is given, C is inserted in empty fields. Here is a typical use of the functions:

```
_put_record "${record_vals[@]}"
db[$rec_num]=$_PUT_RECORD
```

The Script

```
_put_record()
{
    local NULL=
    local IFS=${DELIM:-$TAB}
    case $1 in
        -n*) NULL=${1#-n} ## no space after the option letter
            shift
            ;;
        -n) NULL=$2 ## space after the option letter
            shift 2
            ;;
        *) _PUT_RECORD="$*"
            return
            ;;
    esac
    _PUT_RECORD=$(
        for field in "$@"
        do
          printf "%s${DELIM:-$TAB}" "${field:-$NULL}"
        done )

}
```

247

```
put_record()
{
    _put_record "$@" && printf "%s\n" "$_PUT_RECORD"
}
```

12.6 put_csv—Assemble Fields into a CSV Record

Assembling a CSV array involves enclosing non-numeric fields in quotation marks and inserting commas between the concatenated fields.

How It Works

Each field is tested to see whether it contains non-numeric characters (the period and minus sign are considered numeric). If one does, it is enclosed in quotation marks before being added to the record.

Usage

```
_put_csv "${ARRAY[@]}" ## store record in $_PUT_CSV
put_csv  "${ARRAY[@]}" ## print the record
```

The array is placed on the command line as arguments to either form of the put_csv function. The syntax used in the preceding examples presents each element of the array as a single argument, even if it contains whitespace.

The Script

```
_put_csv()
{
    for field in "$@" ## loop through the fields (on command line)
    do
      case $field in
          ## If field contains non-numerics, enclose in quotes
          *[!0-9.-]*)
                  _PUT_CSV=${_PUT_CSV:+$_PUT_CSV,}\"$field\"
                  ;;
          *)
                  _PUT_CSV=${_PUT_CSV:+$_PUT_CSV,}$field
                  ;;
      esac
    done
    _PUT_CSV=${_PUT_CSV%,} ## remove trailing comma
}

put_csv()
{
    _put_csv "$@" && printf "%s\n" "$_PUT_CSV"
}
```

12.7 db-demo—View and Edit a Password File

To maintain a database, a user must be able to modify individual fields in a record, and add and delete records.

How It Works

Use load_db from the shdb-funcs library to load the entire file into an array. A loop displays one record at a time, allowing the user to select from options displayed on a menu bar, as shown in Figure 12-3. For demonstration purposes, this script makes a copy of the password file so that it can be edited safely. (I don't recommend it, but you can use this script to edit your /etc/passwd file.)

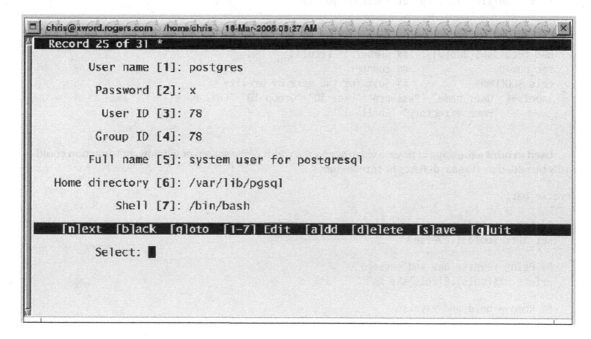

Figure 12-3. *Data entry using db-demo*

Usage

db-demo

The user can move through the file one record at a time, or go to any record by selecting a number after pressing g. Pressing a number from 1 to 7 brings up a prompt to enter a new value for the field at the bottom of the screen. Pressing the up arrow (or Ctrl-P) will bring up the current value, which may be edited.

The Script

```
#! /bin/bash

. screen-funcs-sh      ## load screen manipulation functions
. shdb-funcs-sh        ## load database functions
```

By changing the values in the db_init function, this script can be used with other databases. Just changing the file name and changing the values in the labels[] array will allow another colon-separated file to be used. For more general use, command-line options could be used to specify the parameters. If there are many more than seven fields, the show_record function may have to be adjusted.

```
db_init()
{
    DELIM=:                   ## field delimiter
    cls                        ## clear the screen
    ## We'll work with a copy of the password file
    dbfile=$HOME/etc_passwd ## data file
    [ -f "$dbfile" ] || cp /etc/passwd "$dbfile"

    load_db "$dbfile"        ## store file in array

    num_records=${#db[@]}    ## number of records
    rec_num=0                 ## counter
    cols=$COLUMNS             ## just for the sake of brevity
    labels=( "User name" "Password" "User ID" "Group ID" "Full name"
             "Home directory" "Shell" )
}
```

Used to print a message in reverse video across the width of the screen or window, this function could easily be added to standard-funcs or screen-funcs.

```
reverse_bar()
{
    ## Set to bold reverse
    set_attr $bold $reverse

    ## Print reverse bar and message
    printf "%${cols}.${cols}s\r %s" " " "$*"

    ## Remove bold and reverse
    set_attr 0
}
```

The show_record function prints a record on to the screen. When dealing with a database that has more fields per record, it may be necessary to change the line spacing (lsp) from 2 to 1. For very long records (such as in the Toronto Free-Net database form shown at the beginning of the chapter), a different function will be needed.

```
show_record()
{
    lw=15                             ## Label width
    lm=3                              ## Left margin
    lsp=2                             ## Line spacing
    fmt="%${lw}.${lw}s [$B%d$NA]: %s$cle" ## Format string for fields

    printat 1 1        ## position cursor at top left of screen

    ## Display record number and total number on reverse bar
    reverse_bar " Record $(( $rec_num + 1 )) of $num_records $db_mod"
```

```
  field=0
  while [ $field -lt ${#labels[@]} ]
  do
    printat $(( $field * $lsp + 3 )) $lm
    printf "$fmt"  "${labels[$field]}" \
                   $(( $field + 1 )) \
                   "${record_vals[$field]}"
    field=$(( $field + 1 ))
  done

  menubar=$(( $field * $lsp + 5 - $lsp ))
  printat $menubar 1

  ## Print user options on reverse bar
  reverse_bar \
    "  [n]ext [b]ack [g]oto [1-7] Edit [a]dd [d]elete [s]ave [q]uit"

  prompt_line=$(( $menubar + 2 ))
  prompt_col=$(( $lm + $lw - 8 ))
  printat $prompt_line $prompt_col "$cle"
}
```

The main loop of db-demo waits for single-key user input and performs actions based on the key pressed.

```
db_main()
{
    db_init               ## Initialize the database
    while :               ## loop until user quits
    do
      ## break the current record into its constituent fields
      split_record "${db[$rec_num]}"

      show_record

      ## read a single keystroke
      read -sn1 -p "Select: " x
      case $x in
          q) break ;; ## quit; TODO: add query to save if modified

          a) ## Add new record
             rec_num=${#db[@]}
             db[${#db[@]}]="$DELIM$DELIM$DELIM$DELIM$DELIM$DELIM"
             num_records=${#db[@]}
             db_mod=*                 ## Modified flag
             ;;

          b) ## move to previous record (wrap around if at first record)
             rec_num=$(( ($rec_num + $num_records - 1) % $num_records ))
             ;;
```

```
d) ## Delete current record
   unset db[$rec_num]
   db=( "${db[@]}" )
   num_records=${#db[@]}
   db_mod=*                        ## Modified flag
   ;;

g) ## display a specific record (by number)
   printat $prompt_line $prompt_col "$cle"
   read -ep " Record number: " rec_num

   ## check for valid record number
   if [ $rec_num -gt $num_records ]
   then
     rec_num=$(( $num_records - 1 ))
   elif [ $rec_num -le 1 ]
   then
     rec_num=0
   else
   rec_num=$(( $rec_num - 1 )) ## arrays count from 0
   fi
   ;;

s) ## Save the database
   printf "%s\n" "${db[@]}" > "$dbfile"
   db_mod= ## Clear modified flag
   ;;

[1-7]) ## User selected a field number; prompt for data entry
   in_field=$(( $x - 1 ))

   ## Place field's current value in history
   history -s "${record_vals[$in_field]}"

   ## Place the cursor at the entry line and clear it
   printat $prompt_line $prompt_col "$cle"
   _getline "${labels[$in_field]}" INPUT

   ## If something has been entered, and it is not the same as before
   ## then replace the record with the modified version
   [ -n "$INPUT" ] && [ "$INPUT" != "${record_vals[$in_field]}" ] && {
       record_vals[$in_field]=$INPUT    ## Store entry in field
       db_mod=*                         ## Modified flag
       _put_record "${record_vals[@]}"  ## Rebuild record
       db[$rec_num]=$_PUT_RECORD        ## Place new record into array
   }
   printat $prompt_line 1 "$cle"
   ;;
*) ## display next record (wrap around if at end)
   rec_num=$(( ($rec_num + 1) % $num_records )) ;;
esac
```

```
              ## check for valid record number
              if [ $rec_num -ge $num_records ]
              then
                  rec_num=$(( $num_records - 1 ))
              elif [ $rec_num -lt 1 ]
              then
                  rec_num=0
#             else
#                 rec_num=$(( $rec_num - 1 )) ## arrays count from 0
              fi
      done
      printf "\n\n"
}
```

After all the functions have been defined, all the script needs to do is call the main loop:

```
db_main     ## Enter the main loop
```

PhoneBase: A Simple Phone Number Database

While there are many databases for contact information, phone numbers, and other basic information about people, most are far more complicated than necessary. A Rolodex may be efficient on a physical desktop, but it does not take full advantage of the capabilities of a modern computer. For most uses, all one needs is a simple text file with unstructured records, and methods to search for, add, and remove records.

How It Works

Simplicity and ease of use are the hallmarks of this little database system, PhoneBase, which was born on my Amiga computer in the 1980s, grew up under Linux a few years ago, and is in use on various operating systems today. Its features include the following:

- A command-line interface eliminates waiting for a GUI to load.

- Searching is case-insensitive; you don't need to remember whether your contact's name is Macdonald or MacDonald.

- You can store arbitrary information along with names and phone numbers.

- You can add comments that will not be displayed when searching the database.

- Searching can be done for any information entered.

- Phone books can be edited with any text editor.

- You can use multiple database files.

Until I was half way through writing this section, PhoneBase had only three commands, ph, phadd, and phdel. Now it has four; I added phx, a graphical interface.

12.8 ph—Look Up a Phone Number

The workhorse of the PhoneBase system is ph, the command that searches the database for the requested name.

Usage

```
ph [OPTIONS] STRING
```

While ph takes no options of its own, it will pass any options, along with everything else on the command line, to egrep. As a result, the permissible options are those that your system's egrep will accept. In addition, you can use a regular expression instead of a STRING.

Most of the time, all you would need to use is a simple search:

```
$ ph colin
Colin Johnson, C & J Solutions 555-8341
Colin McGregor 416-555-1487 (Toronto Free-Net)
```

If you want to find numbers for more than one person, you can pass multiple search strings with -e options:

```
$ ph -e michael -e rosalyn
Rosalyn Johnson 555-0878
Michael Smith 555-2764
Michael Johnson 555-6528, cell 555-4070
```

If you want to find *John*, but not *Johnson*, you can use the -w option since my system has GNU egrep:

```
$ ph -w John
Bayliss, John~555-6460
```

With other versions of egrep, you would use this:

```
ph '\<John\>'
```

For more information on other possibilities, read the egrep manual page.

By default, ph searches /var/data/phones and $HOME/.phones, but this can be overridden by putting other files in the phbase variable. Use this to search $HOME/contacts:

```
$ phbase=$HOME/contacts
$ export phbase
$ ph someone
```

The Script

The script loops through the files in $phbase, or the default /var/data/phones and $HOME/.phones, and builds a list of those files that do exist. If any files are in the resulting list, they are searched by egrep.

```
[ -z "$*" ] && exit 5 ## If no query, exit

## If the $phbase variable is not set,
## place the default files in $_phbase
for f in ${phbase:-/var/data/phones $HOME/.phones}
do
    [ -f "$f" ] && _phbase="$_phbase $f"
done

## Search files listed in $_phbase, ignoring comments
[ -n "$_phbase" ] && egrep -ih "$@" $_phbase 2>/dev/null | grep -v '^#'
```

12.9 phadd—Add an Entry to PhoneBase

Additions to the database can be made with any text editor or word processor (be sure to save it as a text file), or with the phadd command.

Usage

```
phadd [OPTION] "DATA"
```

With the -s option, phadd will save DATA to the system's phone list, /var/data/phones, rather than to the user's own file.

```
phadd -s "J. Jonah Jameson 555-444-3210"
```

The -f option takes the path to a file as an argument and appends DATA to that file:

```
phadd -f $HOME/my_phone_list "Perry White 324-597-5263"
```

The Script

Since only one option can be used, getopts would be overkill; instead, a case statement examines the first argument to see whether it is an option.

```
case $1 in
    ## Add to the system list instead of your own list
    -s) phlist=/var/data/phones
        shift
        ;;

    ## Use file supplied on the command line
    -f) phlist=$2
        shift 2
        ;;
```

```
    -f*) phlist=${1#-f}
        shift
        ;;
    ## Use personal list
    *) phlist=$HOME/.phones
esac

## Append all non-option arguments to the file
printf "%s\n" "$*" >> "$phlist"
```

12.10 phdel—Delete an Entry from PhoneBase

Before using phdel to delete a record from your database, it is a good idea to use ph with the same pattern to make sure that you will delete only the record or records you don't want. Or you can use a text editor.

Usage

```
phdel [-s] PATTERN
```

If you use the -s option, phdel will delete from the system phone list rather than your personal file.

The Script

As with phadd, there is no need to use getopts for a single option. A temporary file stores the output of grep -v and is then moved over the original file.

```
if [ "$1" = "-s" ] ## Check for option in first argument
then
    phlist=/var/data/phones ## Use the system-wide list
    shift                   ## Remove option from command line
else
    phlist=$HOME/.phones    ## Use personal list
fi

tmpfile=$HOME/phdel$$      ## Store modified file in temporary location
grep -iv "$1" $phlist > $tmpfile ## Remove entry
mv $tmpfile $phlist        ## Replace data file
```

12.11 phx—Show ph Search Results in an X Window

When Chris started writing this PhoneBase section, there were only three commands; half an hour later, he decided to look into the possibility of displaying the results in a new window. Now there are four commands, and PhoneBase can be used without a terminal.

Usage

```
phx [OPTIONS] PATTERN
```

Since phx just hands the output of ph to Xdialog, all the options are exactly the same as for ph. The results for this script are shown in Figure 12-4.

```
$ phx segovia
```

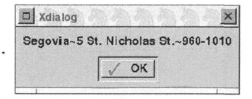

Figure 12-4. *The ouput of phx*

The Script

This script requires the Xdialog utility. It is available for most Unix systems, though it may be called xdialog. If neither is available for your system, you may be able to find equivalent utilities on the Internet.

```
Xdialog --left --msgbox "`ph "$@"`" 0 0
```

Summary

Besides presenting one complete, though simple, application (PhoneBase), the functions we have provided here are the building blocks for serious database manipulation. The demonstration script can easily become the basis for a general-purpose database viewer and entry program that accepts command line arguments for the file and the delimiter.

If you have experience with scripting, you would know the pros and cons of using a script based database vs using a Relational database (RDBMS). However, the way things are coming around full circle, the commonly used popular databases are of the NoSQL genre. These are similar to our script databases but ususaly reside on the web/cloud and are accessed via REST interfaces. Maybe in the next edition of this book, we might be using a No SQL database instead.

CHAPTER 13

■ ■ ■

Home on the Web

"What else is there?" a friend asked when I said the World Wide Web was the part of the Internet that I used least. I explained that I use e-mail, FTP, Usenet newsgroups, and telnet or SSH far more than I use the Web. Despite the fact that I use it the least, the WWW, and its standard file format, HTML, are indispensable.

The gazillions of badly constructed pages on the Web do not negate the fact that HTML is the best format for viewing text (and illustrations) across different platforms and different hardware configurations. A well-constructed page will be as legible on a 640×480 monochrome display as on a 1600 ×1200 24-bit color screen, and everything in between.

A browser is the only tool you need to view HTML files, but what if you want to dissect them or create them on the fly? This chapter contains scripts that build as well as pull apart HTML files.

There are a lot of options today to work with HTML and Web technologies, such as PHP, and Ruby. For some users, Bash would be considered a bit outdated in comparison to other languages and tools.

Playing with Hypertext: The html-funcs Library

Most of the time, I use the functions in the html-funcs library at the command line. When viewing the source of HTML pages created by HTML Editors or other programs that write long lines, with many elements on a line, the function split_tags makes them legible. These functions also work with XML files.

13.1 get_element—Extract the First Occurrence of an Element

The mk-htmlindex script that appears later in this chapter creates an HTML page with links to all the files in a directory. Wherever possible, it would help to include more information about a file than just its name. A well-formed HTML file will contain a <title> tag. You would need a method of extracting that element.

How It Works

A number of tools for manipulating HTML files are available as C source code from the World Wide Web Consortium (W3C) at http://www.w3.org/Tools/HTML-XML-utils/. One of these utilities is extract, which prints all instances of a given tag that are contained in a file. If you plan to do a lot of work with HTML or XML files, I recommend getting and compiling these tools.

For the occasional, relatively simple task, a shell script can do the job. The get_element function will print the first occurrence of an element, including the opening and closing tags, all on a single line.

Usage

```
get_element < FILE
COMMAND | get_element
```

A file must be supplied to get_element on its standard input, not as a command-line argument, and the tag variable must be set to the name of the element you want. An empty tag variable will return the first element. For get_element to work, an element must have both opening and closing tags.

My current directory has an index file created by the mk-htmlindex script. We can extract the title with

```
$ . html-funcs     ## this is assumed for all the examples in this section
$ tag=title
$ get_element < index.html
<title>chris/tmp</title>
```

To get a tag from a remote page, one could use lynx -source, wget -O -, or curl -s, and pipe the page to get_element:

```
$ curl -s http://www.apress.com | tag=title get_element
<title>A P R E S S . C O M | Books for Professionals, by Professionals ...</title>
```

The shell page on my web site has an h2 element. I can retrieve that with

```
$ tag=h2
$ lynx -source -nolist http://cfaj.freeshell.org/shell | get_element
<h2>The Unix Shell</h2>
```

If no instance of the element is found, get_element returns 1; otherwise, it returns 0.

The Script

```
get_element()
{

    ## Read until the opening tag is found, and print the line
    while read -r line
    do
      case $line in
        *\<"$tag"*)
            ## Line contains opening tag,
            ## so remove any preceding text
            line=${line#${line%<"$tag"*}}

            case $line in
              *\</"${tag}"*)
                  ## Line contains closing tag,
                  ## so remove trailing text
                  line=${line%${line#*</"$tag"*>}}
```

```
                        ## print line and return from the function
                        printf "%s " ${line} "${NL:=`printf "\n"`}"
                        return
                        ;;

                *) ## No closing tag in this line,
                   ## so print it and move on
                   printf "%s " $line
                   break
                   ;;
            esac
    esac
done

## Continue reading and printing lines
## up to and including the closing tag
while read -r line
do
   case $line in
        *\</"${tag}"*)
                ## Line contains closing tag so remove trailing text
                line=${line%${line#*</"$tag"*>}}

                ## print line and move on
                printf "%s " ${line} "$NL"
                break
                ;;
        *) printf "%s " ${line} ;; ## Line contains text; print it
   esac
done
}
```

Notes

This script will have a problem when a tag is nested within another instance of the same tag. This should not normally be a problem, as most tags are not nested within themselves.

When you are working with large files, and the tag you are looking for is near the end of the file, the following version of get_element may be faster. It uses the split_tags function, which appears next. This version can take one or more filenames on the command line, or read the standard input.

```
get_element()
{
    split_tags "$@" |
        sed -ne "/<$tag/,/<\/$tag/p" -e "/<\/$tag/q" | tr -d "$NL"
    printf "\n"
}
```

The pure shell version of get_element may be the fastest way to retrieve a title, if one exists, because it will be at the top of the file, and the function stops reading the file as soon as it has retrieved the file. On the other hand, if the element is missing, the function will read through the entire file.

13.2 split_tags—Put Each Tag on Its Own Line

For many functions, putting each HTML tag on its own line makes extracting information a lot simpler. If every tag is on a line of its own, extracting text, for example, is just a matter of grep -v "<".

How It Works

Using awk's global substitution command, gsub, a newline is inserted before every < and after every >.

Usage

```
split_tags [FILE ...]
```

One or more filenames may be specified on the command line, or split_tags can read its standard input.

```
$ html='<ul class="index">
<li><a href="my_file">My file</a></li>
</ul>'
$ echo "$html" | split_tags

<ul class="index">

<li>
<a href="my_file"> My file
</a>
</li>

</ul>
```

Since the output will usually be processed further, elimination of empty lines is not built into this function. For example, to print all the tags in a file, the output of split_tags can be piped through grep:

```
$ echo "$html" | split_tags | grep -e '<'
<ul class="index">
<li>
<a href="my_file">
</a>
</li>
</ul>
```

To extract all the opening tags, grep finds lines with an open bracket that is not followed by a slash:

```
$ echo "$html" | split_tags | grep -e '<[^/]'
<ul class="index">
<li>
<a href="my_file">
```

All of the closing tags are printed with this pipeline:

```
$ echo "$html" | split_tags | grep -e '</'
</a>
</li>
</ul>
```

The text of an HTML file can be extracted by excluding all tags:

```
$ echo "$html" | split_tags | grep  -v -e '^<' -e '^ *$'
My file
```

Many much more complex utilities for converting HTML to text are available on the Web (search for html2text) or included with your operating system. For some tasks, these utilities are overkill; for others, they are inadequate. If you cannot find a utility that does just what you want, the split_tags function may be the tool you need to roll your own.

The Script

The first awk command inserts a newline before an open bracket, <; the second inserts a newline after a closing bracket, >. The third command removes consecutive newlines, and the fourth prints the result without a trailing newline, so that the only newlines are those surrounding a tag. A newline is appended at the very end, and the whole thing is piped through tr to delete multiple spaces.

```
split_tags()
{
  awk '/</ { gsub(/</, "\n<") }  ## Add a newline before "<"
      />/ { gsub(/>/, ">\n") }  ## Add a newline after ">"
          { gsub(/\n\n/, "\n")  ## remove double newlines
            printf "%s ", $0 }  ## Print without trailing newline

      ## Print final newline and remove multiple spaces
      END { printf "\n" }' "$@" | tr -s ' '
}
```

13.3 html-title—Get the Title from an HTML File

A well-formed HTML file always has a title element in its header. When building an index page, you'll want to include the titles from the linked pages.

How It Works

The get_element function will return the title with its tags. This function retrieves the title element and removes the tags.

Usage

```
html_title [FILE]
```

If a filename is not given on the command line, html_title will read the file from its standard input.

On Chris's web site, he has a section devoted to the novels of Dick Francis. To create the index.html file, he used this short script at the command line:

```
$ for page in *_novel.html
do
  title=$(html_title $page)
  printf "<li><a href=\"%s\">%s</a></li>\n" "$page" "${title% }"
done
<li><a href="10-lb.Penalty_novel.html">10-lb. Penalty</a></li>
<li><a href="Banker_novel.html">Banker</a></li>
```

The resulting file looked like this (though it was much longer, as the page has files for all 37 of Francis's novels), before adding the rest of the information using a text editor:

```
<li><a href="BloodSport_novel.html">Blood Sport</a></li>
<li><a href="Bolt_novel.html">Bolt</a></li>
<li><a href="Bonecrack_novel.html">Bonecrack</a></li>
<li><a href="BreakIn_novel.html">Break In</a></li>
<li><a href="ComeToGrief_novel.html">Come to Grief</a></li>
<li><a href="Comeback_novel.html">Comeback</a></li>
<li><a href="DeadCert_novel.html">Dead Cert</a></li>
<li><a href="Decider_novel.html">Decider</a></li>
```

The Script

```
html_title()
{
   NWSP="[!\\$SPC\\$TAB]" ## Pattern to match non-space characters

   ## The title tag may be in upper- or lowercase, or capitalized,
   ## therefore we try all three. Other mixtures of case are very rare
   ## and can be ignored. If you need them, just add them to the list
   for tag in title TITLE Title
   do
     set -f
     get_element *< ${1:-/dev/tty} |     ## Extract the tag to a single line
     {
         read line
         line=${line#*<"${tag}"*>}    ## Delete up to and including opening tag
         line=${line%</"${tag}"*}     ## Delete from closing tag to end of line
         case $line in                ## If the line still contains anything
            *$NWSP*)                  ## other than whitespace
```

```
            printf "%s " $line ## print it, without multiple spaces,
            printf "\n"          ## and print a newline
            break
            ;;
      esac
   }
   done
}
```

HTML on the Fly: The cgi-funcs Library

Common Gateway Interface (CGI) programs create web content when the page is requested; they can be written in any language. Apart from a few places where extra speed is necessary, all mine are shell scripts. Most are no different from any other shell script, but they may need a front end to deal with information passed on by the web server and to provide the necessary context header.

The library uses the _substr function, so it must source string-funcs, which appeared in Chapter 3:

```
. string-funcs
```

13.4 x2d2—Convert a Two-Digit Hexadecimal Number to Decimal

The first step in converting a $QUERY_STRING variable or POST data to a usable format is to convert the hexadecimal (hex) sequences to characters. This involves an intermediate step of converting them to decimal integers.

How It Works

The hex sequences are always two digits, so a simple lookup table will suffice.

Usage

```
_x2d2 XX  ## store result in $_X2D2
x2d2 XX  ## print the result
```

This pair of functions follows the same protocol as many other such pairs in this book: one stores the result in a variable, and the other calls the first and prints the contents of that variable.

```
$ _x2d2 ff
$ echo $_X2D2
255
$ x2d2 7F
127
```

The Script

```
x2d2()
{
    _x2d2 "$@" && printf "%s\n" "$_X2D2"
}

_x2d2()
{
    ## Split argument on the command line into individual digits
    x2d2_n1=${1%?} ## first digit
    x2d2_n2=${1#?} ## second digit

    ## Look up value of first digit
    case $x2d2_n1 in
        [0-9]) _X2D2=$(( $x2d2_n1 * 16 )) ;;
        a|A) _X2D2=160 ;;   ## 16 * 10
        b|B) _X2D2=176 ;;   ## 16 * 11
        c|C) _X2D2=192 ;;   ## 16 * 12
        d|D) _X2D2=208 ;;   ## 16 * 13
        e|E) _X2D2=224 ;;   ## 16 * 14
        f|F) _X2D2=240 ;;   ## 16 * 15
        *) _X2D2= ; return 5 ;;
    esac

    ## Look up value of second digit and add to value of first digit
    case $x2d2_n2 in
        [0-9]) _X2D2=$((  $_X2D2 + $x2d2_n2 )) ;;
        a|A) _X2D2=$((  $_X2D2 + 10 )) ;;
        b|B) _X2D2=$((  $_X2D2 + 11 )) ;;
        c|C) _X2D2=$((  $_X2D2 + 12 )) ;;
        d|D) _X2D2=$((  $_X2D2 + 13 )) ;;
        e|E) _X2D2=$((  $_X2D2 + 14 )) ;;
        f|F) _X2D2=$((  $_X2D2 + 15 )) ;;
        *) _X2D2= ; return 5 ;;
    esac
}
```

13.5 dehex—Convert Hex Strings (%XX) to Characters

Web applications, such as servers and browsers, transmit nonalphanumeric characters as two-digit hexadecimal codes preceded by a percent sign (%). These codes need to be translated to their character equivalents.

How It Works

The string-funcs and char-funcs libraries (from Chapter 3) provide the means to chop up the string and then convert a decimal number to an ASCII character.

Usage

```
_dehex STRING     ## store result in $_DEHEX
dehex STRING      ## print the result
```

A space is encoded as %20, and quotation marks are %22:

```
$ dehex %22The%20quick%20brown%20fox%22
"The quick brown fox"
```

The Script

```
dehex()
{
    _dehex "$@" && printf "%s\n" "$_DEHEX"
}

_dehex()
{
    dx_line=$1
    _DEHEX=
    while :
    do
      case $dx_line in
              *${dx_prefix:=%}[0-9A-Fa-f][0-9A-Fa-f]*)

                        ## Store the portion of the string, up to,
                        ## but not including, the hex string, in $left
                        left=${dx_line%%${dx_prefix}[0-9a-fA-F][0-9a-fA-F]*}

                        ## Everything except $left and the percent sign
                        ## is stored in $right
                        right=${dx_line#${left}?}

                        ## The two hex digits are the first two characters
                        ## of $right; extract them with _substr
                        _substr "$right" 1 2

                        ## Remove the hex digits from $right
                        right=${right#??}

                        ## Convert the hex digits to decimal
                        _x2d2 "$_SUBSTR"

                        ## Add $left and the converted decimal number
                        ## to the result string, $_DEHEX
                        _DEHEX=$_DEHEX$left$(chr -n "$_X2D2")
```

```
                    ## Store $right in $dx_line for further processing
                    dx_line=$right
                    ;;
                *) ## No more hex; add rest of line to $_DEHEX, and exit
                    _DEHEX=$_DEHEX$dx_line; break;;
        esac
    done
}
```

13.6 filedate—Find and Format the Modification Date of a File

One of the most annoying things on many web sites (animations, frames, and ads are in a different class altogether!) is the absence of a date for an article. Does the article's information still apply? To help web site visitors determine a page's timeliness, consider including the date somewhere on the page. How do you do that?

How It Works

This function uses ls and a method of converting the name of a month to a number that was not shown in Chapter 8, which dealt with dates.

Usage

```
filedate FILE
```

The actual formatting is dictated by the contents of a style sheet; filedate supplies the necessary tags:

```
$ filedate index.html
<span class="filedate">index.html updated 2004-12-11</span>
```

The Script

```
filedate() {
    ## Split the date and place into the positional parameters
    set -- $(ls -l "$1")

    ## Extract the month string up to the given month
    mm=JanFebMarAprMayJunJulAugSepOctNovDec
    idx=${mm%%$6*}

    ## Calculate the number of the month from the length of $idx
    month=$(( (${#idx} + 4 ) / 3 ))
    day=$7
    case $8 in
        ## If the output of ls shows the time instead of the year,
        ## calculate which year it should be
        *:*) eval $(date "+y=%Y m=%m")
            [ $month -gt $m ] && year=$(( $y - 1 )) || year=$y ;;
        *) year=$8 ;;
```

```
    esac
    printf "<span class=\"filedate\">${9%.cgi} updated "
    printf "%d-%02d-%02d</span>\n" $year $month $day
}
```

Creating HTML Files

Every web site I have created since I started writing them in 1996 has made use of shell scripts to generate at least some of the pages. A page may be static—created and then left for posterity— or it may be created dynamically when a reader requests it. A third category is somewhere in between: the page is updated only when a change in circumstances warrants it. Generation of the third type is triggered by a request via the Web, a command from a remote or local shell, or a cron job. The first script in this section is of the third type; it creates an index of the files in a directory.

13.7 mk-htmlindex—Create an HTML Index

A directory listing as produced by a web server when there is no index.html file is not very attractive and is disabled by many sites. While it is easy to create a simple HTML index for a directory, producing a standards-compliant page is a little harder.

This simple script produces a very basic index file:

```
for file in *
do
  printf "<a href=\"%s\">%s</a><br>\n" "$file" "$file"
done > index.html
```

A better script would produce a proper header for the file. It would identify the type of file, and perhaps even extract a title from the file itself. It should be able to create indexes in an entire directory tree.

■ **Tip** An alternative way is to use the for file in `ls` command, which would list all the files.

How It Works

If the formatting is done by a cascading style sheet (CSS), the script can assign a class to the entry for each file. You have the option to include dot files, or leave them out; to descend into subdirectories, or just index the current directory; as well as to specify various other features.

Usage

```
mk-htmlindex [OPTIONS] [DIR]
```

By default, `mk-htmlindex` will index the current directory, identifying file types by extension. The header will include the user's name and the creation date and time; the name of the directory will become the title. For certain types of files—HTML, XML, PostScript, and some shell scripts—it will try to find a title or description, and use it in the file's entry. The options are

- `-d`: Include dot files in the index.

- `-f`: If no title is generated for the file, use the `file` command to get the type of file and use that instead of a title.

- `-i FILE`: Use FILE as the name of the index file.

- `-l`: Include the index file being created in the index itself.

- `-R`: Recursively descend the directory tree.

- `-v[v]`: Use verbose mode. Additional vs increase the level of verbosity. At present, two levels are implemented: in level 1, the names of any directories entered in recursive mode will be printed, and in level 2, the names of all files will be printed as they are processed.

The working directory for this chapter contains

```
$ ls
4711ch16d1.doc   index.css     info.cgi         pretext-sh
cgi-funcs-sh     index.html    mk-htmlindex-sh  text2html-sh
html-funcs-sh    index.htmlx   mkhtmlindex-sh   toc.html
```

The default HTML file produced by the script is as follows (long lines have been wrapped):

```
$ mk-htmlindex
<!DOCTYPE HTML PUBLIC  "-//W3C//DTD HTML 4.01 Transitional//EN">
<html lang="en">
<!-- : index.html, 2004-12-14_17.06.56, Chris F.A. Johnson $ -->
 <head>
  <meta http-equiv="Content-Type" content="text/html;  charset=ISO-8859-1">
  <title>Documents/ch16</title>
  <link rel="stylesheet" type="text/css" href="index.css"
 </head>
 <body class="html">
  <span class="h2">Listing of /home/chris/Documents/ch16</span>
  <div class="main">
   <ul>
    <li class="doc"><a href="4711ch16d1.doc">4711ch16d1.doc </a></li>
    <li class="shell"><a href="cgi-funcs-sh">cgi-funcs-sh </a></li>
    <li class="shell"><a href="html-funcs-sh">html-funcs-sh </a></li>
    <li class="symlink"><a href="index.css">index.css </a></li>
    <li class="html"><a href="index.html">index.html &mdash;
              <span class="title">Documents/ch16 </span></a></li>
    <li class="symlink"><a href="index.htmlx">index.htmlx </a></li>
    <li class="cgi"><a href="info.cgi">info.cgi </a></li>
    <li class="shell"><a href="mk-htmlindex-sh">mk-htmlindex-sh &mdash;
   <span class="title">"Create index.html for directory"</span></a></li>
    <li class="shell"><a href="mkhtmlindex-sh">mkhtmlindex-sh &mdash;
```

```
  <span class="title">"Create index.html for directory"</span></a></li>
    <li class="shell"><a href="pretext-sh">pretext-sh </a></li>
    <li class="shell"><a href="text2html-sh">text2html-sh </a></li>
    <li class="html"><a href="toc.html">toc.html </a></li>
   </ul>
  </div>
 </body>
</html>
```

This is the style sheet that is in use with these indexes. It uses a different background color for each type of file (more types could be added):

```
.main {
     line-height: 150% ;     background-color: #aacccc;
     margin-left: 5%;        margin-right: 5%;           margin-top: 3em;
     color: black;
}


.h2 {
    width: 100%;              position: fixed;
    top: 0;                   margin: 0;
    padding-left: 5%;         border-bottom: 1pt solid black;
    background-color: white;  font-size: 150%;
    line-height: 1.5;         font-weight: bold;
}

li { width: 100%; background-color: #aacccc; padding-left: 1em; }
a { padding-left: 4px; padding-right: 4px; }
a:hover { color: red; border:outset; background-color: white; }
ul { background-color: white; }
.txt  { background-color: #dddddd; color: black; }
.dir  { background-color: #bbbbbb; color: black; }
.cgi  { background-color: #999999; color: black; }
.html { background-color: #888888; color: black; }
.xml  { background-color: #777777; color: black; }
.pdf  { background-color: #666666; color: black; }
.css  { background-color: #555555; color: black; }
.file { background-color: #eeddff; color: black; }
.doc  { background-color: #aaaaaa; color: black; }
.shell { background-color: #ffffff; color: black; }
.title { color: black; font-weight: bold; }
.ps,.eps,.epsi { background-color: #ddffcc; }
```

There is a leaning towards the use of shades of gray in this style sheet since the figures in this book are not printed in color.

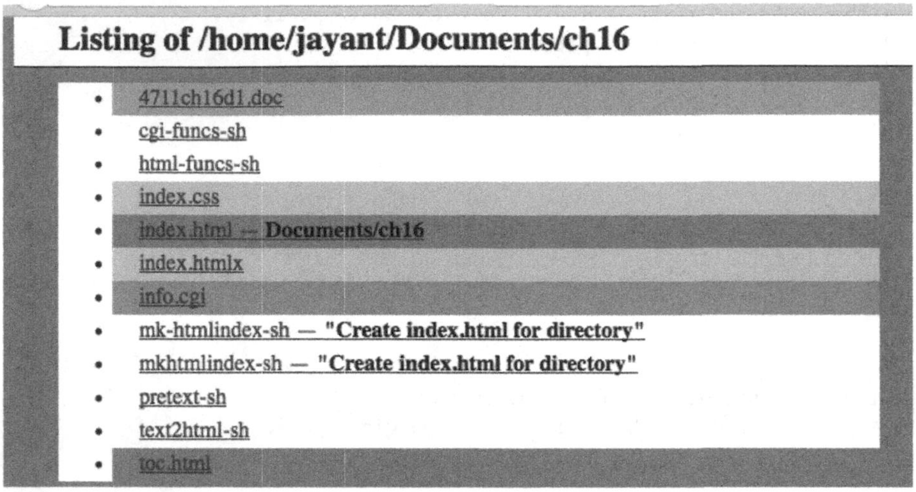

Listing of /home/jayant/Documents/ch16

- 4711ch16d1.doc
- cgi-funcs-sh
- html-funcs-sh
- index.css
- index.html — **Documents/ch16**
- index.htmlx
- info.cgi
- mk-htmlindex-sh — **"Create index.html for directory"**
- mkhtmlindex-sh — **"Create index.html for directory"**
- pretext-sh
- text2html-sh
- toc.html

Figure 13-1. *Web page created by* `mk-htmlindex`

The Script

```
mk_htmlheader()
{
    date_vars ## from standard-funcs which is sourced by html-funcs

    ## Look up user's full name in /etc/passwd (see Chapter 15)
    name=$(lookup -f: -v5 $USER /etc/passwd)

    ## Use name of current directory as the title
    title=${PWD#${PWD%/*/*}}

    ## Form the name of the CSS file from the name of the index file
    css_file=${filename%.html}.css

    ## If the CSS file is not in the current directory,
    ## but it is in the parent directory, link to it
    [ -f "$css_file" ] ||
        { [ -f "../$css_file" ] && ln -s "../$css_file" . ; }

    ## Print the header
    printf "%s\n" \
    '<!DOCTYPE HTML PUBLIC "-//W3C//DTD HTML 4.01 Transitional//EN">' \
    '<html lang="en">' \
    "<!-- $Id: $filename, $datestamp, ${name:-$USER} $ -->" \
    '  <head>' \
    "    <title>${title#/}</title>" \
    "    <link rel=\"stylesheet\" type=\"text/css\" href=\"$css_file\"" \
    '  </head>' \
```

```
    "   <body class=\"${filename##*.}\">" \
    "    <span class=\"h2\">Listing of $PWD</span>" \
    '    <div class="main">' \
    '        <ul>'
}

mk_htmlfooter()
{
    ## Close all the open tags
    printf "%s\n" " </ul>" " </div>" " </body>" "</html>"
}

## Defaults; these may be changed by command-line options
verbose=0               ## Don't print any progress reports
recursive=0             ## Don't descend into directories
filename=index.html     ## Filename for generated HTML file
vopts=                  ## Verbose options, used for recursive operation
listfile=0              ## Exclude the index file itself from the listing
dotfiles=               ## Do not include dot files
usetype=0               ## Do not use file type if there is no title

progname=${0##*/}
. html-funcs     ## Load functions

## Parse command-line options
while getopts vRdi:lf var
do
  case $var in
      d) dotfiles=.* ;;
      f) usetype=1 ;;
      i) filename=$OPTARG ;;
      l) listfile=1 ;;
      R) recursive=1 ;;
      v) verbose=$(( $verbose + 1 ))
         vopts=${vopts}v ;;
      *) die 5 "Invalid option: $var" ;;
  esac
done
shift $(( $OPTIND - 1 ))

## Change to directory on the command line, if any
[ -d "${1:-.}" ] && cd "${1:-.}" || exit 5

## Set $PWD if the shell doesn't
[ -z "$PWD" ] && PWD=$(pwd)

## To avoid corrupting a page that may be loaded into a browser
## while the indexing is in progress, it is saved to a temporary
## file. That file is then moved in place of the original file.
tempfile=$(mktemp $filename.XXXXXX)
```

```
{
    mk_htmlheader ## Print the HTML header and top of <body>

    for file in * $dotfiles
    do

        ## If dot files are enabled, the current directory and parent
        ## directory will show up. The script ignores them.
        case $file in
            .|..) continue ;;
        esac
        ## The file we are creating will be ignored unless
        ## the -l option has been selected
        [ "$file" = "$filename" ] && [ $listfile -eq 0 ] && continue

        ## Clear variables
        title=
        class=

        ## In very verbose (-vv) mode, print the name of every file
        [ $verbose -ge 2 ] && printf "%s\n" "$PWD/$file" >&2

        if [ -d "$file" ]
        then
          ## Recursive mode; descend into directories
          ## by calling the script with the directory as the argument
          if [ $recursive -eq 1 ]
          then

            ## Verbose mode: print name directory being descended into
            [ $verbose -ge 1 ] &&
              printf "\nDescending into %s..." "$PWD/$file" >&2
            ## Call the same program with options from the command line
            $0 -${vopts}Ri "$filename" "$file"
          fi

          ## Information for listing
          class=${class:+$class }dir ## $file is a directory, so add "dir" to class
          title=""
          file=$file/
        else

          ## The file's extension is used to determine the class; if the
          ## file type may contain a title, it is searched for and used
          ## in the listing
```

```
    case $file in
        *.html|*.shtml)
            class=${class:+$class }html
            title=$(html_title "$file")
            ;;
        *.xml)
            class=${class:+$class }xml
            title=$(html_title "$file")
            ;;
        *[-.]sh)
            title=$(head "$file")
            class=${class:+$class }shell
            case $title in
                *'# DESCRIPTION:'*)
                    title=${title#* DESCRIPTION: }
                    title=${title%%$NL*}
                    ;;
                *description=*) title=${title#*description=}
                    title=${title%%$NL*}
                    ;;
                *) title= ;;
            esac
            ;;
        *.ps|*.eps|*.epsi)
            title=$(head "$file")
            case $title in
                *%%Title:\ *)
                    title=${title##*%%Title: }
                    title=${title%%$NL*}
                    class=${file##*.}
                    ;;
                *) title= ;;
            esac
            ;;
        *)
            title=
            if [ -L "$file" ]
            then
              class="$class symlink"
            elif [ -x "$file" ]
            then
              class="$class exe"
            else
              case $file in
                *.*) class="$class ${file##*.}" ;;
                *) class="$class file" ;;
              esac
            fi
            ;;
    esac
fi
```

```
     ## If a title has been generated, use <span class=""> to display it
     if [ -n "$title" ]
     then
       title=${title:+&mdash; <span class=\"title\">$title</span>}

     ## Otherwise do nothing unless the user has requested the
     ## file type as a default.
     elif [ $usetype -ge 1 ]
     then
       title=$(file "$file")
       title=" &mdash ${title#*:}"
     fi

     class=${class# } ## Remove leading space, if any

     ## Print listing
     printf "    <li class=\"%s\"><a href=\"%s\">%s %s</a></li>\n" \
                 "${class:-file}" "$file" "$file" \
                 "$title"
   done

   ## Print footer
   mk_htmlfooter

} > "$tempfile"
chmod a+r "$tempfile"
mv "$tempfile" "$filename"
```

13.8 pretext—Create a Wrapper Around a Text File

When a text file needs to be displayed in a web browser, but its formatting needs to remain the same, it should be wrapped in <pre> tags.

How It Works

Besides enclosing the file in <pre> tags, this script inserts a standards-conformant header, translates open brackets (<) to <, and appends the correct closing tags. It also gives the text some style, with margins on both sides for better readability.

Usage

```
pretext [OPTIONS] [FILE]
```

A title can be specified with -t, and an output file can be specified with the -i option. If no FILE is given, the standard input is used.

The Script

```
## By default, output goes to the standard output where it can be
## redirected to a file
htmlfile=/dev/tty

while getopts t:h: opt
do
  case $opt in
      h) htmlfile=$OPTARG ;; ## output file
      t) title=$OPTARG ;;    ## title
  esac
done
shift $(( $OPTIND - 1 ))
{
    printf "%s\n" \
    '<!DOCTYPE  HTML PUBLIC "-//W3C//DTD HTML 4.01 Transitional//EN">' \
    '<html lang="en">' \
    ' <head>' \
    "   <title>${title:-$1}</title>" \
    ' </head>' \
    ' <body>' \
    "   <h2>${title:-$1}</h2>" \
    '       <pre style="margin-left: 10%; margin-right: 10%;">'

    sed 's/</\&lt;/g' "$@" ## convert '<' to '&lt;'
    printf "</pre>\n</body>\n</html>\n"
} > "${htmlfile}"
```

13.9 text2html—Convert a Text File to HTML

A regular text file needs to be converted to HTML. It is a straightforward file, with paragraphs separated by blank lines.

How It Works

The perfect tool for this job is awk. A short script can read through the file, inserting paragraph tags on blank lines, and converting open angle brackets to <. The <blockquote> tag indents the text for readability.

Usage

```
text2html [OPTIONS] [FILE] [> HTMLFILE]
```

A title can be specified with -t, and an output file can be specified with the -i option. If no FILE is given, the standard input is read.

The Script

```
## default is the terminal
htmlfile=/dev/tty

while getopts t:h: opt
do
  case $opt in
      h) htmlfile=$OPTARG ;;    ## output file
      t) title=$OPTARG ;;       ## title
  esac
done
shift $(( $OPTIND - 1 ))
{
    printf "%s\n" \
      '<!DOCTYPE  HTML PUBLIC "-//W3C//DTD HTML 4.01 Transitional//EN">' \
      '<html lang="en">' \
      ' <head>' \
      "   <link rel=\"stylesheet\" type=\"text/css\" href=\"main.css\"" \
      "   <title>${title:-$1}</title>" \
      ' </head>' \
      ' <body>' \
      "   <h1>${title:-$1}</h1>" \
      "<blockquote><p>"

    ## insert closing and opening paragraph tags on blank lines,
    ## and convert open brackets to &lt;
    awk '/^$/ { printf "</p>\n<p>\n"; next }
         /</ { gsub(/</,"\\&lt;") }
             {print}' "$@"
    printf "</p></blockquote>\n</body>\n</html>\n"
} > "${htmlfile}"
```

13.10 demo.cgi—A CGI Script

When the POST method is used in an HTML form or parameters are added after the URL on a browser's address line, they show up in the $QUERY_STRING variable. Spaces and some other characters are translated to hexadecimal. The query string needs to be parsed and the hex translated to ASCII characters.

How It Works

The first part of the script uses Unix commands to show the date and variables set by the web server. Then the script parses the information passed as part of the URL, or in the POST action of a web form, and displays the results.

Usage

I used a text browser to view the page, using the following commands:

```
$ x='http://cfaj.freeshell.org/demo.cgi?book=%22Shell Scripting Recipes%22&a=1&666'
$ elinks "$x"
```

```
                        Wed Dec 15 01:06:00 UTC 2004

                   You are connected from: 192.168.0.2

                           Your browser is:
              ELinks/0.9.2rc4 (textmode; Linux 2.6.8.1-12mdk i686; 74x51)

                 You have appended the following QUERY_STRING:

               book=%22Shell%20Scripting%20Recipes%22&a=1&666:
                      VARIABLE                VALUE
                      book         "Shell Scripting Recipes"
                      a            1
                      --           666
```

The Script

A CGI script needs a shebang on the first line to tell the web server what interpreter to use to execute the script. On a POSIX system, #!/usr/bin/env bash will invoke the bash shell wherever it is. On other systems, it must be replaced with the path to the executable. It need not be bash, but it must be a POSIX shell.
#!/usr/bin/env bash

```
## Load functions
. cgi-funcs

## The content-type header must be followed by a blank line
printf "Content-type: text/html\n\n"

## Print page head element
printf "%s\n" "<html>" " <head>" "<title>Welcome</title>" \
              " </head>" " <body>"
printf "%s\n" " <center>"

## Print various bits of information
date
printf   "<h3>You are connected from: %s</h3>\n" "$REMOTE_ADDR"
printf   "Your browser is:<br>%s<br>\n" "$HTTP_USER_AGENT"
printf   "<br>You have appended the following QUERY_STRING:<br>\n"
printf   "<br>%s:\n" "$QUERY_STRING"

printf   "<br><br>%s\n" "<table><th>VARIABLE<th>VALUE"
```

```
## Parse the QUERY_STRING
## Elements of QUERY_STRING are separated by ampersands
IFS='&'
set -- $QUERY_STRING
for arg    ## Loop through the elements
do
    _dehex "$arg
    case $_DEHEX in
        *=*) ## Split into VARIABLE and VALUE
            var=${_DEHEX%%=*}
            val=${_DEHEX#*=}
            ;;
        *) var=; val=$_DEHEX ;;
    esac
    printf "<tr><td>%s</td><td>%s</td></tr>\n" "${var:---}" "$val"
done
printf "%s\n" "</table>"
## Tidy up
printf "</body>\n</html>"
```

Summary

A single chapter can hardly do justice to the possibilities of using shell scripts in conjunction with HTML files. Nevertheless, there is a good deal to chew on in this chapter, and the tools presented lay the groundwork for more advanced scripts.

CHAPTER 14

■ ■ ■

Taking Care of Business

Chris loves composing cryptic crossword puzzles, teaching chess and writing computer programs. He has a large collection of scripts to help you to do those things well.

Record keeping is a tedious chore, and the computer should help me do my bookkeeping with less effort than without it. Using shell scripts at the command line, One could enter an invoice and move on to something else in less time than it would take to open a spreadsheet or an accounting program.

The two scripts in this chapter form the basis of a bookkeeping system. First `prcalc`, to consolidate a pocketful of receipts into a single ledger entry. The script allows the user to comment each entry (if you feel conscientious) and save it to a file for future reference.

All the transaction records are stored in a file named for the year in which the transaction occurred—`GL.2004` and `GL.2005`, for example. Most of the invoices are generated by other scripts, and they enter the transaction record without any intervention on my part. When a crossword puzzle is finished, one command (`gt G200503`, for example) generates a text file with the clues, encapsulated PostScript files with the grid and the solution, and an invoice, all of which it e-mails to the *Good Times* magazine. It also adds a transaction record to my ledger. When you need to enter a transaction manually, you could use the second script in the chapter, `gle`.

■ **Note**   The scripts are based on solutions that work personally for Chris. Your requirements might be different and there could be off-the-shelf solutions that may help in generating invoices and managing finances.

14.1 prcalc—A Printing Calculator

The `calc` script in Chapter 5 calculates a single expression entered on the command line. For long calculations, such as totaling a pile of receipts from the proverbial shoebox, entering one amount per line is easier. Sometimes a record is needed of all the entries. A program that works like a desktop printing calculator would be useful.

How It Works

The metaphor of a desktop printing calculator is a useful one, but it shouldn't be carried too far. A computer is capable of doing far more than a printing calculator. The entries can be stored in a file, and they can be combined with other sessions. The files can be edited and reprocessed through `prcalc`. The results, with or without the history, can be stored in a variable for later use in a script. There are other possibilities floating around in my head, and no doubt you can come up with many more not thought of.

Usage

```
[COMMAND |] prcalc [> FILE]|[ | COMMAND]
```

The basic operation of prcalc is to add the entries as they are entered. These are stored in a history file whose name is printed when the program is invoked. The running total and a prompt are printed to the standard error channel at the beginning of each line. Entering a blank line terminates the script, and the result is printed to the standard output. In these sample runs, the user's input is printed in bold:

```
$ prcalc
History file is /home/chris/prcalc.history.27224
       0 : 23
      23 : 14.5
    37.5 :

37.5
```

For an operation other than addition, the arithmetic operator is entered before the number:

```
$ prcalc
History file is /home/chris/prcalc.history.27628
         0 : 666
       666 : / 2
       333 : * 1.333
   443.889 : % 10
   44.3889 : s
0 + 666
666 / 2
333 * 1.333
443.889 * 10 / 100
   44.3889 : q

44.3889
```

The standard arithmetic operators, +, -, *, and /, for addition, subtraction, multiplication, and division, respectively, are accepted along with x (when followed by a number) for multiplication and % for percentage. The percent sign can be placed after the number; either %15 or 15% will work. There are also a number of commands that can be entered at the prompt. In the last example, s (save) and q (quit) are used. Here are all the commands:

- h: History; display the operations entered in the current session on the standard error so that the history appears on the terminal even when the standard output is redirected.

- s: Save the history by printing it to the standard output, which may be redirected to a file or a printer. If STDOUT is not redirected, the history will be displayed on the terminal.

- v: Verbose mode; each operation performed is printed against the right margin.

- q, x: Exit the script.

- =: Print the current total to STDOUT, delete the history, and start a new history file.

- #: Enter a comment to be saved in the history file. A comment may also be entered after an operation.

Because prompting and ongoing information is sent to STDERR, the result of an interactive session can be placed in a file or a variable:

```
$ result=$(prcalc)
History file is /home/chris/prcalc.history.28697
        0 : 2.3
      2.3 : v
      2.3 : 1.5%
   0.0345 : * 12                              2.3 * 1.5 / 100   =  0.0345
    0.414 : 3.14159265 * 2                    0.0345 * 12       =  0.414
  6.69719 : 42 ## The universal answer  0.414 + 3.14159265 * 2 =  6.6971
  48.6972 : h              6.69719 + 42 ## The universal answer = 48.6972
0 + 2.3
2.3 * 1.5 / 100
0.0345 * 12
0.414 + 3.14159265 * 2
6.69719 + 42 ## The universal answer
   48.6972 :

$ echo $result
48.6972
```

When the input is not coming from a terminal, the prompts are not printed:

```
$ printf "%s\n" 2.45 3.79 "*2" "s" | prcalc > calc.txt
$ cat calc.txt
0 + 2.45
2.45 + 3.79
6.24 * 2
12.48
```

The Script

The sh_read function prompts the user for input and reads that input. If the script is being run under bash (version 2 or later), the readline library is used, and full command-line editing may be done. Previous entries may be recalled in the same way as they can at the command prompt, by pressing the up arrow key or Ctrl-P.

```
sh_read()
{
    [ -n "$x" ] && printf "%s\n" "$x" >> $HF
    case $BASH_VERSION in
        ## If this is bash, take advantage of history and command-line editing
        [2-9]*|[[0-9][0-9]*)
                [ -n "$x" ] && {
                    history -c      ## Clear the history
                    history -r $HF ## Read history from file
                }
```

```
            read -ep " : " ${1:-x}
            ;;
     *) printf " : " >&2; read ${1:-x} ;;
   esac
}
```

The initialization of variables and the history file is placed in a function, as it may be called when the total is reset with the = command.

```
prc_init()
{
    ## Initialize variables
    NL='
'
    total=0
    PR_N=0
    x=
    op=

    set -f      ## turn off pathname expansion

    ## The history file is re-created every session,
    ## or whenever the total is reset with =
    HF=$HOME/$progname.history.$$
    n=
    ## add increment if file exists
    while [ -f "$HF${n:+.$n}" ]
    do
       n=$(( ${n:-0} + 1 ))
    done
    HF="$HF${n:+.$n}"
    > $HF
    [ -t 0 ] && printf "History file is %s\n" "$HF" >&2

    ## If standard input is not connected to a terminal,
    ## send prompts and progress info to the bit bucket
    [ -t 0 ] || exec 2>/dev/null
}

progname=${0##*/}
prc_init

## The main loop of the script reads the user's input,
## parses the operator and operand,
## and passes it to awk in much the same way as in the calc script.
while :
do
    printf "%10s" "$total" >&2
    sh_read
```

```
case $x in
    *%) ## Percentage sign can go after the number
        op=%
        num=${x%?}
        ;;
    ""|q|x) break ;; ## Quit, exit, etc...
    h|s) ## A subshell is used to prevent the change to IFS,
         ## or the redirection of STDERR, affecting the rest of the script.
        (
            IFS=$NL
            [ $x = s ] && exec 2>&1 ## Send history to standard output
            printf "%s\n" $history >&2
        )
        x=
        continue
        ;;
    x*) op=*; num=${x#x} ;;
    v) ## Toggle verbose mode
        [ ${verbose:-0} -eq 1 ] &&
            verbose=0 ||
            verbose=1

        continue
        ;;
    [a-zA-Z]*) ## Ignore invalid input
            x=
            continue ;;
    =) ## print result and reset total to 0
        printf "%s\n" "$total"
        prc_init
        continue
        ;;
    *) ## Separate operator and operand
        op=${x%%[.0-9]*}
        num=${x#"$op"}
        ;;
esac

## Adjust operator and operand for percentage calculation
case $op in
    *%*)
        op=*
        num="$num / 100"
        ;;
esac

## Add current operation to history
history="$history$NL$total ${op:-+} $num"
PR_N=$(( $PR_N + 1 ))
old=$total
```

```
    total=$(awk " BEGIN { OFMT= \"%f\"
                          printf \"%s\n\", $total ${op:-+} $num
                          exit }")

    ## In verbose mode, print operation (against right margin)
    [ ${verbose:-0} -ge 1 ] && {
        w=$(( ${COLUMNS:-80} - 1 ))
        printf "%${w}.${w}s\r" "$old ${op:-+} $num = $total" >&2
    }
done
printf "\n" >&2
printf "%s\n" "$total"
```

14.2 gle—Keeping Records Without a Shoebox

I have been self-employed for more than 15 years, and for 20 years before that I usually did freelance work even when I had a full-time job. In the days before personal computers, I conscientiously kept records in account books. When I got my first computer, I thought that it would all be so much easier. Boy, was I wrong!

I tried different accounting and bookkeeping packages, but all seemed like even more work than writing the information down on paper. I never reached the point of usefulness with any of the packages. Perhaps it was just impatience on my part, but every piece of software I tried required too much time to set up before I could begin using it.

I tried writing my own bookkeeping systems, but I got bogged down in the details. It was a few years before I solved the problem. This could be true for others, despite the many options available. Surprisingly things have not changed much in terms of record keeping and a shoebox full of receipts.

How It Works

The proverbial shoebox that is delivered to one's accountant every year at tax time may be adequate for some self-employed workers, but most need to keep better track of their finances. A computerized accounting system that is too difficult or cumbersome to use efficiently is worse than a pen and an account book. My previously well-kept, handwritten accounts degenerated into a half-forgotten mess, and my computer did little or nothing to take up the slack.

I don't remember what led to the breakthrough, but in retrospect, the solution I came up with seems eminently logical, if not downright obvious. All I needed was a data format that included all the necessary information about a transaction and a means of entering that information. Once the information was stored in a structured format, other programs could be written to analyze it as and when necessary.

The transactions would be stored in a text file, one to a line. I originally used tilde-delimited records, but those eventually gave way to tab-separated fields. The fields have undergone some transformation since the first implementation, but there's not a lot of difference. I now use the fields shown in Table 14-1.

Table 14-1. *Fields in the General Ledger File*

Field	Description
Transaction number	A unique number generated sequentially from the last number used.
Account	An abbreviation for the name of the account; AR for accounts receivable and OS for office supplies, for example. The full names can be looked up in a chart of accounts.
Transaction date	The date, in international YYYY-MM-DD format, on which the transaction took place.
Amount	The amount of the transaction expressed in cents, so that integer arithmetic can be used for calculations.
Client or supplier	An abbreviation for the name of the client or supplier.
Details	Information about the transaction. This can include a reference to another transaction (as when a check is received to pay off an invoice) or an invoice number for a payable amount.
Date of entry	The date on which the transaction was added to the database.
Action taken	For accounts receivable, this is usually "e-mailed." Other actions include "cash payment," "check deposited," and "invoice received."

Somewhat abbreviated, and with tabs reduced to two spaces, here is an excerpt from the file GL.2004. The transaction records for invoices are created automatically by the same scripts that e-mail my crossword puzzles along with their invoices:

```
10411  AR  2004-01-01  50000  SS  5 Puzzles, Jan 2004 2004-01-01  E-mailed
10412  RE  2004-01-01  50000  TL  January office rent 2004-01-01  Check sent
10413  PR  2004-01-21  50000  SS  INV: 10411          2004-01-22  Check deposited
10414  AR  2004-01-27  40000  GT  Puzzles G200403     2004-01-27  E-mailed
10415  AR  2004-02-01  40000  SS  4 Puzzles, Feb 2004 2004-02-01  E-mailed
10416  RE  2004-02-01  50000  TL  Rent for February   2004-02-01  Check mailed
10417  OS  2004-02-11   1979  BB  Printer paper       2004-02-13  Debit card
10418  PR  2004-02-18  40000  GT  INV: 10414          2004-02-18  Check deposited
10419  AR  2004-02-24  40000  GT  Puzzles G200404     2004-02-24  E-mailed
```

You can easily import this file into a spreadsheet, or you can write scripts to organize and print the data. For extracting information from this file, awk is the ideal tool. For example, to find how much I am owed in accounts receivable, I would use this:

```
awk '$2 == "AR" {ar += $4}
     $2 == "PR" {ar -= $4}
   END {
      print "Accounts Receivable: " ar/100
     }' GL.2004
```

To extract all the transactions from April 2004 and write them to a file that can be processed further, I would use the following:

```
awk '$3 ~ /2004-04/ {print}' GL.2004 > 2004-02.tmp
```

The format has changed a few times over the last 15 years, and I started using the current version last year. By the time you're reading this, I'll have had to write a script to produce the statement of income and expenses that the tax department wants.

■ **Note**   You might want to ensure that the data sent to the government complies with all requirements.

This system is not sophisticated enough for most businesses, but a self-employed person may well need nothing more than this and a few report-writing scripts.

Usage

gle [-t]

With the -t option, gle uses a test directory ($HOME/.testing) instead of the regular set of books ($HOME/books). (It really is meant for testing, not a clandestine set of accounts.)

When invoked, gle clears the screen and prints an empty record, with the fixed fields, transaction number and entry date, filled in. A default transaction date (today's date) is also entered:

TR#: **10649**   Entry Date: **21 Dec 2004**

    Date [1]: **21 Dec 2004**

 Account [2]:

  Amount [3]: **0.00**

  Client [4]:

 Details [5]:

  Action [6]:

Select 1-5, [s]ave, [n]ew [q]uit:

A single keypress brings up a prompt or executes a command. The numbers 1 to 6 are for changing the corresponding field in the current transaction, and s, n, and q save the current transaction, bring up a new transaction, and exit the program. If the current transaction has been modified, n or q will print a prompt asking whether you want to save the transaction, discard it, or cancel the command. This prompt will also appear if you exit with Ctrl-C.

This script will work in any POSIX shell, but if you are using bash2+, the history can be loaded with responses appropriate for the field. These are stored in files named accounts, clients, amounts, details, and actions. The up and down arrow keys (or Ctrl-P and Ctrl-N) will move back and forth through the entries in the file. The accounts and clients files are tables with abbreviations and their expansions. This is a cut-down version of the accounts file:

```
AR    Accounts Receivable
AP    Accounts Payable
PR    Payment Received on invoice
OS    Office Supplies
```

```
RE    Office Rent
IR    Income Received
CE    Capital Expenditure
PC    Petty cash
DE    Depreciation
```

The amounts file is generated each time gle is started. The amounts are extracted from the GL file and sorted by frequency, so that the amount most often used appears first when the up arrow is pressed. The same is done for the details file.

The Script

```
progname=${0##*/}
clear
. screen-funcs
. math-funcs
. date-funcs
```

After the function libraries are loaded, gle's own functions are defined, starting with main. The libraries are loaded first in case any functions they contain are redefined, as is the case with cleanup, which is in standard-funcs. A modified version is used in this script.

```
main()
{
    gle_init    ## Load functions and set programwide variables
    while :
    do          ## Endless loop (exit from within get_form)
      tr_init   ## Initialize transaction record
      get_form  ## Display record and get user entry
    done
}
```

The current transaction is printed by tr_form. The fixed fields are printed at the top, on the second line (defined by the line variable), and each changeable field is printed on its own line. These are double spaced, the spacing being governed by the value of $linespace.

```
tr_form()
{
    line=2
    linespace=2

    printat $line 1
    ## Use_show_date from standard-funcs (Chapter 1)
    _show_date "$e_date"
    printf "    TR#: $B%s$UB   Entry Date: $B%s$UB$cle" "$tr_num" "$_SHOW_DATE"

    _show_date "${tr_date:=$DATE}"
    tr_field Date    1 "$_SHOW_DATE"

    [ -n "$acct" ] && lookup "$acct" "$GLDIR/accounts" && acct_name=$_LOOKUP
```

```
    tr_field Account 2 "$acct${acct_name:+ - $acct_name}"
    _fpmul ${amount:-0} .01 ## Convert cents to dollars
    case $_FPMUL in
        *.?)  _FPMUL=${_FPMUL}0 ;;
        *.??|*.*) ;;
        *)   _FPMUL=${_FPMUL}.00 ;;
    esac
    tr_field Amount  3 "$_FPMUL"

    tr_field Client  4 "$client${client_name:+ - $client_name}"
    tr_field Details 5 "$details"
    tr_field Action  6 "$action"
    info_line=$(( $line + $linespace ))
    entry_line=$(( $info_line + $linespace ))
    printat $info_line 1 "$cle"
    printat $entry_line  1 "$cles"
}
```

The positioning and printing of each line of the transaction is done by tr_field, which takes three arguments: field name, selection number, and field contents.

```
tr_field()
{
    line=$(( $line + $linespace ))     ## Move down $linespace lines...
    printat $line 1                    ## ...at left margin
    tr_w=$(( ${COLUMNS:-80} - 20 ))    ## space on line for contents of field
    printf " %12s [%d]: $B%-${tr_w}.${tr_w}s$UB$cle\n$cle" "$1" "$2" "$3"
}
```

All the user interaction is handled within the get_form function, which loops until the user saves the current transaction, clears the transaction, or quits.

```
get_form()
{
    while :
    do
      HF=/dev/null                  ## Reset history file
      tr_form                       ## Display transaction
      printat $info_line 1 "$cles" ## Clear bottom of screen
      printat $entry_line 1 "     Select 1-5, [s]ave, [n]ew : "
      get_key
      case $_KEY in

          1) ## Change transaction date
              info_data=
              prompt="Enter transaction date: "
              sh_read && _parse_date "$_SH_READ" && tr_date=$_PARSE_DATE
              ;;
```

```
2) ## Enter account info_data=$accts
   prompt="Enter account code: "
   HF=$GLDIR/accounts            ## For use with bash history
   sh_read && acct=${_SH_READ%%$TAB*}
   HF=
   ;;

3) ## Enter amount
   info_data="Enter amount in dollars and cents (e.g., $123.45)"
   prompt="       Enter amount: "
   sort_amounts
   HF=$GLDIR/amounts             ## For use with bash history
   sh_read && {
       printf "%s\n""$_SH_READ" >> "$HF.all"
       _fpmul $_SH_READ 100
       _round $_FPMUL amount=${_ROUND} HF=
   }
   ;;

4) ## Enter client
   prompt="       Enter name (or code) of client: "
   HF=$GLDIR/clients                ## For use with bash history
   sh_read && {
       client=${_SH_READ%%$TAB*}
       [ -n "$client" ] &&
           lookup "$client" "$GLDIR/clients" &&
               client_name=$_LOOKUP
   }
   ;;

5) ## Enter details of transaction
   prompt="       Enter transaction details: "
   HF=$GLDIR/details             ## For use with bash history
   sh_read && details=$_SH_READ
   ;;

6) ## Enter disposition of [paper] record
   prompt="       Action taken with [paper] record: "
   HF=$GLDIR/actions             ## For use with bash history
   sh_read && action=$_SH_READ
   ;;

s) save_transaction ;;
   q|n)  ## Quit/New transaction
   k=$_KEY
   is_changed && query_save
   tr_init
   tr_form
```

```
                case $k in
                    q) printf "\r$cles"
                        break 2 ;;
                esac
                ;;
        esac
    done
}
```

When the user selects new or quit, the script calls is_changed. A successful return from the function indicates that the transaction has been modified.

```
is_changed()
{
    ## Record has been changed if:

    ##...the amount is not 0
    [ ${amount:-0} -ne 0 ] && return

    ##...there is anything in the account, client, details, or action fields
    [ -n "$acct$client$details$action" ] && return

    ##...the transaction date is not today's date,
    [ "$tr_date" != "$DATE" ] && return
    return 1
}
```

If the transaction has been modified, the user will be asked whether or not to save it. The user may respond yes to save it, no to discard it, or cancel to ignore the command and stay in the loop.

```
query_save()
{
    printat $info_line 1 "$cles"
    printat $entry_line 6
    printf "%s" "Save current record [Y/n/c]? "
    get_key
    printat $info_line 1 "$cles"
    case $_KEY in
        n|N) ;;             ## fall through to action
        c|C) continue ;;    ## go back to top of loop (i.e., ignore command)
        *) save_transaction ;; ## default action is to save the record
    esac
}
```

The account and client fields are usually abbreviations for the full name of the field. These are looked up in the appropriate files, and the full name is displayed. This function is a limited version of the lookup command presented in Chapter 12. It always looks up the first field and returns the second.

```
lookup()
{
    code=$1
    file=$2
    [ -f "$file" ] && {
                tmp=$(grep "^$code$TAB" "$file" | cut -f2)
                [ -n "$tmp" ] && _LOOKUP=${tmp#*$TAB}
        }
}
```

The name of the GL file, GL.YYYY, is derived from the transaction date, using split_date from the date-funcs library introduced in Chapter 8. Blank fields are replaced with a single period.

```
save_transaction()
{
    split_date $tr_date y m d
    GL_file=$GLDIR/GL.$y
    printf "%s\t%s\t%s\t%s\t%s\t%s\t%s\t%s\t%s\n" \
        "${tr_num:-.}" "${acct:-.}"      "${tr_date:-.}" "${amount:-.}" \
        "${client:-.}" "${details:-.}" "${e_date:-.}"  "${action:-.}" \
        >> $GL_file
    tr_init
}
```

The user's input is read by sh_read. The function can be called with an argument as the variable to store the input, but in this script it is normally called without any argument, and the value is stored in $_SH_READ. If the function returns successfully, then an entry has been made, and it can be assigned to the proper variable, with some massaging if necessary.

If the shell is bash (version 2 or later), then the contents of the file named in $HF are read into the history buffer, and may be accessed with the up and down arrows and edited, just as at the command line.

```
sh_read()
{
    printat $info_line 1 "$cles$RV"
    printf "        $B%s$NA" "$info_data"
    info_data=
    printat $entry_line 1 "$cle"
    [ -t 0 ] && stty echo
    case $BASH_VERSION in
        ## If this is bash, take advantage of history and command-line editing
        [2-9]*|[[0-9][0-9]*)
                    history -c      ## clear history
                    history -r $HF  ## load history
                    printf "$B"     ## print bold
                    read -ep "      $prompt" _SH_READ
                    printf "$UB"     ## remove bold
                    ;;
        *) ## display $prompt and read input from user
            printf "        $UB%s$B" "$prompt" >&2
            read -r _SH_READ
            ;;
    esac
```

```
    ## If a variable was named on the command line, assign entry to it
    [ -n "$1" ] && eval "$1='$_SH_READ'"

    ## Fail if nothing has been entered
    [ -n "$_SH_READ" ]
}
```

When entering a dollar amount, the history buffer contains all the values that have been previously entered into the ledger. These are sorted by frequency, so that the most often used value will be the first one that appears when the up arrow is pressed. This sorting is done by

```
sort_amounts()
{
    grep '.' "$HF.all" |          ## Extract all nonblank lines from history file
     sort |                       ## Sort amounts
      uniq -c |                   ## Count number of instances of each amount
       sort -n |                  ## Sort numerically by number of instances
        awk '{print $2}' > "$HF"  ## Remove counts, and store in history file
}
```

The gle_init function is run before the main loop is entered. It initializes the date variables, decides whether to use the real ledger or the test version, and builds the amounts and actions files from the existing ledger.

```
gle_init()
{
    date_vars

    ## If the -t option is given, or the program is called with the -sh extension,
    ## use the test ledger file, not the real one
    case $1 in
        -t) testing=1 ;;
        *)
            case $progname in
                *-sh) testing=1 ;;
                *) testing= ;;
            esac
            ;;
    esac
    ## Directory to store General Ledger
    if [ -n "$testing" ]
    then
      GLDIR=$HOME/.testing
    else
      GLDIR=$HOME/books
    fi

    ## Store most-used amounts in $GLDIR/amounts.all
    ## for use with bash history
    awk -F "\t" '{ printf "%.2f\n", $4 / 100 }
                ' $GLDIR/GL.$YEAR > "$GLDIR/amounts.all"
```

```
    ## Store actions for use with bash history
    cut -f8 $GLDIR/GL.$YEAR | sort | uniq -c | sort -n |
        awk "{ print $2 }" > actions
}
```

New records are built with the next transaction number and the current date as the entry date.

```
tr_init()
{
    date_vars ## Initialize date and time variables

    [ -d "$GLDIR" ] || {
        ## Try to create directory if it doesn't exist
        mkdir -p "$GLDIR"
        [ -d "$GLDIR" ] || die 5 "Could not create $GLDIR"
    }

    acct=         ## Account
    acct_name=    ## Look up $acct in $GLDIR/accounts file
    tr_date=      ## Date of transaction
    amount=       ## Amount in cents (12345, for $123.45)
    client=       ## Usually an abbreviation...
    client_name= ## ...which can be looked up in $GLDIR/clients file
    details=      ## Details of transaction
    e_date=$DATE ## Date of entry (today's date)
    action=       ## E.g., e-mailed invoice, received check, etc.
    HF=           ## History file for use with bash

    ## Transaction number is incremented from last number in file
    tr_num=$(( $(cut -f1 ~/books/GL* | sort -r | head -1) + 1 ))
}
```

An EXIT trap, set in standard-funcs, calls the cleanup function. This script redefines that function so that it checks whether the current record has been modified. If it has, the user is asked whether to save or discard it.

```
cleanup()
{
    is_changed && query_save
    [ -t o ] && {
        [ -n "$_STTY" ] && stty $_STTY
        stty sane
    }
    printf "\r$cles"
    exit
}
```

After all the functions have been defined, the main function is called.

```
main "$@"
```

Summary

The bookkeeping needs discussed are small, and the general ledger system described in this chapter is simple for both data entry and reporting. The latter is often done with a one-off script. If you need to expand the database, adding more fields means less than a dozen lines of additional code.

Both scripts will run in any POSIX shell, but they are enhanced when interpreted by bash2+.

CHAPTER 15

■ ■ ■

Random Acts of Scripting

The generation of random numbers is too important to be left to chance.

—Robert R. Coveyou, Oak Ridge National Laboratory

Although it may often seem otherwise, computers are very predictable; they do exactly what they are told (i.e., programmed) to do. Randomness is the antithesis of predictability, and this makes the generation of random number by a computer problematic.

There are two general methods used by computers to generate random numbers: hardware and software. A hardware generator may be a dedicated device, noise from device drivers, or some other source. The software method uses a pseudo-random number generator (PRNG), so called because a mathematical formula produces the numbers. The random numbers generated in this chapter use the second method, a PRNG, which is built into either the shell or awk. This generator uses the last number produced to calculate the next one, unless a new seed is given.

If you toss a coin 92 times, you don't expect it to come up heads every time, but it would be a perfectly reasonable random sequence, and certainly unpredictable. If you roll a die six times, you don't expect each number to come up exactly once, but the more times you roll, the closer the result should be to an even distribution across all the possible values. The PRNGs in modern shells, as well as that in awk, produce very good random sequences that can be used for all but the most exacting tasks.

This chapter presents functions for generating one or more random numbers across a given range, and scripts that take advantage of them.

The rand-funcs Library

Some shells have a $RANDOM variable that returns a different random number between 0 and 32,767 inclusive each time it is referenced. Since this variable is not required by the POSIX standard, there are shells within the scope of this book that do not include it. To write scripts that are portable, yet take advantage of the variable when it exists, was the random function written. If $RANDOM produces random numbers, then the function is defined to use it. Otherwise, random numbers are generated by awk.

Two functions that make use of random, toss and randstr, are also included in the library.

15.1 random—Return One or More Random Integers in a Given Range

When you want a random number, you usually want more than one, and usually want them in a certain range. For example, if you want to simulate rolling a pair of dice, you would need two numbers each between 1 and 6 inclusive. If you want five cards from a deck of cards, you will need five numbers from 1 to 52.

297

How It Works

If the shell does generate a new random number each time the variable $RANDOM is referenced, then that is used. If not, awk's rand() function is called. A test when the library is sourced determines which version to define. The requested number of values is stored in the $_RANDOM variable.

The interface to these functions is the same whether or not your shell has a $RANDOM variable, although two of the options are ignored when it does.

Usage

```
random [OPTIONS]
```

The first four options are used by both versions of the function. They determine the number of values to return, the upper and lower bounds (the defaults are 0 and 32,767), and a seed for the PRNG.

- -l LOWER: Set the lowest possible value to be generated. The default is 0.

  ```
  $ random -l 32765; echo $_RANDOM
  32766
  ```

- -n NUM: The number of values to be generated is defined by NUM. If this option is not given, one value will be returned in $_RANDOM.

  ```
  $ random -n 5; echo $_RANDOM
  10135 173 26521 17731 2589
  ```

- -s SEED: Use SEED as the basis for all following calculations. This is useful for debugging a script, as a seed always generates the same sequence of numbers.

  ```
  $ random -n5 -s49152; echo $_RANDOM
  15058 18347 29836 13746 985
  $ random -n5 -s666; echo $_RANDOM
  7657 12002 28194 4940 3905
  $ random -n5 -s49152; echo $_RANDOM
  15058 18347 29836 13746 985
  ```

- -u UPPER: Set the highest possible value to be generated. When the shell generates $RANDOM, the highest number is (in all the shells I have used) 32,767; this is the default for both versions of random.

  ```
  $ random -n6 -u6; echo $_RANDOM
  6 5 3 2 1 3
  ```

The last two options are ignored when the function is using the shell's $RANDOM variable.

- -b NUM: Set the number of values to store in $_random. By generating as many numbers as you are likely to need on the first call to random, the number of external calls (to awk) is reduced. The default is 200.

  ```
  $ random -rb 18 -u 12; echo $_random
  6 2 11 10 4 11 4 2 12 0 1 11 3 4 11 1 11
  ```

- -r: Remove any numbers stored in $_random. This is used when a different set of parameters is needed—for example, if the stored values are in the range of 1 to 6, and you need numbers between 24 and 36.

```
$ random -l 24 -u 36 -n 4; echo $_RANDOM
6 2 11 10
```

Because the values from the previous call were still stored in $_random, no new numbers were generated. The -r option wipes out those values:

```
$ random -r -l 24 -u 36 -n 4; echo $_RANDOM
31 28 33 36
```

The Script

If the shell generates random numbers in $RANDOM, the chance of two successive numbers being the same is extremely small, if not nil; it didn't happen in several million tries in three different shells. Therefore, if $RANDOM equals $RANDOM, the function that uses awk will be used.

```
if [ "$RANDOM" = "$RANDOM" ]
then
  random()
  {
    ## Set defaults
    rnd_num=1                 ## Number of values to generate
    rnd_lower=0               ## Lowest value of range
    rnd_upper=32767           ## Highest value of range
    rnd_bank=200              ## Number of values to store
    rnd_seed=                 ## Seed for random number generator
    _N=0
    _RANDOM=

    ## Parse command-line options, if any
    case $* in *?*) rand_opts "$@" || return 5 ;; esac

    set -- $_random ## Use remainder of previously generated numbers

    ## The number to be generated must be as large as the number to be returned
    [ $rnd_bank -lt $rnd_num ] && rnd_bank=$rnd_num
    ## If there are not enough numbers stored (in $_random), generate more
    if [ $# -lt "$rnd_num" ]
    then
      rnd_bank=$(( $rnd_bank - $# ))
      set -- $_random $(echo "" | ${awk:-awk} '
          {
            if (length(seed) > 0) srand(seed)
            else srand()
            while ( n++ < bank )
              printf "%s ", int(rand()*(upper - lower + 1)) + lower
          }' bank=$rnd_bank seed="$rnd_seed" lower=$rnd_lower upper=$rnd_upper)
    fi
```

```
          ## Build $_RANDOM with desired number of numbers
          while [ $_N -lt $rnd_num ]
          do
            _RANDOM="${_RANDOM:+$_RANDOM }$1"
            _N=$(( $_N + 1 ))
            case ${1+X} in X) shift ;; esac
          done

          ## Assign remaining numbers to $_random for reuse
          _random=$*
  }
else
    random()
    {
          ## Set defaults
          rnd_num=1        ## Number of numbers to generate
          rnd_lower=0      ## Lowest number of range
          rnd_upper=32767 ## Highest number of range
          rnd_seed=        ## Seed for random number generator
          _N=0
          _RANDOM=

          ## Parse command-line options, if any
          case $* in *?*) rand_opts "$@" || return 5 ;; esac

          ## Seed random number generator if a seed has been given
          [ -n "$rnd_seed" ] && RANDOM=$rnd_seed

          rnd_mod=$(( $rnd_upper - $rnd_lower + 1 ))
          while [ $_N -lt $rnd_num ]
          do
            _RANDOM="${_RANDOM:+$_RANDOM }$(( $RANDOM % $rnd_mod + $rnd_lower ))"
            _N=$(( $_N + 1 ))
          done
    }
fi
rand_opts()
{
    OPTIND=1
    while getopts b:n:l:u:s:r var
    do
      case $var in
          b) rnd_bank=$OPTARG ;;   ## Number of values to generate
          l) rnd_lower=$OPTARG ;; ## Lower end of range
          n) rnd_num=$OPTARG ;;    ## Number of values to return
          r) _random= ;;          ## Reset
          s) rnd_seed=$OPTARG ;;   ## Seed the random number generator
          u) rnd_upper=$OPTARG ;; ## Highest number to generate
          *) return 5 ;;          ## Invalid option
      esac
    done
}
```

Notes

When using random in a shell without its own PRNG, the function will continue to use previously generated values unless $_random is emptied (manually, or with the -r option), or the "bank" is never set larger than the number of values to be returned.

15.2 toss—Simulate Tossing a Coin

To simulate tossing a coin, you want a function that succeeds half the time, and fails the other half, so that you can base further action on its return code.

How It Works

Since tossing a coin is a random action with one of two possible results, the random function with a lower bound of 0 and an upper bound of 1 will do the trick.

Usage

```
toss [NUM]
```

The optional number, NUM, is how many tosses to perform. The return value is determined by the first number, and the entire throw is stored in $_RANDOM:

```
$ toss 12; echo $_RANDOM
0 1 0 0 1 1 0 1 1 0 1 0
```

A more common use is to test a single flip:

```
$ toss && echo HEADS || echo TAILS
HEADS
$ toss && echo HEADS || echo TAILS
TAILS
$ toss && echo HEADS || echo TAILS
TAILS
```

The Script

This function saves and removes any previously stored values, sets the range of number to 0 and 1, and, after restoring any existing values, tests the result.

```
toss()
{
    _toss=$_random              ## Save any previously generated values
    random -r -l0 -u1 ${1:+-n $1}   ## Toss
    _random=$_toss              ## Restore previous values
    [ ${_RANDOM%% *} -eq 1 ]    ## Test
}
```

15.3 randstr—Select a String at Random

To create a random word, whether for a password, a temporary filename, or any other purpose, you need a script that will select one letter or word from a list of several.

How It Works

Using the positional parameters as an array, a random number from 1 to the number of parameters is used to select one of them.

Usage

```
_randstr STR STR ...    ## Result in $_RANDSTR
randstr STR STR ...     ## Result is printed
```

This function can be used to choose a month at random:

```
$ randstr Jan Feb Mar Apr May Jun Jul Aug Sep Oct Nov Dec
Mar
```

It can also be used to build a random word:

```
$ word= _random=
$ for l in 1 2 3 4 5 6 7
do
  _randstr a b c d e f g h i j k l m n o p q r s t u v w x y z
  word=$word$_RANDSTR
done
$ echo $word
izyqjty
```

The Script

```
_randstr()
{
    random -l 1 -u $#
    eval _RANDSTR=\${$_RANDOM}
}
randstr()
{
    _randstr "$@" && printf "%s" "$_RANDSTR"
}
```

A Random Sampling of Scripts

In the old days, when a Commodore 64 graced my desktop, I wasted many an hour playing some simple, but nonetheless interesting games. I converted three of these to shell scripts: maxit, an arithmetical game where two players select numbers on a grid, one player selecting from the current row, the other from the current column; yahtzee, a dice game that members of the Toronto Free-Net can play online by telnetting to `torfree.net`); and `tic-tac-toe` (which I knew from childhood as Noughts and Crosses). I would have included one of them in this book, but my editor would have had a fit: they range from 500 to 1,000 lines. Instead, here are a few simpler examples of using the `rand-funcs` library.

15.4 rand-date—Generate Random Dates in ISO Format

When testing some of my scripts, I needed a method of generating a lot of random dates. For some scripts, I needed to be able to give a range of years.

How It Works

Since each date required random numbers in three different ranges, rather than using the `random` function to constrain the numbers, the script generates three numbers for each date and performs the modulus operation on each one itself.

Usage

```
rand-date [-n NUM] [-y YEAR] [-Y YEAR]
```

The `-n` option indicates the number of dates to generate, and the `-y` and `-Y` options set the first and last years of the range to include. The default is a single date in the range 1900 to 2100:

```
$ rand-date
1908-11-02
```

The next example produces three dates between 2000 and 2005 inclusive:

```
$ rand-date -n3 -y2000 -Y2005
2003-05-26
2002-04-08
2001-02-06
```

The Script

```
## Load functions
. standard-funcs ## For is_num and other functions
. rand-funcs

## Defaults
n=1
first_year=1900
last_year=2100

## parse command-line options
opts=n:y:Y:
while getopts $opts opt
do
  case $opt in
     n) is_num $OPTARG || exit 5
```

```
            n=$OPTARG
            ;;
      y) is_num $OPTARG || exit 5
         first_year=$OPTARG
            ;;
      Y) is_num $OPTARG || exit 5
         last_year=$OPTARG
            ;;
      *) exit 5 ;;
  esac
done
shift $(( $OPTIND - 1 ))

## Calculate the modulus for the year
rd_mod=$(( $last_year - $first_year + 1 ))

## Generate each date
while [ $n -gt 0 ]
do
  random -rn3      ## Get 3 numbers in the range 0 to 32767
  set -- $_RANDOM  ## Place them in the positional parameters

  ## Calculate year and month
  year=$(( $1 % ${rd_mod#-} + $first_year ))
  month=$(( $2 % 12 + 1 ))

  ## Find maximum number of days in month
  ## (leap years are not acknowledged; see Notes)
  set 31 28 31 30 31 30 31 31 30 31 30 31
  eval max=\${$month}

  ## Calculate day of month
  day=$(( $3 % $max + 1 ))

  ## Print date in ISO format
  printf "%d-%02d-%02d\n" $year $month $day

  ## Count down to 0
  n=$(( $n - 1 ))
done
```

Notes

For my purposes, the exclusion of February 29 was not important. If you want to use this script and include February 29 in leap years, source date-funcs (from Chapter 8) at the beginning of the script, and use these lines to place the number of days in the month in max:

```
_days_in_month $month $year
max=$_DAYS_IN_MONTH
```

15.5 randsort—Print Lines in Random Order

The order of chess players on a round-robin tournament table (a chart that shows who plays whom in which round) is chosen at random. A script to randomize the names could also be used to deal or shuffle a deck of cards, or set the order in which to ask a round of trivia questions.

How It Works

The list to be randomized is given to randsort one to a line. By putting a random number at the beginning of each line and sorting on that, the original lines, whether from a file or standard input, will be in random order once those numbers are removed.

Usage

```
randsort [FILE ...]
```

The randsort script takes no options, and reads the standard input if no files are given on the command line. Here, the world's top ten chess players are shuffled randomly for a tournament pairings table:

```
$ names='Kasparov Anand Topalov Kramnik Leko
         Morozevich Adams Svidler Bacrot Shirov'
$ printf "%s\n" $names | randsort
Adams
Topalov
Svidler
Anand
Morozevich
Kramnik
Shirov
Kasparov
Leko
Bacrot
```

In the next example, a deck of cards generated by the brace expansion found in some shells (e.g., bash2+ and ksh93) is dealt to four bridge players:

```
$ {
printf "\t %-11s\t %-11s\t %-11s\t %-11s\n" West North East South
printf "\t%s %-9s\t%s %-9s\t%s %-9s\t%s %-9s\n" $(
    printf "%s\n" \
    {1,2,3,4,5,6,7,8,9,J,Q,K,A}\ {Hearts,Spades,Diamonds,Clubs} |
    rndsort)
}
```

	West		North		East		South
7	Diamonds	7	Spades	2	Clubs	9	Spades
7	Hearts	2	Spades	J	Hearts	K	Clubs
6	Clubs	5	Diamonds	K	Hearts	1	Diamonds
A	Spades	4	Hearts	Q	Spades	3	Diamonds
4	Diamonds	Q	Diamonds	8	Hearts	5	Hearts
A	Hearts	6	Diamonds	1	Spades	9	Hearts
Q	Hearts	6	Hearts	A	Diamonds	9	Diamonds

8 Diamonds	5 Clubs	5 Spades	7 Clubs
3 Hearts	K Spades	4 Spades	J Clubs
A Clubs	J Diamonds	6 Spades	K Diamonds
4 Clubs	J Spades	1 Clubs	9 Clubs
2 Diamonds	3 Clubs	8 Clubs	2 Hearts
3 Spades	1 Hearts	8 Spades	Q Clubs

The Script

```
awk '## Seed the random number generator
    BEGIN { srand() }

    ## Put a random number in front of each line
    { printf "%.0f\t%s\n", rand() * 99999, $0 }' "$@" |
        sort -n | ## Sort the lines numerically
        cut -f2- ## Remove the random numbers
```

15.6 randomword—Generate Random Words According to Format Specifications

The generation of a random series of letters can easily be done with the randstr function from the rand-funcs library presented earlier in this chapter; an example is given in the "Usage" section. Sometimes I want a word that is a little more like a word, perhaps using a certain set of letters, or letters and punctuation. These words may be useful as passwords or temporary filenames.

How It Works

The randomword script lets the user select the number of words, the characters or character classes to be included in the words, and a single length or range of lengths. This version requires a shell that generates its own random numbers, but as there are only two places where $RANDOM is used, it would be a simple task to convert it to using the random function from rand-funcs. I'll leave that as an exercise for you, the reader, if you feel so inclined.

Usage

```
randomword [OPTIONS]
```

The unadorned command randomword prints one word containing letters, numbers, and punctuation marks, six to eight characters long:

```
$ randomword
J11}X%
```

The -n option specifies the number of words to print, and the -l option specifies the length of the words, either as an absolute value or a range, for example, to produce three words of five letters:

```
$ randomword -n3 -l5
NLnnK
nr8Ie
OiiiQ
```

Five words of from 5 to 12 characters can be generated with

```
$ randomword -n5 -l5,12
3U)uLIA
eUvZV
US70o1
KIAvBl
a?i6Jcmi
```

A list of allowable characters can be specified by class with the -a option. Characters that do not match a class are taken literally. The character classes are

- c: Lowercase consonants

- C: Uppercase consonants

- d: Digits, 0 to 9

- l: Lowercase letters, a to z

- p: Punctuation marks

- P: POSIX portable filename punctuation (period, hyphen, and underscore)

- u: Uppercase letters, A to Z

- v: Lowercase vowels

- V: Uppercase vowels

The following prints two words (-n2, using only uppercase consonants -a C):

```
$ randomword -n2 -a C
YHBNJXX
LVTPVL
```

The next command prints two words using numbers (d), lowercase consonants (c), and uppercase vowels (V):

```
$ randomword -n2 -a dcV
j3q800
2UUA4IOr
```

The -f option accepts a specific format string; the words will follow the format exactly. Here, the format is an uppercase vowel, followed by a consonant, vowel, and another consonant, all in lowercase:

```
$ randomword -n2 -f Vcvc
Igup
Agif
```

Anne McCaffrey could have produced names for her dragon riders of Pern with this command:

```
$ randomword -n6 -f "C'cvc"
H'noc
D'lug
Y'zad
```

```
C'rar
G'zig
B'cuz
```

The -f option takes a number specifying the length of a format string that will be generated randomly. All words will use the same format:

```
$ randomword -n4 -F 7
CM@t)oI
WO=r?uO
GB)l}dA
XJ(d>cI
```

The Script

Very similar to _randstr in the rand-funcs library, _randletter defaults to selecting a random letter (selected from both upper- and lowercase) or digit, storing the character in $_RANDLETTER.

```
_randletter() {
    [ -z "$1" ] && set -- $upper $lower $digits
    eval "_RANDLETTER=\${$(( $RANDOM % $# + 1 ))}"
}
```

The character set passed to _randletter needs to be separated by spaces. When the -a option is used to select a character set, interspace is called to insert spaces between letters if they are not already there.

```
interspace()
{
    echo $* | sed 's/./& /g'
}
```

_randword generates a random word (of length $rw_len) from the characters in $charset; this word is used as a format string by _rand_word when none is supplied.

```
_randword()
{
    rw_len=${1:-8}                      ## Default to 8 characters
    _RANDWORD=                          ## Clear the variable
    ## Build the string with characters chosen by _randletter
    while [ ${#_RANDWORD} -lt $rw_len ]
    do
      _randletter ${charset:-$upper$lower$digits}
      _RANDWORD=$_RANDWORD$_RANDLETTER
    done
}
```

The workhorse of this script is _rand_word, which selects the character set for each letter in the word based on the characters in the format string, $fmt, which may be set with the -f command-line option.

```
_rand_word()
{
    ## Create format string if not specified
    [ -z "$fmt" ] && charset=$format _randword ${1:-8}
    rp_fmt=${fmt:-$_RANDWORD}
    _RAND_WORD=
    set -f ## Disable filename expansion
    while [ ${#rp_fmt} -gt 0 ]
    do
      rp_=${rp_fmt#?} ## Remove first character from format string
      rp_char=${rp_fmt%"$rp_"} ## Get first character of format string
      case $rp_char in ## Get random letter from appropriate char. set
          c) _randletter $consonants ;; ## Lowercase consonants
          d) _randletter $digits ;; ## Digits, 0 to 9
          l) _randletter $lower ;; ## Lowercase letters, a..z
          p) _randletter $punct ;; ## Punctuation marks
          P) _randletter $ppunct ;; ## Portable filename punct.
          u) _randletter $upper ;; ## Uppercase letters, A..Z
          v) _randletter $vowels ;; ## Lowercase vowels
          C) _randletter $CONSONANTS ;; ## Uppercase consonants
          V) _randletter $VOWELS ;; ## Uppercase vowels
        ## Use the next character literally, not as a class designation
          \\) rp_fmt=$rp_
              rp_=${rp_fmt#?}
              rp_char=${rp_fmt%"$rp_"}
              _RANDLETTER=$rp_char
              ;;
        *) _RANDLETTER=${rp_fmt%"$rp_"} ## Use the literal character
              ;;
      esac
      _RAND_WORD=$_RAND_WORD$_RANDLETTER ## Build word
      rp_fmt=$rp_ ## Reset format string without first character
    done
    set +f ## Turn filename expansion back on
}
rand_word()
{
    _rand_word "$@" && printf "%s\n" "$_RAND_WORD"
}
```

Several different subsets of the alphabet are provided to make producing somewhat realistic words possible. If you wanted to go further, you could subdivide the consonants into phonetic types, such as labials, sibilants, and fricatives.

```
lower='a b c d e f g h i j k l m n o p q r s t u v w x y z '
upper='A B C D E F G H I J K L M N O P Q R S T U V W X Y Z '
digits='0 1 2 3 4 5 6 7 8 9 '
punct='% # ! @ ? > } | \ = - _ ) ( + * & ^ $ <'
```

```
ppunct=' . - _ '
format='u l d u l p ' ## Superseded below; kept just in case.

## These are to help make plausible words
vowels='a e i o u '
consonants='b c d f g h j k l m n p q r s t v w x y z '
VOWELS='A E I O U '
CONSONANTS='B C D F G H J K L M N P Q R S T V W X Y Z '
format='u l d u l p v c V C ' ## Characters for format string

## Defaults
fmt=                        ## Format string
num=1                       ## Number of words to generate
length=                     ## Length of word
len_lower=6                 ## Lower range for length of word
len_upper=9                 ## Upper range for length of word
charset=$lower_$upper_$digits_$punct ## Default characters

## Parse command-line options
opts=n:f:F:l:a:
while getopts "$opts" opt
do
  case $opt in
      ## classes of characters allowed
      a) case $OPTARG in
             *[!\ \ ][!\ \ ]*) format=$(interspace $OPTARG) ;;
             *) format=$OPTARG ;;
         esac
         ;;

      ## -l LL,UU lower and upper no. of characters
      l) len_lower=${OPTARG%[!0-9]*}
         case $len_lower in *[!0-9]*) exit 5 ;; esac
         len_upper=${OPTARG#*[!0-9]}
         case $len_upper in *[!0-9]*) exit 5 ;; esac
         [ $len_lower -gt $len_upper ] && {
             len_lower=$len_upper
             len_upper=${OPTARG%[!0-9]*}
         }
         ;;
      ## number of words to generate
      n) case $OPTARG in *[!0-9]*) exit 5 ;; esac
         num=$OPTARG ;;

      ## format string, e.g., -f ucClvVdpp
      f) fmt=$OPTARG ;;

      ## All words use same (random) format string of the given length
      F) case $OPTARG in *[!0-9]*) exit 5 ;; esac
         charset=$format _randword $OPTARG
         fmt=$_RANDWORD
         ;;
```

310

```
  esac
done

## Generate requested number of words
while [ $num -gt 0 ]
do
  [ $len_upper = $len_lower ] &&
        length=$len_upper ||
        length=$(( $RANDOM % ($len_upper - $len_lower) + $len_lower ))
  rand_word $length
  num=$(( $num - 1 ))
done
```

15.7 dice—Roll a Set of Dice

For several games, I needed to print dice on the screen at specific locations. These may be standard, six-sided dice, or they may have more (or fewer) sides. The number of dice that need to be shown will also vary, from one to six or more.

How It Works

Using screen-manipulation functions and variables from Chapter 12, a block can be placed anywhere on the screen, using any available colors. The random function, from the rand-funcs library at the beginning of this chapter, supplies the necessary number of rolls. The dice are available with up to 15 sides, though they are inaccurately displayed as if a cube had that many faces.

This script may be used on its own and used in place of physical dice, but it is more a demonstration of how to incorporate dice into larger scripts.

Usage

dice [OPTIONS]

This script is controlled by four options, all of which take arguments. They are -b for the background color of the dice, -f for the foreground color (the dots), -n for the number of dice, and -s for the number of sides on the dice.

For the game of Yahtzee, five standard dice are used, as shown in Figure 18-1.

```
$ dice -n 5 -s 6 -b black -f white
```

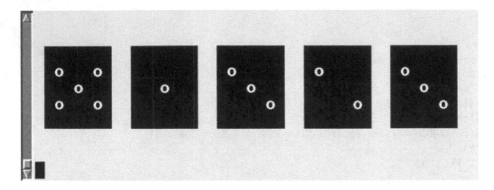

Figure 18-1. *A roll of five dice*

The Script

The dice are defined using variables and functions from screen-funcs and screen-vars in Chapter 12, allowing any die to be placed anywhere on the screen.

```
define_dice()
{
    ## requires screen-vars: $cu_save $cu_restore $cu_d1 $NA
    ## optional $ds, the character to use for the spots
    ## provides variables d_w, dice{1..15}.
    ds=${ds:-o}              ## The character used for the spots
    ds2=$ds$ds              ## Two spots
    ds3=$ds$ds$ds           ## Three spots
    ds3x="$ds $ds $ds"      ## Three spots with spaces
    ds4=$ds$ds$ds$ds        ## Four spots
    ds5=$ds$ds$ds$ds$ds     ## Five spots
    d_w=5                   ## Width, in characters, to allow for spots

    ## Each die comprises 5 rows, the first and last being blank;
    ## the $d_fmt string contains the code to save the cursor position,
    ## print a row, restore the previous cursor position,
    ## and move down one line
    d_fmt="$B$cu_save %-$d_w.${d_w}s $cu_restore$cu_d1"

    ## Each die, from 1 to 15 is stored in its own variable
    dice1=$( printf "$d_fmt" "" ""          "  $ds"     ""           "")
    dice2=$( printf "$d_fmt" "" "$ds"       ""          "     $ds" "")
    dice3=$( printf "$d_fmt" "" "$ds"       "  $ds"     "     $ds" "")
    dice4=$( printf "$d_fmt" "" "$ds  $ds"  ""          "$ds  $ds" "")
    dice5=$( printf "$d_fmt" "" "$ds  $ds"  "  $ds"     "$ds  $ds" "")
    dice6=$( printf "$d_fmt" "" "$ds3x"     ""          "$ds3x"    "")
    dice7=$( printf "$d_fmt" "" "$ds3x"     "  $ds"     "$ds3x"    "")
    dice8=$( printf "$d_fmt" "" "$ds3x"     " $ds $ds"  "$ds3x"    "")
    dice9=$( printf "$d_fmt" "" "$ds3x"     "$ds3x"     "$ds3x"    "")
    dice10=$(printf "$d_fmt" "" "$ds3x"     "$ds2 $ds2" "$ds3x"    "")
    dice11=$(printf "$d_fmt" "" "$ds3 $ds"  "$ds3x "    "$ds $ds3" "")
    dice12=$(printf "$d_fmt" "" "$ds3 $ds"  "$ds2 $ds2" "$ds $ds3" "")
```

```
    dice13=$(printf "$d_fmt" "" "$ds5"          "$ds3x"      "$ds5"        "")
    dice14=$(printf "$d_fmt" "" "$ds5"          "$ds3 $ds"   "$ds5"        "")
    dice15=$(printf "$d_fmt" "" "$ds5"          "$ds5"       "$ds5"        "")
    dice_defined=1
    export dice1 dice2 dice3 dice4 dice5 dice6 dice7 dice8 dice9
    export dice10 dice11 dice12 dice13 dice14 dice15 dice_defined d_w
}
```

The show_die function prints a die at the specified point on the screen, using the defined colors.

```
show_die()
{
    ## First 2 arguments are row and column
    ## Third argument is number on face of die
    ## Requires screen functions printat, set_fgbg
    ## Optional variables: fg and bg (defaults to black and white)
    printat $1 $2
    set_fgbg ${fg:-$white} ${bg:-$black}
    case $dice_defined in "") define_dice ;; esac
    eval "printf \"%s\" \"\$dice$3\"" #>&2
}
```

```
## Clear variables
_random=
dice_defined=
```

```
## Load functions
. rand-funcs
. screen-funcs
```

```
## Defaults
row=3           ## screen row to print dice
sides=6         ## number of sides on dice
bg=$white       ## background color
fg=$black       ## foreground color
num=1           ## default number of dice
## Parse command-line options
while getopts vVhH-:s:n:f:b:c:r:p: var
do
  case $var in
    b) get_colour $OPTARG ## background color
       bg=$colour ;;
    f) get_colour $OPTARG ## foreground color
       fg=$colour ;;
    n) num=$OPTARG ;; ## number of dice
    s) sides=$OPTARG ;; ## number of sides on each die
  esac
done
shift $(( $OPTIND - 1 ))
```

```
## Clear screen to default colors
printf "$NA"
clear

## Generate random numbers for all the dice
random -r -l 1 -u $sides -n $num

## Place dice values in the positional parameters
set -- $_RANDOM

## Print the required number of dice
n=0
while [ $n -lt $num ]
do
  column=$(( $n * ($d_w + 4) + 2 ))
  show_die $row $column $1
  shift
  n=$(( $n + 1 ))
done
printf "$NA\n\n"
```

15.8 throw—Throw a Pair of Dice

When you don't need the image of the dice, just the number, you can write a script for the specific situation. One of the most common requirements is for one or more throws of a pair of six-sided dice.

How It Works

Throwing two six-sided dice is not the same as throwing one twelve-sided die. First, the range with a twelve-sided die is one to twelve; with two six-sided dice, it is two to twelve. Second, the distribution of numbers is different. With a twelve-sided die, each number has an equal chance of being thrown, whereas there is only one possible combination of two dice for each of 2 and 12 (1-1 and 6-6), and six combinations for 7 (3-4, 4-3, 5-2, 2-5, 6-1, and 1-6), making it the most likely number to be thrown. The script therefore uses two random numbers for each throw and adds their values.

Usage

```
throw [NUM]
```

By default, one throw is made, but that can be changed by putting a number on the command line:

```
$ throw 5
5
11
7
7
4
```

The Script

```
. rand-funcs      ## Load random functions

sides=6           ## Number of sides on the dice
sep='\n'          ## String to place between numbers
num=${1:-1}       ## Default to 1 throw if no number on command line

## Generate all the random numbers
random -r -l 1 -u $sides -n $(( $num * 2 ))

## Place numbers in the positional parameters
set -- $_RANDOM

while [ $# -gt 0 ]
do
  printf "%s$sep" $(( $1 + $2 ))   ## Print sum of first two numbers
  shift 2                          ## Remove two numbers
done
```

Summary

The mathematical literature contains a wealth of information and discussion on random numbers. Much of it explains why this method or that method is not good enough to generate truly random numbers. Some papers reject pseudo-random number generators altogether; others allow that they have their uses.

For practical purposes, however, PRNGs are adequate in the majority of cases, and certainly for anything one is likely to do in a shell script. The scripts in this chapter presented methods of generating and manipulating random numbers as well as some applications for them.

They will serve you well for day-to-day use, but please don't use them for encrypting national secrets!

CHAPTER 16

■ ■ ■

A Smorgasbord of Scripts

The scripts in this section are varied. Many are responses to questions in Usenet newsgroups, and may solve a very narrow problem. Some are valid for some operating systems but not others. Some scripts use commands that are not always installed (though they are generally available for Unix systems).

It is often easier to write a script for a specific situation than to write a general solution that can be used in many places. While the latter is more efficient, and should be attempted whenever feasible, one shouldn't rule out the one-time script. Peter Seebach says it well:

> *A good rule of thumb is to start thinking about the design of a utility the second time you have to solve a problem. Don't mourn the one-off hack you write the first time; think of it as a prototype. The second time, compare what you need to do with what you needed to do the first time. Around the third time, you should start thinking about taking the time to write a general utility.*[1]

The first script, `topntail`, went from a one-off one-liner to a general-purpose utility in a matter of hours, with three people contributing to it.

16.1 topntail—Remove Top and Bottom Lines from a File

After saving a report from an application, a poster to the `comp.unix.shell` newsgroup wanted to remove the header and footer (the first three lines and the last three lines) from the file. He knew he could remove the first three lines by using `sed '1,3d'`, but didn't know how to delete the last three.

How It Works

The first three lines can be removed by using `sed` or `tail`, and the GNU utility `tac` (that's `cat` backward) could be used. After the first three lines are removed with `tail`, the output is piped to `tac`, which reverses the order of the lines. This is then piped to `tail` to remove the first three lines (which were formerly the last three), and finally through `tac` again to put the file back in the correct order. This is not a very elegant solution, but for a one-time script, it is acceptable.

```
tail +4 FILE | tac | tail +4 | tac
```

---

[1]"The Art of Writing Linux Utilities," http://www-106.ibm.com/developerworks/library/l-util.html?ca

Another solution would be to count the lines in the file by using wc, and use head to remove the lines from the bottom and tail to remove them from the top:

```
head -$(( `wc -l < FILE` - 3 )) FILE | tail +4
```

I was pondering a prettier solution using awk when Bill Marcum, one of the regulars in the newsgroup, posted his solution:

```
awk 'NR>6{print last3[NR%3]} {last3[NR%3]=$0}'
```

A little later, Janis Papanagnou posted a generalized version of Marcum's script that allowed any number of lines to be deleted:

```
awk -v f=${1:?} -v r=${2:?} 'NR>f+r {print buf[NR%r]} {buf[NR%r]=$0}'
```

With the hard work already done, the script was packaged with command-line options for the number of lines to be removed, and a conditional that uses sed when no lines are to be removed from the tail (without it, there would be a "division by zero" error). The script also checks that arguments to the options are valid, i.e., that they are positive integers.

Usage

```
topntail [-b N][-e N] [FILE ...]
```

By default, topntail removes one line from the top and one line from the bottom of a file. The -b and -e options change the number of lines to remove from the top and bottom, respectively. If no FILE is given, topntail reads from the standard input.

```
$ printf "%s\n" alpha beta gamma delta | topntail
beta
gamma
```

To remove lines only from the bottom of a file, use -b0:

```
$ printf "%s\n" 1 2 3 4 5 6 7 | topntail -b0 -e4
1
2
3
```

The Script

```
b=1 ## No. of lines to remove from beginning
e=1 ## No. of lines to remove from end

## Parse command-line options
while getopts b:e: opt
do
  case $opt in
     b) b=$OPTARG ;;   ## Number of lines to remove from beginning
     e) e=$OPTARG ;;   ## Number of lines to remove from end
  esac
```

```
done
shift $(( $OPTIND - 1 ))
case $b$e in    ## check for non-numeric characters in $b and $e
    *[!0-9]*) exit 5 ;;
esac

if [ $e -eq 0 ]
then
  sed "1,${b}d" "$@" ## just remove from the top
else
  ## The buf[] array is a rotating buffer which contains the last N lines
  ## where N is the number of lines to be removed from the bottom of the file
  ## Printing starts when the line number is equal to the sum of the number
  ## of lines to be removed from top and bottom, and continues to the end
  ## of the file; the earliest line in the buffer is printed.
  ## The last N lines will not be printed.
  awk 'NR > b + e { print buf[ NR % e ] }
                  { buf[ NR % e ] = $0 }' b=$b e=$e "$@"
fi
```

16.2 flocate—Locate Files by Filename Alone

The traditional tool for finding a file by name on a Unix system is find. Unfortunately, it is very slow when searching a large file system. To mitigate this, a database, regularly updated by a cron job, is often used to store all the files on the system, and a command is provided to search the database.

The most common system in current use is locate (which may be a link to slocate). This command searches a database for a string, a file-globbing pattern, or a regular expression. When a string is used, locate will find that string anywhere in the full path to the file. In other words, locate bash will return /usr/share/man/man1/bash.1.bz2 and /home/chris/.bashrc as well as /bin/bash (and probably a lot of other files as well).

How does one locate a file without getting all of the file paths that contain the name?

How It Works

If a search pattern contains an unescaped wildcard character (* or ?), then the pattern must match the entire path to a file. By putting an asterisk at the beginning of the pattern, the pattern on the command line must match the end of a pathname; in other words, it must match the filename.

Usage

```
flocate FILENAME
```

If FILENAME contains a slash, the pattern preceding it must match the entire name of a directory for it to be displayed. For example, this would find executables named cut:

```
$ flocate bin/cut
/usr/bin/cut
/bin/cut
```

The Script

```
locate "*/$1"
```

16.3 sus—Display a POSIX Man Page

Since you might want to use your scripts on various systems, consider using portable options with Unix commands. While not infallible, the POSIX standard (which has been merged with SUS) gives a good indication of what one can expect in most implementations of Unix commands. The man pages for POSIX commands are available on the Open Group web site.[2] Rather than remembering the URL each time, you could have a command to do that for you.

How It Works

The first time you request any particular man page from the Open Group web site, the script saves it to a local directory and uses that on all subsequent requests for that page.

Usage

```
sus [-d] COMMAND
```

Since the pages are marked up with HTML, the logical choice for viewing it is a web browser. From the command line, the logical browser for the script to use is lynx or links. I prefer the former, but feel free to change the script if you prefer the other.

■ **Note**   lynx is not available on Mac OSX by default, you might have to compile it yourself for use.

If the -d option is given, lynx is used to dump the formatted text of the page to the screen.

The Script

```
. standard-funcs ## load functions from library in Chapter 1
dump=0

while getopts d opt
do
  case $opt in
      d) dump=1 ;;
  esac
done
shift $(( $OPTIND - 1 ))
```

---

[2]http://www.opengroup.org/onlinepubs/009695399/utilities/contents.html

```
sus_ldir=$HOME/work/sus          ## Directory for storing HTML pages
[ -d "$sus_ldir" ] ||            ## If directory doesn't exist
mkdir -p "$sus_ldir" || exit 3   ## create it
html_file=$sus_ldir/$1.html      ## Path to stored HTML file

## Location of man pages on Open Group web site sus_dir=http://www.opengroup.org/
onlinepubs/007904975/utilities

## If the file doesn't exist locally, download it
[ -f "$html_file" ] || wget -O $html_file $sus_dir/$1.html > /dev/null 2>&1

case $dump in
    1) ## Dump file with lynx
       lynx -dump -nolist $html_file | ${PAGER:-less}
       ;;
    *) ## View file with lynx
       lynx $html_file
       ;;
esac
```

16.4 cwbw—Count Words Beginning With

A poster in the comp.unix.shell newsgroup asked how to count the words beginning with f in a comma-separated list. The is what the list, in a variable $A, contained:

```
A=qad,security,printq,mfgpro,sugroup,f000000m,f000000r,f000000s,m000000r,m000000s
```

How It Works

The script uses printf and a modified $IFS to replace the commas with newlines and pipe the output to grep -c.

Usage

```
cwbw STRING
```

With the preceding string in variable $A, cwbw counts the number of words beginning with f:

```
$ cwbw "$A"
3
```

The Script

```
IFS=,
printf "%s\n" $* | grep -c "^f"
```

Notes

An alternative script uses tr rather than printf to break the string into separate lines:

```
echo "$@" | tr ',' '\012' | grep -c "^f"
```

This one-off script is simple enough to modify to suit changing requirements. If it turns out to be of general use, either version of the script can be modified to allow specification of different separator and search characters on the command line.

16.5 cci—Configure, Compile, and Install from Tarball

Programs downloaded as source code usually come in packages known as *tarballs*, archives created with tar and then compressed with gzip. They usually include a configure script that builds a Makefile. For most of these packages, the process is as follows:

1. Uncompress the tarball with gunzip.

2. Unarchive the resulting file with tar.

3. Change directory to the one created by tar.

4. Run the configure script.

5. Compile the program with make.

6. Install the program, as root, with make install.

Since these steps are the same for the majority of packages, this is a candidate for a script that does it all with a single command.

How It Works

The only complication in writing this script is knowing which directory to cd into after unarchiving the source code. By using tar's verbose mode, the first line output will be the name of the directory. The script uses set to store tar's output in the positional parameters. The name of the directory will be in $1.

Usage

```
cci PACKAGE.tar.gz
```

Some package names end with .tgz instead of .tar.gz. This script will work with either.

The Script

```
gunzip "$1"                     ## Uncompress the file
case $1 in
    *.gz) file=${1%.gz} ;;       ## File will have no extension
    *.tgz) file=${1%.tgz}.tar ;; ## File will have .tar extension
esac
```

```
## Place the path to the extracted files in the positional parameters
set -- $(tar -xvf "$file")
## The first positional parameter will contain the name of the directory,
## so cd into it, and configure and compile the program
cd $1 && ./configure && make && sudo make install
```

Notes

I wrote this script in answer to a question posted on a Linux newsgroup, although I rarely use it myself. Instead, I usually unpack the file at the command line and cd into the directory thus created. Usually, there is a README file with information about the package, and it often contains instructions on how to prepare and compile it:

```
tar xvzf FILE.tgz ## requires GNU tar; otherwise gunzip the file first
cd <name of directory> ## depends on the package
t README          ## 't' is aliased to 'less -egimQrXF'
```

Then, depending on the contents of the README file, you may make a change in a file, or read the INSTALL file, or perform some other actions before doing ./configure && make.

16.6 ipaddr—Find a Computer's Network Address

The Unix systems I use have a command that shows networking information. The command, ifconfig, includes the machine's IP addresses in its output. On my Linux systems, the output looks like this:

```
eth0      Link encap:Ethernet HWaddr 00:07:95:18:89:2F
          inet addr:192.168.0.49 Bcast:192.168.0.255 Mask:255.255.255.0
          inet6 addr: fe80::207:95ff:fe18:892f/64 Scope:Link
          UP BROADCAST RUNNING MULTICAST MTU:1500 Metric:1
          RX packets:478882 errors:3 dropped:0 overruns:0 frame:4
          TX packets:576878 errors:0 dropped:0 overruns:0 carrier:0
          collisions:1513 txqueuelen:1000
          RX bytes:288668489 (275.2 Mb) TX bytes:299036237 (285.1 Mb)
          Interrupt:11 Base address:0xd400

lo        Link encap:Local Loopback
          inet addr:127.0.0.1 Mask:255.0.0.0
          inet6 addr: ::1/128 Scope:Host
          UP LOOPBACK RUNNING MTU:16436 Metric:1
          RX packets:614904 errors:0 dropped:0 overruns:0 frame:0
          TX packets:614904 errors:0 dropped:0 overruns:0 carrier:0
          collisions:0 txqueuelen:0
          RX bytes:97049241 (92.5 Mb) TX bytes:97049241 (92.5 Mb)
```

The output can be limited to a single interface (in this example, either eth0 (IP address 192.168.0.49) or lo (127.0.0.1). Each section contains the machine's IP address for that interface. That address may be the Internet address, or a LAN address, with the Internet address controlled by a network address translation (NAT) gateway.

A common question in the newsgroups is, How do I find the machine's IP address?

How It Works

With the output of `ifconfig` stored in a variable, parameter expansion can extract the IP address. Different systems use different formats, and this script will give results for Linux, FreeBSD, and NetBSD.

Usage

```
ipaddr [-n] [interface]
```

If `ipaddr` is used without any option or argument, it will return the first IP address it finds. If the name of a network interface is given, `ipaddr` returns the first IP address for that interface.

The `-n` option tells the script to find the Internet address, which will not be returned by `ifconfig` if the computer is on a local network behind a NAT. Instead, the script will use `lynx` to get the address from a CGI script (see the next script, `ipaddr.cgi`) on my web site.

The Script

```
if [ "$1" = "-n" ]
then        ## Get the address externally with lynx
  ip=$(lynx -dump http://cfaj.freeshell.org/ipaddr.cgi)
else
  if=$1            ## Name of interface (optional)
  system=$(uname)  ## What system is being used?
  case $system in
      ## Set the string appropriate to the OS
      FreeBSD|NetBSD) sep="inet " ;;
      Linux) sep="addr:" ;;
      *) printf "System %s is not yet supported\n" "$system"
         exit 1
         ;;
  esac
  temp=$(ifconfig $if) ## Get the information
  temp=${temp#*"$sep"} ## Remove everything up to the IP address
  ip=${temp%% *}       ## Remove everything after the IP address
fi

printf "%s\n" "$ip"    ## Print the IP address
```

16.7 ipaddr.cgi—Print the Remote Address of an HTTP Connection

My Internet connection has a dynamic IP address; it can change anytime my service provider wants. How can I find the current network address for my Internet connection?

How It Works

I have a web site on which I can run CGI scripts, and the address of computers that access it is stored in `REMOTE_ADDR`. The `ipaddr.cgi` script prints the contents of that variable (after sending the necessary header).

Usage

The script must be placed in a directory from which the user has permission to run CGI scripts, and the execute bit must be set.

The Script

```
#!/bin/sh
echo "Content-type: text/plain

"
echo "$REMOTE_ADDR"
```

16.8 iprev—Reverse the Order of Digits in an IP Address

From time to time in the Unix or Linux newsgroups, someone has obtained an IP address with the digits reversed (for example, 49.0.168.192 instead of 192.168.0.49) and wants to put them back in the correct order. These *reverse dotted quad* numbers are used by domain name servers for reverse look-ups to find the name of a host given its IP address. (An explanation of how it works can be found at http://howtos.linux.com/guides/nag2/x-087-2-resolv.howdnsworks.shtml.)

How It Works

By changing the field separator (IFS) to a period, set can assign each element of the dotted quad number to a positional variable. All that remains is to print them in the reverse order.

Usage

```
iprev    NN.NN.NN.NN
```

The Script

```
IP=$1              ## The address to be reversed is in the first argument
IFS='.'            ## Set the field separator to a period
set -- $IP         ## Split the address into its components
echo "$4.$3.$2.$1" ## Print the result in the reverse order
```

Notes

Instead of changing IFS, parameter expansion could be used:

```
IP=$1
ab=${IP%.*.*}
cd=${IP#*.*.}
echo "${cd#*.}.${cd%.*}.${ab#*.}.${ab%.*}"
```

16.9 intersperse—Insert a String Between Doubled Characters

A poster on `comp.unix.shell` asked how to convert this string:

```
123 | 456 || abc ||| cdef |||| end
```

into this one:

```
123 | 456 |\N| abc |\N|\N| cdef |\N|\N|\N| end
```

I've had to do similar things to a database file when the utilities have a problem with empty fields and interpret two or more consecutive separator characters as a single separator, rather than boundaries of empty fields. For example, in a file with tab-separated fields, the following record (with literal tab characters instead of ${TAB}) would cause problems in some shell scripts:

```
field=13023${TAB}${TAB}2002-11-03${TAB}20599${TAB}STA
```

After splitting this record with `set`, there are only four fields instead of five. A placeholder must be inserted between consecutive tabs.

How It Works

The poster already had a solution, but wanted a more efficient one. His solution was this:

```
cat some_file | sed 's/|||/|\\N|\\N|/g' | sed 's/||/|\\N|/g'
```

Besides the unnecessary use of `cat` (see Chapter 1), two invocations of `sed` are unnecessary, as `sed` can take multiple commands on the command line. All that is needed is one call to `sed` with two commands (using the `-e` option).

The algorithm can be generalized. For every two consecutive instances of X, insert Y between them, then do it again. This allows any character or string to be given on the command line for either element.

Usage

```
intersperse BOX CONTENTS [FILE ...]
```

The CONTENTS will be placed inside all consecutive instances of the BOX. If no FILE is given, `intersperse` will use the standard input. For example, to insert an underscore in the empty field in the preceding `$field` variable, use this:

```
$ printf "$field" | intersperse "$TAB" "_"
13023    _        2002-11-03      20599$ STA
```

The Script

```
[ $# -lt 2 ] && exit 1       ## Check that there are at least two arguments
box=$1                       ## Enclosing character or string
contents=$2                  ## Character or string to be inserted
shift 2                      ## Remove first two positional parameters

## Two commands are necessary; the first will convert (for example)
## "||||" to "|X||X|", and the second will take care of any remaining doubles
sed -e "s/$box$box/$box$contents$box/g" \
    -e "s/$box$box/$box$contents$box/g" "$@"
```

16.10 ll—Use a Pager for a Directory Listing Only If Necessary

When displaying a list of files in a terminal, you would like to use a pager when the list is longer than a screenful, but only then. If the list is shorter than the number of lines on the screen, you can prefer it to be printed directly. While less is very configurable, you have not been able to get it to do this. The -F option tells less to exit if there is less than one screen, but it prints at the bottom of the screen rather than starting at the current cursor position.

How It Works

The ll script stores the output of ls -l in a variable and counts the lines. If it is more than the number of lines on the screen, it pipes the variable through less; otherwise, it echoes the result to the screen.

Usage

```
ll [OPTIONS] [FILE ...]
```

Since all of its arguments are passed to ls, you may use any options that your version of ls accepts. If you want any options to be used by default, assign them to the ls_opts variable in the script.

The Script

```
IFS='
'
ls_opts=          ## Assign options as default behavior; I use "-lA"
list=$(ls $ls_opts "$@")
set -- $list
if [ $# -lt $LINES ]
then
  printf "%s\n" $list
else
  ## Your version of less may not have all these options, so adjust to taste
  printf "%s\n" $list | ${PAGER:-less -egimQrXF}
fi
```

16.11 name-split—Divide a Person's Full Name into First, Last, and Middle Names

A person's full name may be just first and last names, or it may also contain one or more middle names or initials. When the entire name is in a single variable, a method is needed to split it into its components.

How It Works

If the first and last words are the first and last names respectively, then everything else is the middle name (or names, or initials). The name is split using set, which places the elements of the name in the positional parameters.

Usage

```
name-split
```

The name is read from the standard input. If that is a terminal, the user is prompted for a name:

```
$ name-split
 Enter name: Christopher Frederick Arnold Johnson

   Last name: Johnson
  First name: Christopher
Middle name: Frederick Arnold
```

If either the first or last name contains a space, it must be escaped. Escaping can be done by preceding the space with a backslash:

```
$ name-split
 Enter name: Ralph Vaughan\ Williams
   Last name: Vaughan Williams
 First name: Ralph
Middle name:
```

Alternatively, the entire name may be enclosed in single or double quotes:

```
$ name-split
 Enter name: Alicia "de la Rocha"

   Last name: de la Rocha
 First name: Alicia
Middle name:
```

The Script

```
## Use the bash readline library if it's available
case ${BASH_VERSION%%.*} in
    [2-9]|[0-9][0-9]) read_opt='-rep' ;;
    *) read_opt=-r ;;
esac
```

```
## The prompt will only be displayed if the standard input
## is connected to a terminal; bash does this automatically
## when read's -p option is used; other shells need to test for it
prompt=" Enter name: "
[ -n "$read_opt" ] && read $read_opt "$prompt" name || {
  [ -t 0 ] && printf "%s" "$prompt"
  read $read_opt name
}

set -f                   ## Turn off pathname expansion
eval "set -- $name"      ## Put the name into the positional parameters
first=$1                 ## First name is $1
eval "last=\${$#}"       ## Last name is the last parameter
shift                    ## Remove the first parameter
middle=$*                ## Middle name is what's left, after
middle=${middle% $last}  ## removing the last name

## Adjust output to your own needs
printf "\n Last name: %s\n" "$last"
printf " First name: %s\n" "$first"
printf "Middle name: %s\n" "$middle"
```

16.12 rot13—Encode or Decode Text

By no means a cryptographically sophisticated code, rot13 is intended to make text unintelligible at a glance. It is often used in the Usenet newsgroups to encode the answer to a puzzle so that the answer is not given away immediately, but can still be easily converted to plain text.

How It Works

Most Usenet news readers have rot13 encoding and decoding built in, but for other uses, tr can do the job. Since the code is symmetrical (A becomes M, and M becomes A), the same script both encodes and decodes the text.

Usage

```
tr [FILE ...]
```

If no files are supplied on the command line, rot13 reads the standard input:

```
$ printf "%s\n" "The quick brown fox" | rot13
Gur dhvpx oebja sbk
$ printf "%s\n" "Gur dhvpx oebja sbk" | rot13
The quick brown fox
```

The Script

```
## Ranges of characters are used; [a-m] expands to abcdefghijklm
## and will be replaced by the corresponding character in the range [n-z]
## Each letter in the first half of the alphabet is replaced by
## a letter from the second half, and vice versa.
cat "$@" | tr '[a-m][A-M][n-z][N-Z]' '[n-z][N-Z][a-m][A-M]'
```

Notes

If you prefer to encode the arguments on the command line rather than use the standard input, use this script instead:

```
printf "$*\n" | tr 'a-zA-Z' 'n-za-mN-ZA-M'
```

16.13 showfstab—Show Information from /etc/fstab

In the alt.linux newsgroup, someone suggested a new format for the /etc/fstab file, which tells the mount command how and where to mount disk partitions. Each device entry would be on six lines instead of one line as it is now. Each line would be labeled, and the entries would be separated by a blank line:

```
device /dev/hda1
       mountpoint      /
       type     ext3
       options defaults
       dump     1
       pass     1

device /dev/hda2
       mountpoint      /home
       type     ext3
       options defaults
       dump     1
       pass     2
```

Other people suggested that the difficulty of conversion to and from the new format would be a stumbling block to its adoption. I had no strong feelings about the format either way, but I didn't think the conversion would be hard to program. It occurred to me that the more verbose format would be a good way to view the information in /etc/fstab, so this script exists to view the file in this format.

How It Works

Since it was designed for reformatting its input, awk is the logical tool to use. If the line begins with an octothorpe (#), it is a comment, and it is printed unchanged. Other lines are printed field by field, with the name of the field preceding its value.

Usage

```
showfstab [FILE ...]
```

If no file is supplied on the command line, showfstab uses /etc/fstab.

The Script

```
awk '/#.*/ { print; next }
    { printf "device %s\n", $1
      printf "\tmountpoint\t%s\n", $2
      printf "\ttype\t%s\n", $3
      printf "\toptions\t%s\n", $4
      printf "\tdump\t%s\n", $5
      printf "\tpass\t%s\n\n", $6
    }' "${@:-/etc/fstab}"
```

Notes

Assuming that the fields remain in the same order as they appear in /etc/fstab, the verbose format can be restored to its original terseness with

```
awk '/#.*/ { print; next }
        NF { printf "%s\t", $2; next }
           { print }
'
```

If the lines modified by showfstab are piped through this snippet, the output is suitable for inclusion in etc/fstab:

```
/dev/hda1       /       ext3    defaults        1       1
/dev/hdb7       /data   ext3    defaults        1       2
```

16.14 unique—Remove All Duplicate Lines from a File

All Unix systems have the uniq command, which deletes consecutive identical lines, but there is no standard command to remove duplicate lines without first sorting the file.

How It Works

Associative arrays in awk can remember previous lines and can be used to suppress printing of lines that have already been seen.

Usage

```
unique [FILE ...]
```

One or more files may be supplied on the command line, and the standard input will be used if no file is given:

```
$ printf "%s\n" 1 2 3 2 4 5 4 2 6 | unique
1
2
3
4
5
6
```

The Script

The pattern increments a variable after testing whether the array element whose key is the current line is zero. If it is zero, the line has not been seen before, and the default action for lines that match the pattern, print, is used.

```
awk 'x[$0]++ == 0' ${1+"$@"}
```

Summary

The scripts in this chapter are generally less polished than in the rest of the book, and some work in limited environments. More than in other chapters, the code here is often more interesting than the script itself. All the scripts do solve a problem expressed by someone at one time or another, but some are included mostly because the techniques used can be applied to solving other problems.

■ ■ ■

## CHAPTER 17

Script Development Management

The need for a script development system becomes obvious when you want to modify scripts that are in use on a regular basis by you, other users, or `cron` jobs. You can't afford to have a script fail; that could result in anything from users not being able to access the system, to an invoice not being sent out.

If like the original author you are writing scripts for a couple of operating systems, a development machine for each is out of the question (though you can have the options of VM's and Docker). The solution that he came up with was using three different directories, one for developing the script and one for deploying and one for backing up each version as a new one replaced it. This is a suggestion only; there could be other solutions that might work for you.

The scripts under development have an extension, `-sh` by default, to distinguish them from production versions. The backups are renamed with a numbered extension that is incremented with each successive replacement. The extension is zero-padded, with three digits as the default.

To access the scripts from the terminal, you would also need a configuration file that specifies the directory where to find the scripts. The configuration file is called `script-setup.cfg` and placed in the `$HOME/.config` directory as the other configuration files have been placed throughout this book. The directories are created by the `script-setup` script.

17.1 script-setup—Prepare the Scripting Environment

To set up the directories for a scripting system, the user needs the ability to override the default names. A playwright might already have a directory called `scripts` in his home directory. A user's `bin` directory may be laden with anything but scripts (though if no other files use the `-sh` extension, there may be no conflict).

A setup script needs to present a user with the default directories and file suffixes, and allow them to be changed according to one's wishes.

How It Works

Since a user is not likely to run this script more than once or twice, this is a straightforward traditional shell script with no special formatting. It presents two menus in succession, each offering the user the opportunity to change either the defaults or the current settings.

Usage

```
script-setup
```

The first menu presents the directories. The user may change any or all of them by pressing the appropriate number.

```
==============================================================================
  Directories for Script Development
==============================================================================

  1. Script development: /home/cfaj/scripts
  2.        Installation: /home/cfaj/bin
  3.              Backup: /home/cfaj/scripts/bak
==============================================================================

  Select 1 to 3 to change directory or <ENTER> to accept:
```

The second menu prompts for the suffixes on the three types of file: development, production, and backup. The production scripts have no suffix, and the backups are padded with zeroes: script-setup-001, script-setup-002, and so forth.

```
==============================================================================
  Suffixes
==============================================================================

  1. Development suffix: -sh
  2.    Installed suffix:
  3.       Backup padding: 3

==============================================================================

  Select 1 to 3 to change suffix or <ENTER> to accept:
```

The Script

The contents of $defaults will be written to the user's script-setup.cfg file. By using eval, variables entered by the user will be expanded; in other words, if user enters ~/scripts, or $HOME/scripts, then /home/user/scripts will be placed in the file.

```
set_defaults()
{
    defaults="
## Directory for development copy of script
ScriptDir=${ScriptDir:-$HOME/scripts}

## Directory for production copy of script
InstalDir=${InstalDir:-$HOME/bin}
```

```
## Directory for old versions of script
BackupDir=${BackupDir:-$HOME/scripts/bak}

## Directory for configuration files
ConfigDir=${ConfigDir:-$HOME/.config}

## Suffix for development version of script
devel_suffix=-sh

## Suffix for production version of script (by default, none)
bin_suffix=

## Backup suffixes will be padded with zeroes to $VERSION_WIDTH
VERSION_WIDTH=3

## Verbose sets level of progress and error reporting
verbose=0

## Copyright statement
copyright_blurb='
    This is free software, released under the terms of the GNU General
    Public License. There is NO warranty; not even for MERCHANTABILITY or
    FITNESS FOR A PARTICULAR PURPOSE.'
"
    eval "$defaults"
}

write_config()
{
    set_defaults                             ## Expand variables
    printf "%s\n" "$defaults" > $configfile   ## Write to config file
}
```

When a user is asked to enter a value, and we don't want any previous value to be replaced by an empty string, set_var reads the input into a different variable and only assigns it to the destination if it is not empty.

```
set_var()
{
    var=$1
    prompt=$2
    printf "\t%s: " "$prompt"
    read _var
    [ -n "$_var" ] && eval "$var=\"$_var\""
}
```

335

The configuration file is read, and the four directories used in this chapter (or the default values, if there is no `script-setup.cfg` file) are displayed. The user can accept these or enter new values. The directories are created if they do not already exist.

```
set_dirs()
{
    while :
    do
      set_defaults
      dirx="Directory exists"

      ## Check whether the directories already exist
      [ -d "$ScriptDir" ] && sde="[$dirx]" || sde=
      [ -d "$InstalDir" ] && bde="[$dirx]" || bde=
      [ -d "$BackupDir" ] && kde="[$dirx]" || kde=

      ## Print directory information
      printf "\n\n%s\n" "$eq_bar"
      printf " %s\n" "Directories for Script Development"
      printf "%s\n\n" "$eq_bar"
      w=-25 ## Display width for directories
      printf " 1. Script development: %${w}s%s\n" "$ScriptDir" "${sde}"
      printf " 2.        Installation: %${w}s%s\n" "$InstalDir" "${bde}"
      printf " 3.              Backup: %${w}s%s\n" "$BackupDir" "${kde}"
      printf "\n%s\n\n" "$eq_bar"
      printf " %s: " "Select 1 to 3 to change directory or <ENTER> to accept"

      read _var
      case $_var in
          "") break ;;
          0|q) exit ;;
          1) set_var ScriptDir "Script development directory"
             mkdir -p "$ScriptDir" || printf "\a"
             ;;
          2) set_var InstalDir "Installation directory"
             mkdir -p "$InstalDir" || printf "\a"
             ;;
          3) set_var BackupDir "Backup directory"
             mkdir -p "$BackupDir" || printf "\a"
             ;;
      esac
    done

    ## Create directories that don't yet exist
    for dir in $ScriptDir $InstalDir $BackupDir
    do
      [ -d "$dir" ] && continue || mkdir -p "$dir" || exit 1
    done
}
```

The user is prompted to enter suffixes to use for development and production scripts, as well as the amount of zero-padding for backup versions. By default, development scripts use `-sh`, and production scripts have no suffix. The default padding width is 3.

```
set_suffixes()
{
    while :
    do
      printf "\n\n%s\n" "$eq_bar"
      printf " %s\n" "Suffixes"
      printf "%s\n\n" "$eq_bar"
      printf " 1. Development suffix: %s\n" "$devel_suffix"
      printf " 2.   Installed suffix: %s\n" "$bin_suffix"
      printf " 3.     Backup padding: %s%s\n" "$VERSION_WIDTH"
      printf "\n%s\n\n" "$eq_bar"
      printf " %s: " "Select 1 to 3 to change suffix or <ENTER> to accept"
      read _var
      echo
      case $_var in
          "") break ;;
          0|q) exit ;;
          1) set_var devel_suffix "Development suffix" ;;
          2) set_var bin_suffix "Installed suffix" ;;
          3) set_var VERSION_WIDTH "Backup padding" ;;
      esac
    done
}

progname=${0##*/} ## Extract filename of script from $0

## Decorative line
eq_bar========================================================================
configfile=$HOME/.config/script-setup.cfg ## Configuration file

set_defaults ## Populate default variables
[ -f "$configfile" ] && . "$configfile" ## Load configuration if file exists

set_dirs        ## Get directory names from user
set_suffixes    ## Get suffixes from user
write_config    ## Write the settings to the configuration file
printf "\n\n"   ## Keep things tidy (since there are no newlines after prompts)
```

Notes

It is left to the user to add the script development directory to the $PATH variable. This should be done in whichever startup file your interactive shell sources. For bash, this would be $HOME/.bashrc. If you use the addpath function from Chapter 7, the command to insert is this:

```
addpath $HOME/scripts
```

Adjust the path if you didn't use the default directory. If you do not have addpath installed, add the following (adjusting as necessary):

```
PATH=$PATH:$HOME/scripts
```

17.2 cpsh—Install Script and Make Backup Copy

When a script is ready to be deployed, the old version (if any) needs to be backed up with an incremented suffix, and the new script must be copied to the production directory without the development suffix.

How It Works

The configuration file $HOME/.config/script-setup.cfg is sourced for the locations of the script directories and the suffixes used. Parameter expansion is used to remove any suffix, if necessary, and shell arithmetic and the _zpad function from standard-funcs in Chapter 1 are used to create the incremental backup suffix.

Usage

cpsh [-c CFG] SCRIPT ...

Apart from the -c option, which specifies a different configuration file, the only complication to using this script, apart from supplying the command names, is that it may need to be run as root if you do not have permission to write to the production directory. If a script is to be deployed to /usr/local/bin, for example, you could get an error message:

```
$ cpsh cpsh
touch: cannot touch `/usr/local/bin/cpsh': Permission denied
```

To install in such a location, you need to become root, either with su or sudo.

The Script

```
install_script()
{
    filename=${file%$devel_suffix}          ## Command name, without suffix
    dest=$InstalDir/$filename$bin_suffix    ## Path to installed file
    source=$ScriptDir/$filename$devel_suffix ## Path to development file
    _uniqfile $BackupDir/$filename          ## Increment backup filename
    bak=$_UNIQFILE                          ## ... and store as $bak

    ## Check that source file exists
    [ -f "$source" ] || return 2

    ## Create destination file to check permissions (if it doesn't already exist)
    [ -f "$dest" ] || touch "$dest" || exit 5

    if cmp "$source" "$dest" >/dev/null
    then ## The files are identical; do nothing
      echo "$source and $dest are the same" >&2
    else
      ## Copy the production file to the backup directory
      [ -s "$dest" ] && cp -p "$dest" "$bak"
      ## Copy the development script to the production directory
      cp -p "$source" "$dest"
```

```
        ## Remove write permissions
        chmod +rx,-w "$dest"
    fi
}

progname=${0##*/}
. standard-funcs ## load standard functions

## Use the script-setup configuration file
configfile=$HOME/.config/script-setup.cfg

## If the configuration file doesn't exist, run script-setup
[ -f $configfile ] || script-setup || exit 5

## Source configuration file
. $configfile

## Parse command-line options
while getopts c: arg; do
    case $arg in
        c) configfile=$OPTARG
           [ -f "$configfile" ] && . "$configfile"
           ;;
        *) exit 1 ;;
    esac
done
shift $(( $OPTIND - 1 ))

## This is only necessary when a hand-rolled config file is used
checkdirs $HOME/.config $ScriptDir $BinDir $BackupDir ||
           die $? "Could not create $dir"

## Install all commands given on the command line
for script
do
    install_script "$script"
done
```

17.3 shgrep—Search Scripts for String or Regular Expression

When writing a new function, you might want to check that it will not crash with any previous function. If you are even thinking of deleting a function from the library, you need to check if other scripts are using it. Find out if the script exists and where it resides.

For these situations and others, you will require a script that will search all your scripts for a string or regular expression.

How It Works

The `script-setup.cfg` file is sourced to get the location of the scripts, and the suffix used on the development versions. By using the suffix, any stray files (backups, accidental redirections, or whatever) will be ignored.

Usage

```
shgrep [GREP_OPTIONS] REGEXP
```

The `shgrep` script itself takes no options, but will pass all its arguments to `grep`; in this way, you can use whatever features your version of `grep` supports.

The Script

```
## Use the script-setup configuration file
configfile=$HOME/.config/script-setup.cfg

## If the config file doesn't exist, run script-setup
[ -f $configfile ] || script-setup || exit 5
. $configfile

grep "$@" $ScriptDir/*$devel_suffix
```

17.4 shcat—Display a Shell Script

Rather than have to hunt for the location of a shell script, you might like to have a command that will display it for you when you just provide the name.

How It Works

In `bash`, the `type` command has an option, `-p`, that tells it just to print the path to the file that would be executed, without any other verbiage. In other shells, the `$PATH` variable is examined with the `cmdpath` function. The result of either `type` or `cmdpath` is displayed with the user's default `$PAGER`, or `less`, if that variable is not defined.

Usage

```
shcat SCRIPT
```

If the command entered is not a script, `less` (if that is your `PAGER`) will ask whether you really want to see it:

```
$ shcat ls
"/bin/ls" may be a binary file. See it anyway?
```

Entering n will abort the command; y will display a lot of nonsense.

The Script

```
cmdpath()
{
    _CMD=${1##*/}
    oldIFS=$IFS
    IFS=:
    set -- $PATH
    IFS=$oldIFS
    for _DIR
    do
      if [ -x "$_DIR/$_CMD" ]
      then
        cmd=$_DIR/$_CMD
        return
      fi
    done
}

if [ -n "$BASH_VERSION" ]
then
  cmd=$(type -p "$1")
else
  cmdpath "$1"
fi

${PAGER:-less} "$cmd"
```

Summary

There's not a great deal to the suggested system for managing script development, but it is enough to save a lot of work and worry. The most important part of it is cpsh, which takes care of installing and backing up the scripts. But isn't something missing? For a long time I thought so: Where is the script to revert the installed copy to an earlier version?

For a long time I planned to write the reversh script, but finally came to the conclusion that it really wasn't necessary. Being able to run the development version means that a bad script hardly ever gets installed. I've only had to use the backups two or three times in the years I've used this system. In addition, you could simply use GIT from the command line to back up your scripts, or to revert to an earlier version.

■ ■ ■

Internet Scripting Resources

A vast amount of information about shell scripting is on the Internet. One of the most useful, and where one can learned a great deal, is the Usenet newsgroup `comp.unix.shell`. Its archives can be searched at `http://groups-beta.google.com/group/comp.unix.shell`, but for posting, using your own newsreader is recommended over the Google form. There's no shortage of newsreaders, both text based and GUI: `tin`, `slrn`, and `pan` to name a few, as well as combined mail and newsreaders, such as `pine` and Mozilla Thunderbird.

Listed here are a number of useful web sites. The WWW is notorious for changing locations, and these links were all valid at the time of writing; many should be stable for a long time. Chris has them all posted on his web page at `http://cfaj.freeshell.org/shell`, where he shall try to keep them current and add new pages.

Introductions to Shell Scripting

- `http://www.linuxcommand.org/writing_shell_scripts.php`: *Writing shell scripts*, by William Shotts, Jr.

- `http://steve-parker.org/sh/sh.shtml`: Steve Parker's *Bourne/Bash shell scripting tutorial*.

- `http://www-128.ibm.com/developerworks/linux/library/l-bash.html`: *Bash by example: Fundamental programming in the Bourne again shell (bash)*, by Daniel Robbins.

- `http://www.ibiblio.org/mdw/HOWTO/Bash-Prog-Intro-HOWTO.html`: *BASH Programming - Introduction HOW-TO*, by Mike G.

- `http://www.icon.co.za/~psheer/book/node10.html.gz`: *Rute User's Tutorial and Exposition: Shell Scripts*, by Paul Sheer.

Intermediate and Advanced Scripting

- `http://www.grymoire.com/Unix/`: Bruce Barnett's tutorials on UNIX shell programming.

- `http://www.tldp.org/LDP/abs/html/index.html`: *Advanced Bash-Scripting Guide*, by Mendel Cooper.

- `http://home.comcast.net/~j.p.h/cus-faq.html`: *The* comp.unix.shell *FAQ*, compiled by Joe Halpin.

- `http://code.dogmap.org/lintsh/`: Paul Jarc's shell constructs page.

Collections of Scripts

- `http://www.shelldorado.com`: Heiner's SHELLdorado; links, tutorials, and a lot of scripts.

- `http://www.mtxia.com/fancyIndex/Tools/Scripts/Korn/`: Dana French's Korn Shell scripts.

Home Pages for Shells

- `http://cnswww.cns.cwru.edu/~chet/bash/bashtop.html`: Chet Ramey's Bash home page.

- `http://kornshell.com`: The KornShell home page.

- `http://www.cs.mun.ca/~michael/pdksh`: pdksh—the Public Domain Korn Shell.

Regular Expressions, sed, and awk

- `http://www.linuxfocus.org/English/July1998/article53.html`: *Regular Expressions*, by Guido Socher.

- `http://etext.lib.virginia.edu/services/helpsheets/unix/regex.html`: *Using Regular Expressions*, by Stephen Ramsay.

- `http://sitescooper.org/tao_regexps.html`: *A Tao of Regular Expressions*, by Steve Mansour.

- `http://www.amk.ca/python/howto/regex`: *Regular Expression HOWTO*, by A.M. Kuchling. This is Python-specific, but the principles apply to other languages, as well.

- `http://www.faqs.org/faqs/computer-lang/awk/faq`: *The awk FAQ*, maintained by Russell Schulz.

- `http://www.student.northpark.edu/pemente/sed`: Eric Piment's sed page.

Miscellaneous Pages

- `http://www.gnu.org/software/textutils/manual/textutils/html_chapter/textutils_10.html`: *Opening the software toolbox*, by Arnold Robbins.

- `http://www-128.ibm.com/developerworks/linux/library/l-util.html`: *The art of writing Linux utilities*, by Peter Seebach.

- `http://www.gnu.org/software/autoconf/manual/autoconf-2.57/html_node/autoconf_114.html#SEC114`: *Portable Shell Programming*.

History of the Shell

- `http://www.cnop.net/staticpages/index.php/intro-unix`: Steven Bourne's *An Introduction to the Unix Shell*. A description of the original Bourne shell, by its author.

- `http://www.in-ulm.de/~mascheck/bourne`: *The Traditional Bourne Shell Family*, by Sven Maschek.

- `http://www.faqs.org/faqs/unix-faq/faq/part3/section-16.html`: *Why do some scripts start with #! ... ?*

- `http://groups-beta.google.com/group/alt.folklore.computers/msg/a176a30b54f92c99`: *History of Unix shells*, by John Mashey.

- `http://groups.google.com/groups?hl=en&lr=&ie=UTF-8&selm=1994Feb23.235836.15874%40sq.sq.com`: *Unix before sh*, by Mark Brader.

Index

Get the eBook for only $5!

Why limit yourself?

Now you can take the weightless companion with you wherever you go and access your content on your PC, phone, tablet, or reader.

Since you've purchased this print book, we're happy to offer you the eBook in all 3 formats for just $5.

Convenient and fully searchable, the PDF version enables you to easily find and copy code—or perform examples by quickly toggling between instructions and applications. The MOBI format is ideal for your Kindle, while the ePUB can be utilized on a variety of mobile devices.

To learn more, go to www.apress.com/companion or contact support@apress.com.

Printed in the United States
By Bookmasters